OXFORD STUDIES IN
SOCIAL AND CULTURAL ANTHROPOLOGY

THE FEMALE BRIDEGROOM

The Female Bridegroom

A Comparative Study of Life-Crisis Rituals in South India and Sri Lanka

ANTHONY GOOD

CLARENDON PRESS · OXFORD

1991

$ 39—

Oxford University Press, Walton Street, Oxford OX2 6DP
Oxford New York Toronto
Delhi Bombay Calcutta Madras Karachi
Petaling Jaya Singapore Hong Kong Tokyo
Nairobi Dar es Salaam Cape Town
Melbourne Auckland
and associated companies in
Berlin Ibadan

Oxford is a trade mark of Oxford University Press

Published in the United States
by Oxford University Press, New York

British Library Cataloguing in Publication Data
Good, Anthony
The female bridegroom: a comparative study of life crisis rituals in South India and Sri Lanka
1. Rites and ceremonies
I. Title
392
ISBN 0–19–827853–5

Library of Congress Cataloging in Publication Data
Good, Anthony.
The female bridegroom: a comparative study of life-crisis rituals in South India and Sri Lanka / Anthony Good.
p. cm.
Includes bibliographical references and index.
1. Rites and ceremonies—India—Tirunelveli (District)
2. Rites and ceremonies—India, South.
3. Rites and ceremonies—Sri Lanka. 4. Tirunelveli (India: District)—Social life and customs. 5. India, South—Social life and customs. 6. Sri Lanka—Social life and customs. I. Title.
GN635.14G66 1991 392′.0954–dc20 90–45585
ISBN 0–19–827853–5

Typeset by Hope Services (Abingdon) Ltd
Printed in Great Britain by
Biddles Ltd,
Guildford & King's Lynn

To Alison, Emily, and Harriet

Preface

This book arises out of fifteen months of fieldwork in South India during 1976–7, but it is not a conventional ethnographic monograph, still less a 'village study'. Although it first describes and analyses one set of life-crisis rituals marking female puberty, marriage, birth, and death, to show how these fit into one particular local framework of intra-caste and inter-caste relationships, it then goes on to set these practices into broader context by way of a regional comparison.

Such a comparison could in principle be conducted across South Asia as a whole. That is not attempted here, and in fact not all the necessary data are available as yet. Instead, a more modest comparison is carried out across southern India and Sri Lanka. The region concerned corresponds roughly to that within which Dravidian languages are spoken by people who mostly have a so-called 'Dravidian' relationship terminology (Trautmann 1981); within which up to 25 per cent of marriages involve first cousins and/or elder sister's daughters (Beck n.d.; 1972: Table 5.9); and within which the gender imbalance in the total population is comparatively slight, in sharp contrast to the situation further north (Dyson and Moore 1983). It would be pointless to try to bound the region more precisely, and indeed these criteria themselves are by no means perfectly congruent.

Many people have participated in, or advised on, the work leading up to the present book. I thank them all, but certain people deserve specific mention.

Palanimurugan Chettiar, MA was an invaluable research assistant during the first half of my 1976–7 fieldwork. My gratitude also goes to Fr. Thomas Malayampuram SJ, Director of the Tirunelveli Social Service Society, for his whole-hearted assistance then, and to Br. Job, my guide in selecting a fieldwork location. In 1983–4 I owed a great deal to the assistance of Dr D. Venkatesan, and had very fruitful contacts with the staff of the Anthropology Department at Madras University, under Professor N. Subba Reddy.

My warm thanks go to all the residents of Terku Vandanam, Vadakku Vandanam, and Kalinkapatti, especially our landlord, Mekalinka Konar; his son, my friend Sankarapandi; Vijaya and Ravi; and my *sittappā*, Suppaiya Konar.

The staff of Kalugumalai temple, especially K. G. Subramania Pattar and K. G. Paramesvara Pattar, shared their knowledge with enthusiasm. The temple Trustee, E. Thangaswami, and Executive Officer, R. Tamilanandan, were always courteous and helpful. Many other friends in India cannot be mentioned here, but their names and ideas recur in the text which follows.

Some parts of the book have been presented at departmental seminars and conferences over the past ten years. I am grateful to all these audiences for their comments, and especially to Mike Carrithers, Chris Fuller, Liz Nissan, Johnny Parry, Martin Southwold, Jock Stirrat, and to Penny Logan, whose generosity in supplying vital unpublished data of her own is acknowledged at appropriate places in the text. I also thank Nick Allen for his advice during my preparation for field-research, and Alan Barnard for thoughtful criticism on kinship matters.

Some material in this book has already appeared elsewhere. The early part of Chapter 4 was published in *Man* (NS) 17 (1982), 23–41; much of Chapters 5 and 6 was published in *Journal of Anthropological Research*, 36 (1980), 474–500, and *Man* (NS) 16 (1981), 108–29; and the central argument of the book appeared, in preliminary form, in *Social Analysis*, 11 (1982), 35–55.

The initial fieldwork was done under the auspices of a Conversion Fellowship from the Social Science Research Council: the Durham University Staff Research Fund also made a grant towards research expenses. The final chapter of the book incorporates material from a subsequent field-trip in 1983–4, supported by ESRC Research Grant no. G 00230100.

Finally, and above all, I acknowledge the contributions made by my wife Alison, and our daughters Emily and Harriet. I thank them for their forbearance during the preparation of the book, but especially for their contributions during our stays in India. Alison bore the brunt of our unfamiliar and sometimes difficult living conditions, without even the compensatory satisfactions which arise from the process of field-research. It was her presence and support which enabled me to continue, and without her this book could never have been completed.

Edinburgh,
February, 1990. A.G.

Contents

Plates

I Velar Sadanku (Chapter 7, Example C): Karuppayi in her 'bridal' sari. Her 'groom' Uccimali wears a turban and a boy's shirt. Their relative positions are reversed from those adopted during the preceding ritual.

II Maravar Sadanku (Chapter 7, Example A): Sanmukattay, dressed in a half-sari, seated with her turbaned 'bridegroom', Tamilarasi. Both have holy ash on their foreheads, offered by important relatives and villagers. Female relatives are urging Sanmukattay to raise her head for the camera, but she maintains the demure posture expected of a bride.

III Maravar Temple Kaliyanam (Chapter 8, Example C): The bride and groom, Komati and Muttupandi Tevar, seated on the marriage blanket, just after the offerings of ash and money by important guests. To the left of the picture is the Pasuvandanai temple priest who officiated at the ceremony.

IV Maravar Kaliyanam (Chapter 8, Example B): The bride and groom, Viralaksmi and Muniyasami, seated on the marriage platform near the end of the ceremony. They are related as MBDy to FZSe. Minatci, the Female Officient, stands at the rear, identifiable by the ash on her forehead.

V Asari Funeral (Chapter 10, Example A): The chief male mourners go in procession under a white canopy to fetch water from the temple well. They are led by the band and the Terku Vandanam Barber, Sanmukam, who is carrying a conch-shell.

VI Asari Funeral (Chapter 10, Example A): The body of Aiyan Asari, bathed and decorated for the procession to the cemetery. I was asked particularly to take this picture: a framed print now hangs in the family home.

VII Paraiyar Funeral: The body of Mariyammal, prepared for the funeral cortège. The dead are garlanded and decorated in similar—though less elaborate—ways to the central participants in Sadankus and Kaliyanams.

VIII Divine Wedding (Chapter 16): Two silver *kumpam* pots on a small marriage platform represent the divine couple. The larger pot is Kalukacalamurtti, the smaller Valli.

IX Divine Wedding (Chapter 16): Two Temple Servants take seven steps round the sacred fire, carrying the pots representing the groom and bride. Behind them is the mobile image of the god, decorated and bejewelled like a royal bridegroom. Only the head-dresses of his wives are visible on either side of him.

Figures

Maps

Tables

Relationship Notation

Standard abbreviations are used for kin types, based on the following symbolic equivalences:

F	father	P	parent
M	mother	C	child
B	brother	G	sibling
Z	sister	E	spouse
S	son	e	elder
D	daughter	y	younger
H	husband	ms	man speaking
W	wife	ws	woman speaking

Throughout the book, such abbreviations are used *only* to denote the precise genealogical positions specified, whereas English-language relationship terms written within double quotes are simple-minded translations of Tamil terms, and should not be taken to have precise genealogical significance. Thus, for example, MB denotes the actual mother of Ego's actual brother, whereas "mother's brother" may refer to any or all of those people whom a Tamil would call *māmaṉ* (see Tables 5.1 and 5.2).

1

Life-Crisis Cycles in South India and Sri Lanka

1.1 Introduction

The starting-point for this book is a female 'puberty ritual' practised by Hindus in three Tirunelveli villages— and probably in most of south Tamil Nadu. Its distinctive feature is an episode analogous to a wedding, involving a 'bridegroom' who is, in most cases, a *female* cross-cousin of the pubescent girl. This raises the question of the relationship of this rite to such practices as the *tāli*-tying rites of Kerala, and demands a re-examination of notions about affinity and female sexuality in South India and Sri Lanka generally.

Life-crisis rituals—especially weddings—loom very large in South Asian society. Quite apart from the magnificence and elaboration of the rites themselves, the cost of the ceremonies and the magnitude of the associated prestations make them the largest economic transactions in the lives of many Indians. The findings of this book may help explain why this is so, and why it would be misguided to see here only wasteful ostentation. Quite the contrary, these rituals are essential to the very definition and maintenance of local sub-caste groups.

In South Asia, life-crisis rituals have always been seen as important. The Sanskrit *sāstra* texts called them *saṁskāras*, 'rites that impart fitness' (Kane 1941: ii. 1, 190–1). They were 'the outward symbols or signs of the inner change which would fit human beings for corporate life and they also tended to convey a certain status on those who underwent them' (ii. 192). Not surprisingly, therefore, the number of *saṁskāras* required depended on the social status of the group concerned. More were prescribed for twice-born castes, particularly Brahmans, than for Sudras. For similar reasons, there were more for men than for women. The texts list far more *saṁskāras* than are actually observed in practice, however, and the rituals they describe are very different from those dealt with below, with partial exceptions in the case of Brahmans. Moreover, *non*-literary Indian theories regarding such ceremonies, and the processes of conception and reproduction which they regulate, are extremely varied (David 1973; Barnett 1976; Inden and Nicholas 1977; McGilvray 1982*a*; 1982*b*), rather more so in fact than the practices to which they refer. Even within a given area, the degree of consensus seems to be slight.

The present analysis will therefore concentrate for the most part upon social structure, not merely because the data are generally much more comprehensive, but in the belief that this is the level at which regional comparison has to begin. The next section provides a preliminary justification for this position, and an explanation of the stance taken in this book.

1.2 Problems of Anthropological Comparison

The ultimate aim of this book is to compare life-crisis rituals performed by people in different parts of South Asia, and to correlate these practices with various structural features of their societies. In order to avoid an unacceptable degree of reification, it is assumed that the labels applied to such features—labels like "descent", "marriage", and, indeed, "social structure" itself—are useful for comparative purposes only if nominally and polythetically defined.[1]

This approach to definition assumes that most technical terms in anthropology are what Wittgenstein called 'odd-job' words (Needham 1975: 365), which should be defined only in relation to their signification, or use, not with reference to the alleged essence of the 'thing' signified. In fact, it cannot be assumed that the various phenomena to which they are applied have any attributes universally in common (Southwold 1978*b*: 369).

For example, "descent" is a very widely used index for cross-societal comparison. Yet even if it is distinguished clearly from "inheritance" and "succession" (cf. Rivers 1924: 85–8), and used only to refer to transmission of membership in some group or category, "descent" remains a clearly polythetic notion (Needham 1975: 360). To begin with, it can be understood in three distinct

[1] Nominal and real definitions are contrasted by Southwold (1978*a*; 1978*b*). The case for polythetic classification is made by Needham (1975). I have proposed elsewhere a polythetic definition of "kinship" (Barnard and Good 1984: 187–9), building on the work of Needham (1971*b*) and Leach (1961*a*: 107–8).

senses: (1) as an idiom which people use to classify themselves and others;[2] (2) as a criterion for establishing social status, and allocating jural rights and responsibilities; and (3) as the empirical basis upon which members are recruited to particular corporate groupings (Barnard and Good 1984: 78). Put another way, "descent" can be understood at the categorical, jural, or behavioural levels, respectively.[3]

These three viewpoints have to be kept distinct because the phenomena they embrace are themselves distinct, though not wholly independent.[4] Most writers have tended to see "descent" primarily in jural terms (sense 2) (cf. Fortes 1970: 84), but an account dealing *only* with rules or norms would be seriously inadequate because "descent" in the other two senses may be different in character, or even absent altogether.

Although "descent" rules are likely to reflect both categorization (sense 1) and group behaviour (sense 3) in some way, the degree of congruence need not be as great as is often tacitly assumed. The Nuer provide a famous illustration of this. They have an extremely strong descent ideology (senses 1 and 2), but their villages are actually quite heterogeneous in composition (sense 3) (Evans-Pritchard 1951: 28). Even where congruence *does* potentially exist, it need not actually be realized in particular cases. Thus, one can make demands on others (sense 3) by appealing to norms and values (sense 2) predicated upon common 'blood' (sense 1), but it does not automatically follow that the claimed kinship and/or the obligations which flow from it will be accepted by others. Moreover, rules and norms are often used to justify and rationalize behaviour, rather than being motivating forces in themselves (Bourdieu 1977: 22).

The problems do not end there, however, because at least two of the senses of "descent" are themselves polythetic. The idioms of sense 1 and the rules of sense 2 take such varied forms that it is almost impossible to compare one group of people with another on either count. Moreover, "descent" used in either sense is in effect a translation into anthropological jargon of a set of localized categorizations and norms, rather than a technical term which can be applied to any society whatever in a purely formal, abstract way.

[2] This is the idiom of 'descent constructs' (Scheffler 1966: 544), or descent categories.

[3] These notions are discussed in more detail later (see 5.1).

[4] This point is discussed in more detail later; for kinship in general, and marriageability in particular see 5.1 and 6.9.

Even in sense 3 "descent" may encompass many different sorts of group, and an almost infinite variety of contexts. Not surprisingly, then, it too has often been used as a catch-all descriptive label with any number of varied manifestations, some of which are inevitably borderline or controversial cases. The difference is that "descent" in sense 3 can also be used in another way, a formal, analytical way which is not tied to any one kind of grouping, or any localized form of expression. The word remains the same, but the understanding which lies behind it is radically different. Viewed in this light, "patrilineal descent", say, ceases to be an *ad hoc* descriptive category and becomes instead one of a clearly demarcated set of logical possibilities (as listed at Needham 1971*b*: 10).[5] The possibility *does* then arise of using "descent" in sense 3 as a meaningful index for comparison.

The relevance of this for the present argument can be illustrated by imagining the converse of the Nuer case mentioned earlier. Any settled agricultural community in which sons mostly inherit[6] from their fathers is likely to contain residential units recruited on the basis of "patrilineal descent" in sense 3 (Barnard and Good 1984: 77). This may not be explicitly recognized by community members (sense 1), however, and descent need not be the basis for allocating rights and responsibilities among them (sense 2).[7] This state of affairs might be termed *de facto* patrilineality.

Even such *de facto* "descent" has certain socio-structural entailments, however. If, for example, the society just envisaged contains connubial domestic units, the demands of agriculture make it likely that post-marital residence will be viri-patrilocal, i.e., that a "wife" will leave her natal home, to live with her "husband" in or near the home of his father.[8] Similar arguments apply, though in less straightforward fashion (Fox 1967), to cases of *de facto* "matrilineal descent". *De facto* patriliny and matriliny are bound to be reflected in the

[5] A simple example of the power of this analytical strategy is provided by Goody's typology of sexual offences (1971: 73), which not only solves the problem of how to distinguish "incest", "fornication", and "adultery" cross-culturally, but even manages to identify a fourth logical category of offences—"incestuous adultery". A more conventional analysis would have subsumed this under one of the other three headings, thereby confusing their meanings even further.

[6] "Inheritance" can of course be understood at the self-same three levels as "descent". It is sense 3 which is meant here, i.e., most sons inherit land from their fathers in practice, *whether or not* there is any explicit rule to this effect.

[7] Such a situation is discussed by Sahlins (1965: 105–6).

[8] Marriage has yet to be precisely defined (see 1.3).

"weddings" and other domestic rituals of the community, with regard, for example, to the identities of key participants. This will happen whether unilineal descent is recognized locally or not,[9] although of course the occurrence of descent-based categorizations (sense 1), and/or descent-based rules (sense 2), make it even more likely that unilineality will be manifest in local life-crisis rituals.

These, at any rate, are the kinds of assumptions on which the general argument in this book is based. It was obviously necessary to explain them briefly at this stage, but ultimately, like any other theoretical position, they can only be judged by results. The principal justification for my argument is therefore to be found in Chapters 13 to 15 below.

1.3 The Ritual Cycle

It can be taken for granted that whenever some new technical term is introduced in later chapters, it is to be understood in a nominal, polythetic sense. Certain terms need more explicit and detailed consideration, however, in view of their central role in the argument. Thus, in order to conduct an adequate comparison, it is essential that no substantive distinction be drawn between "puberty rites" and "weddings". For each society, the entire body of ritual dealing with female (and, to a lesser degree, male) sexuality will be treated as a single entity. It will be argued that groups in the region differ mainly in how they emphasize the various implications of this sexuality.

Firstly, the natal relatives of an unmarried female need to protect themselves from the consequences of any sexual activity in which she may engage, particularly with partners of unsuitable status. Secondly, bridegrooms and their families need to be sure of the status and personal purity of their brides. Finally, the status of a woman's offspring must also be beyond question. These concerns are common to all the societies considered, but the precise forms they take reflect the structural particularities of the group in question, such as the presence of unilineality (in either mode) and hypergamy, as well as the rules of inheritance and post-marital residence.

[9] This partly explains why the kind of 'socio-structural' comparison attempted in Ch. 15 is a necessary prerequisite to any 'cultural' account claiming more than purely local validity (cf. 12.2, below).

In their celebrated debate on the definition of marriage, Leach (1961*a*) and Gough (1959*a*) referred to some of the practices considered below, notably the *tāli*-tying rites of Kerala. Although these particular cases are not dealt with until later, it is necessary to raise the problem of definition right at the outset, and adopt a system of nomenclature consistent with the present approach.

Leach (1961*a*: 107–8) defined "marriage" polythetically, as a 'bundle of rights' involving: legitimation of offspring; access to the spouse's sexuality, labour, and property; and affinal linkages between people and between groups. No single case of "marriage" involved all these features, nor was any one feature common to all forms of "marriage". Moreover, other features could be added to the list without compromising it in any way. Gough saw this argument as logically flawed, because 'every ethnographer might extend at will Dr Leach's list of marital rights, and in short define marriage in any way he pleased'. Cross-cultural comparison required a 'single, parsimonious definition, simply in order to isolate the phenomenon we wish to study' (1959*a*: 23). This begged the question of whether there was in fact such a phenomenon to be studied. Leach thought not, hence his subsequent comment that 'all universal definitions of marriage are vain' (1961*a*: 105). In his view, the creation of a class labelled "marriage" was irrelevant to an understanding of social structure (cf. 1961*a*: 4), because such labelling concerned surface form rather than structural relationships.

Structural-functionalism, represented here by Gough,[10] is admirably scrupulous about relating particular cases of "marriage" to their specific social contexts, but as Comaroff points out, its comparative generalizations 'are typically based upon the identification of a synthetic category of largely decontextualized phenomena . . . defined by their surface likenesses' (1980: 31).

Needham, too, saw "marriage" as a polythetic class, based upon sporadic likenesses rather than common structural features. In his view, there 'need not be . . . any one thing that the phenomena of . . . "marriage". . . have in common' (1971*b*: 30) except 'the contractual union of sexual statuses' (1971*b*: 31). If one accepts Leach's and Needham's arguments, it follows that no precise definition of a "puberty rite" is possible either. Although biological puberty is of course definable cross-culturally, it is not a girl's biological condition

[10] Gough later changed her view on Nayar "marriage" (1965: 11).

but her ethno-biological status which is at issue in ritual. The boundary between rites marking this social puberty and those celebrating "marriage" is impossible to draw, as the cases given below illustrate. My own position is that there is *nothing* common to the 'myriad forms of marriage' (Needham 1971*b*: 31). It is therefore fruitless to argue whether the rites to be discussed below are, or are not, "weddings".

The following approach helps overcome such difficulties of definition and nomenclature. Firstly, "female" is used as a generic term to mean anyone of feminine gender. Females may, however, belong to any one of five distinct socio-sexual statuses, namely, "girl", "woman", "wife", "mother", and "widow". These statuses are usually acquired in the order given, but they are not all mutually exclusive; it is obviously possible to be, say, both a "wife" and a "mother".

All these terms must be defined polythetically, and these definitions depend in turn upon polythetic definitions of "marriage", etc. Moreover, they do not necessarily correspond to localized indigenous categories: for example, Reynolds reports that Tamil women are classified as "virgins", "fertile married women", "barren women", or "widows" (1980: 36; see 16.7, below). This does not mean that the five categories are selected arbitrarily, however. On the contrary, their choice stems from the fact that, almost everywhere in South India and Sri Lanka, there are four ceremonial stages in the passage of a female from immature girlhood to widowhood, as follows:

	puberty rite		wedding		birth ritual		H's funeral	
girl	⟶	woman	⟶	wife	⟶	mother	⟶	widow

The terms "girl", "woman", etc., are thus used merely to label the social statuses involved in this cycle, just as "puberty rite", "wedding", etc., are used to label its various ritual stages. This is done purely to avoid circumlocution. No general definitions of "marriage", "wedding", etc., can be assumed, because the contents and purposes of the stages differ from case to case. Certain features occur, say, in the first stage among some peoples of the region, and in the second stage for others. Partly for that reason, I shall argue that these four stages constitute a single cycle which can only be fully understood if it is seen as one long-drawn-out entity.

1.4 The Presentation of the Argument

The first half of the book concentrates on my own ethnographic data from three villages in the Tirunelveli District of Tamil Nadu in South India. Chapters 2 and 3 provide the general social and economic context, and Chapter 4 considers local prestational categories, primarily in inter-caste contexts but also *within* castes. Chapters 5 and 6 examine the local kinship system, from three levels—categorical, jural, and behavioural—which are ultimately synthesized.

The rest of the book concentrates on life-crisis rituals, and Chapters 7 to 10 contain ethnographic descriptions of, respectively, puberty ceremonies, weddings, birth rites, and funerals in the three villages.

The focus then widens, as ceremonies reported from other parts of South India and Sri Lanka are described in Chapter 11. The intention is to examine as wide a range of behaviour as possible, so the examples cited include well-attested cases from the recent past, as well as present-day practices.[11] Previous analyses of such rituals are evaluated in Chapter 12. This provides the framework for the present analysis of the local life-crisis cycle (Ch. 13), and for a comparative study of the social identities of key ritual participants in the region as a whole (Ch. 14). In Chapter 15, the diverse practices from different parts of the region are fitted into a single paradigm. As already mentioned, this starts from the assumption that what is at stake in all these rites is the protection of the group against the status ambiguity and impurity which would result from uncontrolled sexual activity on the part of, especially, its female members.

Finally, Chapter 16 considers the marriage rituals performed for deities in South Indian Hindu temples. It is thereby possible to show that the mythological and ritual treatment of divine sexuality expresses notions central to the human sphere, too. The theological notions revealed by such ceremonies turn out to be more basic than ethnobiology, and much less susceptible to inter- and intra-local variation. They suggest a fruitful path towards understanding the meanings and purposes of the complex, varied, and exotic ceremonies considered below.

[11] This procedure is justified briefly later (11.1).

2
Three Villages

2.1 Fieldwork Location

Tirunelveli[1] District in Tamil Nadu state, at the south-eastern tip of India, lies between the 8,000 foot Western Ghats and the Bay of Bengal. The land is flat, and shelves so gently that the 250-foot contour is 30–40 miles inland. At the 1971 Census the population of the District was 3,200,515. Its main urban centres are Tuticorin port and the Tirunelveli-Palaiyankottai conurbation, but 2,171,019 of its inhabitants are classed as rural (Government of India 1972*b*: i. p. ix). The District is divided into 13 taluks. Kovilpatti Taluk, in the north, has a population of 221,460 (i. 2). Its 145,596 rural inhabitants live in 102 revenue villages,[2] divided among 80 panchayats (i. 54–72), giving an average population of 1,427 per revenue village and 1,820 per panchayat.

About half-way along the road linking the National Highway at Kayattar with the State Highway at Eppodumvendram, a cart track branches off northwards, skirting *Kaliṅkapaṭṭi*[3] village. The track runs below the earth bund of a large irrigation tank, until it reaches *Teṛku Vaṇḍāṉam*,[4] two miles beyond (Map 1). Thence it continues to *Vaḍakku Vaṇḍāṉam*,[5] a mile north of Terku Vandanam, and on to Koppampatti and Kamanayakkanpatti.

My field-research was initially based in Terku Vandanam (TV) village, which met all my prior requirements regarding size and composition. It proved essential to extend my work to Vadakku Vandanam (VV) and Kalinkapatti (KP), however, because, as Chapters

[1] The anglicized form 'Tinnevelly' is found in older works. Tirunelveli District has recently been subdivided, and my discussion here refers to the situation existing up until 1984.

[2] 'Revenue villages' are demarcated for taxation purposes: see 2.3 below for 'panchayats'. There are sometimes two revenue villages in one panchayat.

[3] In the 1971 Census the village is called K. Kumarapuram.

[4] *Teṛku* means 'south', and *vaṇḍāṉam* means 'heron'. Unless otherwise stated, dictionary meanings of Tamil words are taken from Fabricius 1972 or Winslow 1981.

[5] *Vaḍakku* means 'north'.

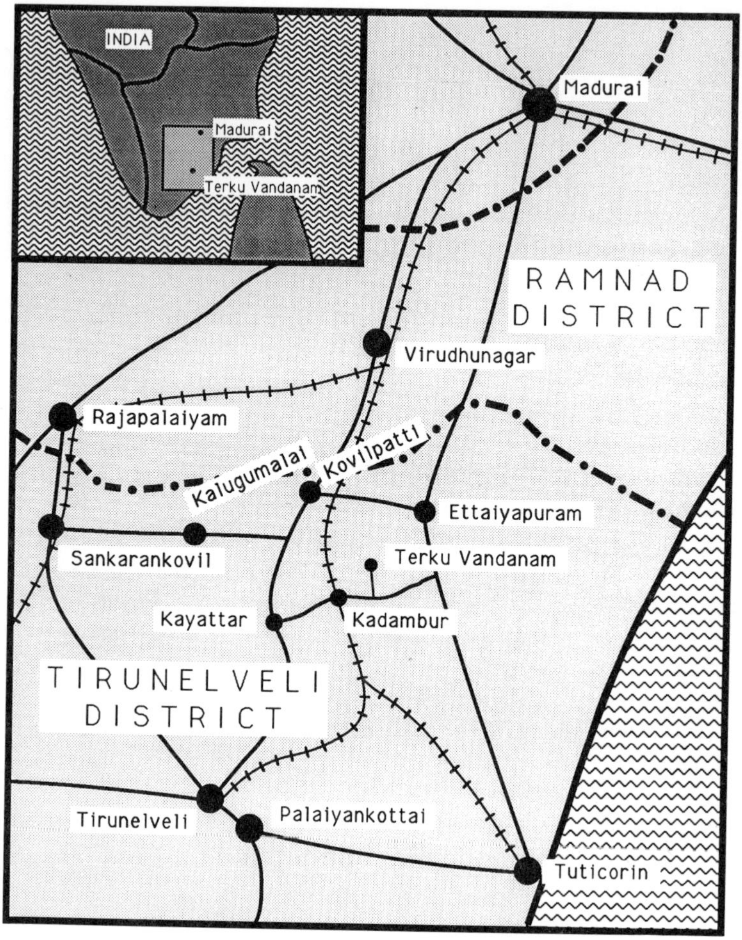

Map 1 Tirunelveli District, south Tamil Nadu

3 and 4 will show, the three villages turned out to be closely interconnected in many ways.

2.2 The Caste Composition of the Local Population

Local villages consist of nuclear settlements surrounded by farmland. These settlements are criss-crossed by streets running north–south and east–west, and most castes live in fairly discrete blocks. Harijan ('Untouchable') castes live outside the settlement proper: locally this applies to the Paraiyars (caste TV 2),[6] Pallars (VV 2), and Cakkiliyars (VV 4).

A caste is an endogamous and occupationally specialized group occupying a more-or-less agreed niche in a status hierarchy justified on the basis of criteria of relative purity and pollution. Most local caste-groups are also groups of fairly closely related genealogical kin. Table 2.1 displays the caste composition of the three villages, in terms of both total population and number of households.[7]

The local population is surprisingly unstable: individuals or whole families return at harvest time; people live for long periods with relatives in other villages; new brides often visit their natal homes, and so on. Those people living locally during the census itself[8] are included in Table 2.1, though not all were fully integrated into village life. For example, some people were living there temporarily because of their jobs: these included the parish priest and headmaster in Vadakku Vandanam; the seed agent, Nayakkar schoolteacher, and Brahman shopkeeper in Kalinkapatti; and a Nayakkar Electricity Board worker in Terku Vandanam. I include them in my calculations, however, because every village contains such outsiders.

No census since 1921 has asked questions about caste, so the available data on the District as a whole are very old. Even before then, each census used different nomenclature, and the District boundaries changed several times. Precise conclusions cannot be

[6] Many Tamil caste names end in *-aṉ*, and have the plural ending *-ar*. I shall, however, write e.g. 'Paraiyars' rather than 'Paraiyar' when referring to caste members in the plural. The caste code numbers for each village are taken from Table 2.1.

[7] A 'household' is defined as a separate cooking unit which maintains its own hearth. In most cases this is a separate property-holding unit, too.

[8] This census was taken in Terku Vandanam during Sept.–Oct. 1976, in Kalinkapatti during Dec. 1976–Jan. 1977, and in Vadakku Vandanam during Feb.–Mar. 1977.

TABLE 2.1. Census Details for the Three Villages

Caste	Hereditary occupation	No. of households	Pop.	Av. size of household	Pop. (%)
Terku Vandanam					
1. Kondaiyankottai Maravar	Watchmen	54	284	5.3	34.8
2. Sampakkamar Paraiyar	Labourers	27	129	4.8	15.8
3. Kammavar Nayakkar	Farmers	19	93	4.9	11.4
4. Sivi Idaiyar Konar	Shepherds	19	92	4.8	11.3
5. Pillaimar	Farmers	16	86	5.4	10.5
6. Taccan Asari	Carpenters	6	30	5.0	3.6
7. Vaniya Cettiyar	Oil Merchants	5	28	5.6	3.4
8. Kollan Asari	Blacksmiths	4	25	6.2	3.1
9. Serman Velar	Potters	4	15	3.8	1.8
10. Sannivan Kavundar	Farmers	2	12	6.0	1.5
11. Pandi Vannar	Washermen	2	12	6.0	1.5
12. Panditar	Barbers	1	6	6.0	0.7
13. Tattan Asari	Goldsmiths	1	2	2.0	0.3
14. Tinda Vannar	Washermen, Barbers	1	2	2.0	0.3
Village Totals		161	816	5.1	100.0
Vadakku Vandanam					
1. Christian Nadar	Toddy-tappers	91	389	4.3	53.5
2. Anjca Pallar	Labourers	28	158	5.6	21.7
3. Kampalattar Nayakkar	Farmers	11	64	5.8	8.8

4. Totti Cakkiliyar	Scavengers	13	57	4.4	7.8
5. Sivi Idaiyar Konar	Shepherds	7	28	4.0	3.9
6. Pandi Vannar	Washermen	1	9	9.0	1.2
7. Maniyakkarar Maravar	Watchmen	2	7	3.5	1.0
8. Sampakkamar Paraiyar	Labourers	1	7	7.0	1.0
9. Maruttuvar	Barbers	1	4	4.0	0.6
10. Headmaster	—	1	3	3.0	0.4
11. Catholic Priest	—	1	1	1.0	0.1
Village Totals		157	727	4.6	100.0
Kalinkapatti					
1. Ayotti Reddiyar	Farmers	29	158	5.4	52.7
2. Kondaiyankottai Maravar	Watchmen	12	49	4.1	16.3
3. Saiva Cettiyar Vellalar	Merchants	5	27	5.4	9.0
4. Kottu Reddiyar	Farmers	4	17	4.2	5.7
5. Pulavar	Drummers	5	15	3.0	5.0
6. Pandi Vannar	Washermen	2	12	6.0	4.0
7. Telunku Asari	Goldsmiths	1	6	6.0	2.0
8. Kammavar Nayakkar	(Teacher)	1	5	5.0	1.7
9. Panditar	Barbers	1	4	4.0	1.3
10. Aiyar Brahman	Priests	1	4	4.0	1.3
11. Govt. Seed Agent	—	1	3	3.0	1.0
Village Totals		62	300	4.8	100.0
Totals for the three villages		380	1843	4.9	

Note: The 1971 Census, taken locally in 1966, gives the populations of Terku Vandanam, Vadakku Vandanam, and Kalinkapatti (alias K. Kumarapuram) as 705, 772, and 294, respectively. The last two figures are reasonable, but it seems most unlikely that the population of Terku Vandanam was so low in 1966, especially given the net emigration which occurred subsequently.

Source: Government of India 1972*b*: i. 64–5.

drawn under such circumstances, but the three villages as a whole seem fairly typical in that the ten most numerous castes in the District are all represented. The caste compositions of the individual villages differ greatly, but this too is typical. Nadars and Maravars are rarely found in the same settlement, for example, because of their long-established mutual hostility (Hardgrave 1969: 109–20).

2.2.1 *Caste Hierarchy*

Several authors have used elaborate techniques to quantify or display data on the minutiae of caste ranking. For example, Mayer's account of caste hierarchy in the northern village of Ramkheri is based on the acceptability of *kaccā* (boiled) and *pakkā* (fried, parched) foodstuffs (1960: 33–41; see also Marriott 1959; 1968; Kolenda 1959; Dumont 1980). Beck, working near Coimbatore in Tamil Nadu, presents detailed scalograms and matrices depicting the rules governing exchanges of rice, curd, and betel; removal of eating leaves after meals; the order in which castes are served; entry into other castes' houses; and orders of precedence at temple festivals (1972: 154–81). Only this last context is relevant here, however.

At domestic ceremonies in Terku Vandanam, all castes are fed by all others in no fixed order and without separation into caste-based lines,[9] except that Vannars and Panditars (TV 11, 12) get food to take home, and Paraiyars (TV 2) and Cakkiliyars (VV 4) are fed in the street afterwards. Wedding feasts comprise boiled rice and curried vegetables, the foods normally most restricted in acceptability, yet no limitations apply to most caste-groups. Only Cakkiliyars cannot go into high-caste houses in Terku Vandanam, though they can enter courtyards on business. Paraiyars can enter house verandas, but always sit on the floor even if chairs are available.

People do say that bodily impurity results from contact with Untouchables,[10] but I never heard of anyone actually purifying themselves because of this. Social forms emphasize avoidance of contact. For example, a shopkeeper will toss change into a Harijan customer's hand, or drop it into the shopping basket. Provided this

[9] This seems to have been so for 50 or 60 years at least. Pillai sub-castes (TV 5) did not interdine until more recently.

[10] Untouchability is expressed by the phrase *toḍu kūḍādu*, literally '[one who] should not be touched'.

etiquette is observed, accidental contact is not taken seriously. We often treated Paraiyars for cuts or wounds, and no one ever suggested that we should bathe afterwards. After funerals, by contrast, I was always told to bathe before re-entering the settlement (see 10.2, below).

Sometimes caste is ignored altogether. On General Election day in March 1977 a stall was set up near the Terku Vandanam polling-station and all male voters were offered free coffee afterwards. Harijans were served cheerfully along with everyone else, although some needed coaxing to accept the drink. The coffee was paid for by the AI-ADMK, one of the main parties.

Only once a year, in fact, does caste hierarchy take on more complex form than a threefold division into 'high' castes/Barbers and Washermen/Harijans.[11] That occasion is the annual goddess festival, when villagers cook *poṅkal*[12] in rows, with the higher castes closer to the temple. The Pillais (TV 5), the only vegetarians in Terku Vandanam, actually cook on the raised plinth of the temple itself (Good 1985*a*: 105).

The arrangement at the festival compares well with Table 2.2, which gives the results of an enquiry into caste ranking in Terku Vandanam. The informants were 3 Konars, 2 Maravars, 2 Pillais, and one Velar, Kollan Asari and Panditar (all men). They were not prompted, and some did not include all local castes in their lists. People seemed proud that castes interacted so freely, and my questions about ranking were greeted with amused condescension ('You won't find any of that here'), yet it seems significant that there was such unanimity. Disagreements usually reflected conflicting ritual criteria. Some ranked the Kavundars higher than sixth place, because 'most of them are Priests'. The Velars were placed first by two informants, because they formerly took water only from Brahmans. One person ranked them only tenth, however, for the curious reason that they eat meat, a characteristic shared by all other castes except the Pillais.

In both Vadakku Vandanam and Kalinkapatti three men of different castes were interviewed, and each time there was almost complete agreement. In Vadakku Vandanam the Nadar ranked his own caste first but otherwise agreed with the Vannar and Pallar

[11] This reflects the higher-caste view: the various Harijan groups never regard themselves as a single entity.

[12] *Poṅkal* is rice boiled in a special, ritualized way. Its cooking is a major rite at all temple festivals.

TABLE 2.2. Caste Hierarchy in Terku Vandanam

Caste	2	3	4	5	6	7	8	9	10	11	12	13
1. Pillai	10/0	8/1	10/0	6/2	8/0	10/0	10/0	10/0	8/0	9/0	9/0	9/0
2. Nayakkar		7/2	9/1	5/3	7/1	10/0	10/0	10/0	8/0	9/0	9/0	9/0
3. Maravar			6/2	5/3	7/1	9/0	9/0	9/0	8/0	9/0	9/0	9/0
4. Konar				5/3	5/3	10/0	10/0	10/0	8/0	9/0	9/0	9/0
5. Velar					4/4	8/0	8/0	8/0	7/1	8/0	8/0	8/0
6. Kavundar						8/0	8/0	8/0	8/0	9/0	9/0	9/0
7. Tattan Asari							3/0	3/0	5/1	9/0	9/0	9/0
8. Kollan Asari								3/0	5/1	9/0	9/0	9/0
9. Taccan Asari									5/1	9/0	9/0	9/0
10. Vaniya Cettiyar										9/0	9/0	9/0
11. Vannar											8/1	9/0
12. Panditar												9/0
13. Paraiyar												—

Note: The number of informants ranking the caste in the row higher than that in the column, is given above the oblique line in each case: the number ranking them lower is given below the line. Not all informants ranked every caste in the list.

informants, while in Kalinkapatti the Maravar put his caste first but otherwise agreed with the Cettiyar and Ayotti informants. The details are given in Table 2.3.

TABLE 2.3. Caste Hierarchies in Vadakku Vandanam and Kalinkapatti according to Informants' Statements

Vadakku Vandanam	Kalinkapatti
1. Nayakkar	1. Saiva Cettiyar Vellalar
2. Konar	2. Kottu Reddiyar
3. Maniyakkarar	3. Ayotti Reddiyar
4. Nadar	4. Panditar
5. Maruttuvar	5. Vannar
6. Vannar	6. Pulavar
7. Pallar	
8. Cakkiliyar	

There are obvious deficiencies in method here, but the ranking I was given for Terku Vandanam did correspond to that observed at the main local temple festival, and given the unimportance of detailed ranking in daily life the matter was not pursued further. In fact there will be little further cause to refer to these systematic rankings, because caste differences play a smaller part in regulating interaction than in many other Indian villages. That is, they involve less separation than usual, although of course they remain essential components of many interpersonal relationships.

Hierarchy is expressed in all relationships through the medium of language. A junior person addresses a senior by a relationship term, while the elder reciprocates with the other's personal name. The second person pronoun *nī* is used to a woman, junior, or inferior, and *nīṅkaḷ* to a man, senior, or superior. This requires both parties in a conversation to make mutually acceptable assessments of their respective rankings.

2.3 History and Administration

Until 1800, semi-independent feudal chieftains flourished in Tirunelveli (Kadhirvel 1977: 30; Ludden 1985). These Poligars (*pāḷaiyakkāraṉ*), mainly Nayakkars or Maravars, were absolute rulers in their territories, though they were notionally liable to pay tribute to the sovereign power (Rajayyan 1974: 23–7). Several Poligars rebelled against the British in 1799, led by Kattabomma Nayakkar, the Poligar of Pancalankuricci, within whose domain the three villages then lay. After defeating him, the British gave his lands to their ally, the Poligar of Ettaiyapuram (Rajayyan 1974: 101). At the same time, the Poligars' military and judicial rights were removed, converting them into Zamindars (1974: 112–13).

Ettaiyapuram estate then comprised 185 villages, of which 79 came from Pancalankuricci (Pate 1917: 374).[13] It grew to become the largest Zamindari estate in Tirunelveli District, and by 1917 comprised 422 villages with a total area of 647 square miles. The estate was taken over by government in 1954. The Zamindar was a Nayakkar, but within Terku Vandanam the main landholders at that time were Pillais. Many of these have now left, however, and there have been increases in the number and proportion of Maravars living in the settlement.

In 1660 the Ettaiyapuram Poligar allowed the Nadars of Kamanayakkanpatti to build a Catholic church (Caldwell 1881: 236). The Vadakku Vandanam Nadars may also have been converted then: they are close relatives, and Vadakku Vandanam was certainly part of that parish in the earliest church records, though it is independent now. The Vadakku Vandanam church school opened in 1905. It is now government-funded and takes children from all three villages for Grades 6–8.

Under Panchayati Raj (village self-government) villages now elect councils (panchayats) with statutory Harijan and woman members. Every panchayat has a President, formerly chosen by panchayat members from among themselves but now elected directly (Saraswathi 1973: 98). Panchayats hold office for five years, though elections were two years overdue by 1977. They have some jurisdiction over roads, drainage, drinking-water, electricity, social services, and hospitals. Funding comes from house, shop, and vehicle taxes, and a share of the land tax. Panchayat boundaries do not always correspond to village boundaries: thus, Terku Vandanam and Kalinkapatti are physically separate but have a joint panchayat.

[13] *Special Tribunal Appeals Nos. 35–122*, in Madras High Court 1958.

The Terku Vandanam members of the joint panchayat are: (1) Madasami Tevar, the President; (2) Lakshmanaperumal Tevar, who is the Kalinkapatti Talaiyari (see below) but resident in and elected from Terku Vandanam; (3) Muttuccami Tevar, his yB; (4) Sanmuka Konar; (5) Suppaiya Pillai; (6) Raman, the Harijan member; (7) Karuppayammal, a Konar, the statutory woman member. The two Kalinkapatti members are (8) Sanmuka Reddiyar, and (9) Naku Reddiyar. The Vadakku Vandanam panchayat comprises: (1) Savarimuttu Nadar, the President; (2) Rajameriyammal, his wife; (3) Innacimuttu Nadar, his BWF; (4) Yakappa Nadar; (5) Yesukani Nadar; (6) Suppa Nayakkar; (7) Muttu Karuppan, a Pallar, the Harijan member.

Savarimuttu Nadar has been President ever since the Vadakku Vandanam Panchayat was constituted in 1960. The Terku Vandanam-Kalinkapatti Panchayat has had two previous Presidents. Ponnu Reddiyar died in office, then Nallaiya Konar resigned when his business in Tirucchi became too time-consuming.[14] As far as I know, there were no opposing candidates in any of these elections: there were certainly none at the election in 1971.

Whereas panchayats are a creation of the modern bureaucratic state, other government officials in the village are hereditary administrators formerly responsible to the Zamindar (Rajayyan 1974: 24). The *muṉsīp* has minor judicial powers and collects the land revenue, the *karṇam* keeps the land register, and the *talaiyāri* assists the Munsip. Nowadays they all get government salaries,[15] but the distinction between them and the President is clearly visible in ritual contexts. They have well-defined rights and duties, whereas the President is merely an honoured guest with no recognized privileges.

The Munsips of Terku Vandanam and Kalinkapatti are Perumalsami Nayakkar and Durairaj Reddiyar (a Kottu Reddiyar), respectively. Srinivasaperumal Nayakkar, who lives in Koppampatti, is both Munsip and Karnam of Vadakku Vandanam. The Karnam of Terku Vandanam and Kalinkapatti is Kumarasamiya Pillai. The Talaiyaris are Muttaiya Tevar (TV), Velccami Maniyakkarar (VV), and Lakshmanaperumal Tevar (KP).

[14] Presidents must chair panchayat meetings every two months (Saraswathi 1973: 12). Karuppayi, the present woman member, is Nallaiya's mother.

[15] Since my first fieldwork, the Tamil Nadu Government has abolished these positions, replacing them by appointed Village Officers. These are often displaced hereditary officials, but do not serve in their native villages.

In this locality, most Karnams are Pillais. Talaiyaris are usually Maravars, a relic of the days when they imposed themselves on villages as paid watchmen (*kāvalkārar*), to guard against the depredations of 'watchmen' from elsewhere (Rajayyan 1974: 30–1). Finally, the Munsips of villages within Nayakkar zamindaris were usually Nayakkars or Reddiyars. The holding of office by such people does not, therefore, necessarily indicate that their caste holds a position of local dominance (cf. 3.3, below).

2.4 Religion

All non-Nadars in the three villages are Hindus. Their Saivite affiliations are more apparent in practices like dabbing holy ash (*vipūti*) and kumkum (*kuṅkumam*, a red cosmetic) on worshippers' foreheads, than in any distinctive points of doctrine. Higher castes tend to be vegetarian, as in the case of local Pillais (TV 5) and Saiva Cettiyars (KP 3). All others, even the priests of vegetarian deities,[16] eat chicken and mutton. Harijans also eat pork—and beef too according to high-caste stereotype. The distinction between meat-eaters and vegetarians appears mostly at festivals when animals are sacrificed, for meat is rarely available otherwise.

The absence of local Brahmans—those in Kalinkapatti are newcomers—is significant, because although non-Brahman villages are in the majority locally (Pate 1917: 373) they have received disproportionately little ethnographic attention. There is a corresponding dearth of temples to 'Brahmanic' gods. The major deities in most villages are the village goddess (*amma<u>n</u>*) and the god Aiyanar (Dumont 1959). Every village also has temples to Pillaiyar (or Vinayakar), the elephant-headed elder son of Siva, and various caste and family deity (*kuladeyvam*) shrines. The main local temples, excluding purely family-deity shrines, are as follows.[17]

In Terku Vandanam, the main temple is that of the goddess Vadakkuvasal Celviyamman, 'Lady of the North Gate' (Dumont 1957*b*: 385). There is daily worship, and the main festival is on the

[16] The question of vegetarian deities is complex. For example, the village goddess of Terku Vandanam eats only vegetarian food inside her temple but emerges to eat meat offerings in the entrance-hall (Good 1985*a*: 135).

[17] The duties and rewards of the various Priests (*pūsāri*) are discussed later (see 4.3.3).

third Tuesday in Pankuni (March–April). The Terku Vandanam Pillaiyar temple lies near the ritual boundary of the village, a spot on the bund of Coconut Tank (see 3.1, below) marked by a small stone (*ellaikkal*). Pillaiyar is worshipped on festival days and before auspicious events like weddings. The Aiyanar temple lies on the road to Kalinkapatti, below Big Tank. The festival is at Pankuni *uttiram* (full-moon in March–April). The temple serves Kalinkapatti as well as Terku Vandanam, and is the family deity shrine of people from elsewhere, too. St Xavier's Catholic church in Vadakku Vandanam is an Indo-Portuguese style building in the Nadar quarter. The main festival is in December. In Kalinkapatti, the temple of the goddess Kaliyamman lies just north of the settlement. The festival is on the third Tuesday in Cittirai (April–May). The Pillaiyar temple faces west along the main street.

Religion is an aspect of all social activity, including agriculture and economics in general. Locally, the ritual and prestational aspects of religion far outweigh the theological and cosmological in importance. The religion of these villages is thus a primarily sociological one, in which the rights and obligations of functionaries are emphasized more than the theological implications of their functions.

3
Caste, Agriculture, and the Local Economy

3.1 Agriculture

There are no permanent rivers in Kovilpatti Taluk, so agriculture depends directly on rainfall. This averages 765 mm. per annum, most of which falls during the north-east monsoon between October and December in heavy, localized downpours. These may cause serious erosion because of the low permeability of the black cotton soil (*karisal*), but can fill irrigation tanks (*kuḷam*) overnight. Rainfall is unreliable, however, and there had been three years of drought before my arrival.

Kalinkapatti has no access to tank water, but Terku Vandanam has sole rights over the shallow Big Tank (*periyākuḷam*), and shares water from Coconut Tank (*teṉnaṅkuḷam*) with Vadakku Vandanam. Both tanks form part of an extensive system of watercourses, which receive excess water from tanks upstream and pass their own over-spill down towards the coast. From the tanks, water passes through sluice-gates into the irrigation channels. The main ones are government-owned and cannot be tampered with, but side-channels are opened and closed as required. I saw no disputes on this account, but in 1976–7 there was enough water for everyone. Under adverse weather conditions it is a great advantage to have land close to the tank, or the power to assert one's claims.

Irrigation wells (*kiṇāṟu*) allow cultivation throughout the year. Formerly a labourer had to be constantly employed, using bullocks to raise a bucket with a leather tube in the bottom (*kavalai*), but increasingly water is raised by electric pump-sets. Wells become an economic proposition[1] for farms of 10 acres upwards (Spate and

[1] It is, however, doubtful whether it is meaningful to reduce income and expenditure to cash equivalences, in a basically subsistence economy (Djurfeldt and Lindberg 1975: 142–6).

Learmonth 1967: 233), and have multiplied over the past twenty years thanks to government loans.

Tank-irrigated land is called 'wet' (*nañcai*), in contrast to rain-watered or 'dry' (*puñcai*) land. Land taxes on wet land are about five times greater than for dry land. Land irrigated by wells is called 'garden' (*tōṭṭam*). It is taxed at the dry rate, plus a levy on the crops grown. Wasteland (*puṛampōkku*) is untaxed, but if villagers own palmyrah or tamarind trees on such land, they pay an annual levy. Few local people own trees, though, and the wasteland is used mainly as common pasture.

The most prized cereal crop is paddy, which is grown on wet or garden land during the monsoon.[2] The fields are ploughed and sown in Purattasi (September–October) and harvested in Tai (January–February). If monsoon rainfall is reasonable, another crop can be grown in the hot season, taking advantage of the erratic showers during the south-west monsoon between June and September. Cotton is a favourite choice because it is a cash crop which ensures a small but steady daily income over several months. It is planted straight after the paddy harvest and yields cotton for two to three months between May and July.

Farmers with wells can operate a three-crop system, growing paddy; *cōlam* (jowar) or *kampu* (bajra); and *kēppai* (ragi). The last three are millets, which are eaten as cereals but seen as inferior to rice. Cash crops like onions, chillies, plantains, or groundnuts can be substituted at the second or third stage. Sugar-cane takes eighteen months to mature, and only large landowners can afford to tie up land for that long. On dry land, rice cannot be grown even during the monsoon. The main crop is kampu or colam, usually inter-sown with pulses of various kinds. Cotton may be grown, either in the hot season as on wet land (though with less success), or as the major crop during the wet season.

[2] One index of its importance is the complex vocabulary applied to it: the plant itself is *nel*, the grain *paḍi*, and the husked grain *arisi*. If parboiled it is *puluṅku*, and when boiled it is *sōṛu* (*poṅkal* at a temple).

3.1.1 *The Organization of Agricultural Labour*

A farmer's nuclear family provides a pool of unpaid labour,[3] but some tasks are always done by larger groups. These include women's jobs like weeding and transplanting; some done by men, like hoeing (ploughing is an individual male activity);[4] and others which are not gender-specific, like harvesting. Some members of these *ad hoc* groups will be working on a relative's land, but most will be paid. Each day fresh groups form, and those who today are working unpaid as family members will tomorrow be paid labourers. Many holdings are too small for subsistence and few are large enough to need full-time attention, so the surplus labour of most families comes on to the market. Year-round work is not available to all, however.[5]

There is thus a continuum stretching from the rich farmer whose womenfolk do no farm work and who supervises work on his lands rather than doing it himself, to the landless labourer whose entire subsistence derives from working for others. Most people occupy an intermediate position, however, so the distinction between 'landowners' and 'labourers' is by-and-large temporary and reversible.

A daily labourer (*kūli*) gets payment in kind as the basic standard.[6] The normal rates are 2 *paḍis* (3 *pakkās* = about 3 kg.) of millet for men, and 1 *paḍi* for women. In November 1976 men were getting Rs 3 and women Rs 1.25 if paid in cash, reflecting the market price of Rs 130 for 100 kg. of millet. Before the State of Emergency then in force, the market price had been Rs 200 and wages had been correspondingly higher too, though still below the official minima of Rs 6 for men and Rs 4 for women.[7] The ending of the black market had thus depressed the cash incomes of both farmers and labourers.

Some tasks are paid at higher rates. A ploughman with his own team gets Rs 10 for an 8-hour day. Men raising well-water using a

[3] This work is unpaid in the sense that no actual wages are given in return: in a subsistence economy, however, subsistence is itself a form of payment (cf. n. 1, above).

[4] In order to emphasize labour scarcity, people in Vadakku Vandanam said that 'even ploughing is done by women'. This was not literally the case.

[5] Conversely, some farmers have occupations which keep them away from the land for part of the time.

[6] This does not apply to Kalinkapatti, where cash crops (cotton) are more common: the established wages there are Rs 3 for men and Rs 1.50 for women, in cash.

[7] Most villagers were unaware of the existence of minimum wages, and few could, in any case, have afforded to pay them.

kavalai get Rs 12 for a 12-hour day if using their own bullocks. Women are paid more for transplanting—Rs 2 plus midday coffee—because of the demand for labour at that time. Labour demand and longer hours also increase rates at harvest time. Men get 4 *paḍis* of paddy, or 3 *paḍis* of husked rice, for 12 hours' harvesting and threshing. Cakkiliyars specialize in winnowing, and are paid 3–4 *paḍis* for a mere 5-hour day.

Sometimes labour is recruited and organized by means of a contract group. Under this system a piece of work is done for a previously agreed fee, irrespective of the time taken. The contract may be negotiated by the whole group of workers or by an individual who undertakes to recruit the labour-force, organize the work, and make the individual payments.

There are no hereditary relationships between families of farmers and labourers. Permanent labourers (*paḍaiyāl*) are often employed over many years, but the link can be severed if either party wishes. Most of the 47 local workers employed in this way are Harijans. They get 1/7 of the yield of dry crops such as millets, but for work on paddy or cash crops the normal wage is 15 *paḍis* of millet per week, or 2 *paḍis* (Rs 3) per day. If paid on a daily rate they get no pay on days when they are not needed, but are then free to work for others.

Some villagers hire out their goats and sheep to manure the fields. This is a major source of income for Konars. They charge 1 *paḍi* of paddy per 20 goats per night, which they collect at harvest time. Herds are usually looked after by the owner's sons or other relatives, so no payment is involved.

Dyadic exchanges between farmers who employ and labourers or groups who are employed are not the only ways of organizing and rewarding labour. Another set of exchanges involves specialists who are not employees but occupy, by virtue of caste and/or inheritance, social niches with well-recognized rights and obligations. Their rewards, which often derive partly from the community as a whole, are dealt with in the next chapter.

3.2 The Distribution of Property

Of the 367 workers in Terku Vandanam, 279 (76 per cent) are classed by the 1971 census as 'cultivators' or 'agricultural labourers'; 42 (11 per cent) keep livestock; and 22 (6 per cent) work in 'household industry', including the Carpenters and Blacksmiths who service the farmers. The 173 workers in Kalinkapatti include 151 (87 per cent) 'cultivators' and 'labourers', and 5 (3 per cent) pastoralists. Vadakku Vandanam's 286 workers include 202 (71 per cent) agriculturalists, 18 (6 per cent) pastoralists, and 4 (1 per cent) workers in household industry (Government of India 1972*b*: i. 64–7). Agriculture is thus so clearly the principal economic activity of most villagers—directly or indirectly—that their relative economic standings may largely be judged by comparing their holdings of land and livestock.

3.2.1 *Land*

The local unit for measuring wet land is the *marakkāl*, which represents one-twelfth of an acre. It is also a measure by volume of grain, i.e., it takes 12 *marakkāls* of paddy to hand-sow one acre. The dry land unit is the *kurukkam* ('diameter'), equivalent to about 97 cents.

Table 3.1 lists the land holdings of each caste-group. It must be remembered that Asaris (TV 6, 8, 13),[8] Vannars (TV 11 and 14, VV 6, KP 6), Barbers (TV 12, VV 9, KP 9), Velars (TV 9), and Cakkiliyars (VV 4), have potential sources of income other than cultivation (see 4.3, below). Urban migration has distorted the picture in other cases: for example, several Cettiyar families with little land had left Terku Vandanam during the drought.

The averages in Table 3.1 are greatly influenced by a few wealthy families. For example, two Konar households own almost 70 acres of land between them, whereas most Konars are below average for Terku Vandanam—not surprisingly, as their main occupation is pastoralism. In Vadakku Vandanam, four Nadar brothers own 158.5 acres of land. The averages for other Nadars are 3.9 acres per household and 0.9 per person. One extended Nayakkar family in Terku Vandanam, totalling 29 people in three households, owns 232 acres (40 wet, 142 dry, and 50 garden). The remaining Nayakkar households have only 7.0 acres per household and 1.7 per person, though this still leaves them well above average.

Most Harijan households own some land, although even the

[8] The Asaris in Kalinkapatti are farmers who have abandoned their hereditary calling.

biggest Paraiyar landowner, who bought 3.5 acres with the proceeds of work on a Kerala plantation, is below average for Terku Vandanam as a whole. The Pallars have below-average holdings too, but their economic position is better, as shown by their livestock holdings (Table 3.2) and the quality of their housing. Even the Cakkiliyars, the lowest-ranking local group, own more land on average than the Paraiyars.

Harijans would not have owned land in the distant past, yet most of the present generation inherited at least part of their holding. The Paraiyars are again the odd ones out: only 4 acres (24 per cent) was inherited. For the populations as a whole, 'acquired land' totals 155.45 acres (16.6 per cent), 138.65 acres (21 per cent), and 289.4 acres (45 per cent), for Terku Vandanam, Vadakku Vandanam, and Kalinkapatti respectively. Altogether, 113 local households acquired land in the present generation, though most also inherited land.

Land prices are low. During the 1976 drought, wet land in Terku Vandanam fetched only Rs 1,250 per acre, and dry land Rs 100–50.[9] After the good harvest in March 1977, wet land rose to Rs 5,000 per acre. As long ago as 1966, even the worst land in rural Coimbatore fetched Rs 4,000 per acre (Beck 1972: 286).

Landownership data in South Asia are notoriously unreliable (Djurfeldt and Lindberg 1975: 82), so it is desirable to have an external check on the figures in Table 3.1. For this purpose it is necessary to consider the three villages as a whole, because many Terku Vandanam residents own land in Vadakku Vandanam or Kalinkapatti, and vice versa. It therefore appears under one village in Table 3.1 and another in the 1971 census. Outsiders own about 26 acres in Terku Vandanam and 95 acres in Vadakku Vandanam (including the Munsip-Karnam's 45 acres). Adding these figures to those in Table 3.1, the total declared area of cultivable land in the three villages comes to 2,354 acres. The 1971 census gives the cultivated areas as 1,099 acres in Terku Vandanam, 459 in Vadakku Vandanam and 1,097 in Kalinkapatti: 2,655 acres in all (Government of India 1972*a*: 28–9).[10] In other words, 89 per cent of local cultivable land is accounted for in my census.[11]

[9] The figures are based on general statements by informants. I have no data on particular transactions.

[10] The Census data are in hectares (1 hectare = 2.47 acres).

[11] Land elsewhere owned by local residents has been excluded: there were only a few acres of this.

TABLE 3.1. Land Holdings in the Three Villages

Caste[a]	Land (acres)	Acres/ household	Acres/ person	Total (%)	Landless households[b]
Terku Vandanam					
1. Maravar	273.11	5.1	1.0	29.2	7
2. Paraiyar	16.40	0.6	0.1	1.8	12
3. Nayakkar	343.24	18.1	3.7	36.7	3[c]
4. Konar	126.78	6.7	1.4	13.6	1
5. Pillaimar	77.55	4.8	0.9	8.3	3
6. Taccan Asari	17.20	2.9	0.6	1.8	—
7. Cettiyar	54.25	10.9	1.9	5.8	—
8. Kollan Asari	10.30	2.6	0.4	1.1	—
9. Velar	4.50	1.1	0.3	0.5	—
10. Kavundar	11.00	5.5	0.9	1.2	—
11. Vannar	—	—	—	—	2
12. Panditar	—	—	—	—	1
13. Tattan Asari	—	—	—	—	1
14. Tinda Vannar	—	—	—	—	1
Village Totals	934.33	5.8	1.1	100.0	31
Vadakku Vandanam					
1. Nadar	493.35	5.4	1.3	74.5	10
2. Pallar	69.35	2.5	0.4	10.5	8
3. Kampalattar	48.60	4.4	0.8	7.3	2

4. Cakkiliyar	15.35	1.2	0.3	2.3	5
5. Konar	11.65	1.7	0.4	1.8	3
6. Vannar	—	—	—	—	1
7. Maniyakkarar	6.00	3.0	0.4	0.9	—
8. Paraiyar	—	—	—	—	1
9. Maruttuvar	8.20	8.2	2.0	1.2	—
10. Headmaster	—	—	—	—	1
11. Catholic Church	10.00	—	—	1.5	—
Village Totals	662.50	4.2	0.9	100.0	31
Kalinkapatti					
1. Ayotti Reddiyar	390.50	13.5	2.4	61.4	1
2. Maravar	26.05	2.2	0.5	4.1	2
3. Saiva Cettiyar	89.00	17.8	3.3	14.0	—
4. Kottu Reddiyar	104.90	26.2	6.2	16.5	—
5. Pulavar	12.75	2.5	0.9	2.0	1
6. Vannar	9.00	4.5	0.8	1.4	—
7. Telunku Asari	4.00	4.0	0.7	0.6	—
8. Schoolteacher	—	—	—	—	1[c]
9. Panditar	—	—	—	—	1
10. Brahman	—	—	—	—	1
11. Govt. Seed Agent	—	—	—	—	1[c]
Village Totals	636.20	10.4	2.1	100.0	8

[a] Full caste-names are given in Table 2.1.
[b] 'Landless households' exclude those headed by married sons whose fathers have yet to partition the property. Widows living separately from landowning sons have also been excluded.
[c] This total includes 1 household with land elsewhere.

TABLE 3.2. Livestock Holdings

Caste[a]	Bullocks	Cows	Buffalo	Sheep and Goats	Chickens	Others
Terku Vandanam						
1. Maravar	46	24	14	166	206	2[b]
2. Paraiyar	2	5	7	27	23	1[b]
3. Nayakkar	17	10	9	51	93	—
4. Konar	19	13	13	385	94	—
5. Pillaimar	2	6	8	21	25	—
6. Taccan Asari	1	—	—	—	6	—
7. Cettiyar	4	—	1	30	9	—
8. Kollan Asari	1	—	—	1	5	—
9. Velar	2	—	1	3	3	—
10. Kavundar	3	—	—	55	12	—
11. Vannar	—	—	—	—	3	4[c]
12. Panditar	—	—	3	2	10	—
Village Totals	97	58	56	741	489	—

Vadakku Vandanam						
1. Nadar	101	31	30	284	235	1[b]
2. Pallar	18	1	7	125	49	8[b]
3. Kampalattar	10	14	4	142	25	—
4. Cakkiliyar	—	—	5	—	11	8[b]
5. Konar	2	—	—	155	22	—
6. Vannar	—	—	—	—	—	3[c]
11. Catholic Church	—	—	—	—	6	8[d]
Village Totals	131	46	46	706	348	—
Kalinkapatti						
1. Ayotti	22	3	5	74	110	—
2. Maravar	3	1	2	22	10	—
3. Saiva Cettiyar	2	1	1	6	—	—
4. Kottu Rediyar	2	5	5	—	20	—
6. Vannar	1	—	—	2	11	2[c]
7. Telunku Asari	—	—	—	1	—	—
Village Totals	30	10	13	105	151	—

[a] Only castes with animals are listed.
[b] Pigs.
[c] Donkeys.
[d] Pigeons.

The average Kalinkapatti household has twice as much land as its Terku and Vadakku Vandanam counterparts, but this gives a misleading impression of relative wealth. Kalinkapatti has much lower proportions of wet and garden land, and even in 1976–7, when the monsoon was good and farmers in Terku Vandanam and Vadakku Vandanam raised bumper paddy crops, some Kalinkapatti fields failed to produce even a single 'dry' crop of millet.

Tenancies are few, and all tenants are also landowners in their own right. All non-cultivating landlords live elsewhere, and only one has local kin. The area of land involved is small, and there is only one long-standing arrangement. All this underlines the unimportance of tenancy to the economy.

3.2.2 *Livestock*

Table 3.2 shows the animals owned by each caste-group. Bullocks are the draught animals: only one farmer used buffaloes for ploughing. Konar and Nayakkar holdings of bullock and buffalo are inflated by the wealthy households discussed above. Konars own disproportionate numbers of sheep and goats. Pillais are not supposed to plough (Thurston and Rangachari 1909: vii. 370–1), and although the ban is not universally observed, several well-off Pillais own neither plough nor bullock.

Again, the low holdings in Kalinkapatti reflect the dryness of its land. Wet land is ploughed many times in the crucial weeks before the monsoon. Dry land needs little ploughing and this is not concentrated into a short period, so there is less need for a farmer to keep his own team of oxen. The lack of grazing land in Kalinkapatti, and the absence of pastoral castes, explain the small herds of cows, buffaloes, and goats.

3.2.3 *Trade and Commerce*

The shops in Terku Vandanam are owned by Pillais (2), a Maravar, and a Nayakkar. Even the largest, Cellaiya Pillai's, has a daily turnover of only Rs 50, two-thirds of which involves credit or payment-in-kind. The shops serve customers from all castes, including Harijans. The Vadakku Vandanam shops belong to Nadars (4), a

Maniyakkarar, and a Nayakkar. Antonimuttu Nadar, yB of the village President, has by far the largest. The three Kalinkapatti shops, all very small, have Brahman, Cettiyar, and Ayotti Reddiyar owners.

Anyone may trade from time to time, given the chance. The shopkeepers Cellaiya Pillai (TV) and Muniyasami Tevar (TV) buy up the local rice crop. Kurusami Konar (TV) trades in charcoal. Rattinasami Reddiyar (KP) deals in cash crops like chillies, though his business is mainly in Tuticorin. Several Nadars have business interests, including the shopkeeper brothers Jesukani and Antonimuttu. Nearly all these people are also farmers, sometimes on a big scale. Their customers, and the suppliers of their commodities, are also mainly local farmers. This again illustrates the prime importance of the land.

3.3 The Dominant Caste

The concept of "dominant caste" was introduced by Srinivas to explain how village unity is maintained in the face of the divisiveness and separation of caste. In the words of his classic definition, a caste

> may be said to be 'dominant' when it preponderates numerically over the other castes, and when it also wields preponderant economic and political power. A large and powerful caste group can more easily be dominant if its position in the local caste hierarchy is not too low. (1955: 18)

Although numerical size and politico-economic power were necessary conditions for dominance, his main diagnostic feature was judicial. The elders of the caste court of the dominant caste administered justice for the entire village population, and thereby represented 'the vertical unity of the village against the separatism of caste' (Srinivas 1955: 34).

Dumont and Pocock criticized the focus on the village in Indian anthropology, yet, paradoxically, they granted even more importance to the "dominant caste" than Srinivas had. They argued that 'India, sociologically speaking, is not made up of villages' (Dumont and Pocock 1957: 25). People's 'loyalty' (Srinivas 1955: 35) was not to the village as such, but to its dominant caste. So-called inter-village disputes were really disputes between the dominant castes of the villages concerned, supported by their dependants. Within the village, the political units were multi-caste factions led by dominant-caste patrons.[12] Moreover, the "jajmani system" (cf. 4.5, below) was focused on the dominant caste 'and only after them do the village servants serve others' (Srinivas, 1955: 31). Finally, they followed Hocart (1968: 8) in correlating the position of the dominant caste with that of the king in the Indian royal court. Srinivas had argued (1959) that a dominant caste-group needed to be big enough to defend its position by force, but Dumont pointed out that a small but wealthy landowning group would not lack supporters if it came to a fight. Moreover, the power of a dominant caste could only be relative. The rights of government were and are pre-eminent (Dumont 1980: 161–2).

Beck takes account of such points when she defines the "dominant caste" as 'the sub-caste community that controls a majority of the local labor force in a given area' (1972: 15). She considers all types of primary resource—not just land, but also animals, minerals, and transportation—and emphasizes *de facto* control rather than mere ownership. When large landholdings are semi-permanently leased out, for example, it is the tenants who control access to them. Dominance cannot therefore be equated with control of land: the latter is simply a useful index of the former. Moreover, it cannot be tied to the village level: a locally dominant group may itself be dominated in some wider context (Beck 1972: 15). This approach allows the notion of "dominance" to apply to any empirical social or territorial entity.[13] It does not stand or fall with the notion of village solidarity, as Srinivas would have it, nor necessarily replace the village sociologically, as Dumont and Pocock suggest. It becomes a *type of relationship*, not the attribute of a particular group.

Beck's account of Coimbatore social structure, at all territorial levels, is validated by her empirical demonstration that a dominant caste *does* exist locally (1972: 269). But there cannot be a dominant caste everywhere, if only on demographic grounds. What, if anything, replaces it as the unifying agency in such cases?

[12] As Srinivas later pointed out, Dumont seems to assume that equality is a prerequisite for community formation, and ignores the possibility that unequal groups might be bound together by common *interests* (1987: 40).

[13] Mayer (1958) made a similar point: in his case the relevant levels were the village, region, and kingdom.

3.4 The Present Case

There is no village-wide judicial institution in any of these three villages at present, nor any memory of one existing in the past. No caste, therefore, fulfils Srinivas's diagnostic criterion of dominance. There are, however, caste groups in every village which would satisfy any reasonable *numerical* requirements for dominance. As for economic power, the Maravars and Nayakkars in Terku Vandanam both control large proportions of land, but only the Nayakkars are also above-average in land per household and per individual. In Vadakku Vandanam the Nadars control so much land that no other caste could possibly be dominant using any of the cited definitions. In Kalinkapatti the Ayotti Reddiyars control by far the most land, and are clearly the group with greatest economic power. With the possible exception of the Nadars in Vadakku Vandanam, no caste-group exerts a preponderant role in trade or commerce.

Srinivas felt that a dominant caste could not be too low in the caste hierarchy (1955: 18). Of the various candidates, only the Nadars would have difficulty satisfying this condition. Though not Harijans, they were once regarded as low. The Terku Vandanam Barber and Washermen said they would not work for Nadars, and this was echoed by the Vadakku Vandanam Washerman.[14] However, the present status of the Nadar community is much higher than this implies.

At village level, formal political power now rests with the panchayat, and executive authority with the hereditary officers (see 2.3 above). Panchayat constituencies do not always correspond to village boundaries, however, and as we saw earlier, Terku Vandanam and Kalinkapatti have a joint panchayat.

Taking all these factors into account the Nayakkars seem to come closest to dominating economically in Terku Vandanam. They also provide the Munsip. Yet they are not represented on the panchayat, and are characterized more by withdrawal from village life rather than by involvement in it. They are less assiduous than others about attending village weddings, and inviting fellow villagers to their own ceremonies. This is not the behaviour expected of dominant groups or patrons. The Maravars are only average economically, but their

[14] The latter *did* actually serve Nadar, but the significant point is that he felt constrained to deny this.

numerical strength gives them three members on the panchayat, including the President. His education to B.Sc. level no doubt helped in his selection, and although I heard whispers of anti-Maravar sentiment among certain other castes, he was elected unopposed.

Ayotti Reddiyars form over half the Kalinkapatti population and own more than their fair share of land. This land is very evenly distributed, however, and no single family or group holds a disproportionate amount. Both Kalinkapatti's panchayat members are Ayottis, but they cannot exert political control because they form a minority on the panchayat as a whole. Their position is further weakened by the fact that the panchayat also includes the Kalinkapatti Talaiyari and his brother, who are relatives of the Kalinkapatti Maravars. Clearly, local economic and numerical strength may count for nothing when the formal political and administrative structure is imposed from without. The fact that the hereditary posts of Karnam and Talaiyari are held by non-residents confirms that Kalinkapatti was subordinate to Terku Vandanam even in the past.

In Vadakku Vandanam only the Nadars come under serious consideration, although as Christians they are cut off from the prestations which express intra-village relationships at temple festivals. Moreover, they owe their position to one family, which provides three panchayat members, owns the two largest shops, and until recently operated a match factory, the only local industry.

Overall, then, wealth and power accrue to individuals rather than to caste-groups as a whole. Both the Nadars and Nayakkars contain a single rich family. Other wealthy and influential persons are the Kottu immigrants in Kalinkapatti, and Nallaiya Konar, who would doubtless be even more prominent if he were permanently resident locally. The fact that he was elected President of Terku Vandanam when his caste-group has none of the prerequisites for dominance, shows that conventional ideas on dominant castes have little relevance here. This does not imply rejection of the notion of "dominance" *per se*, for both Beck and Srinivas have shown how useful such an approach can be. The existence of a "dominant caste" must first be demonstrated empirically, however. As this is not possible here, we must approach the study of these villages in some other way.

4
Inter-Caste Prestations

Analyses in terms of dominance tend to portray inter-caste relationships as focused upon the dominant caste, to whom the service castes are said to owe prime allegiance (Dumont and Pocock 1957: 31; Dumont 1980: 102). In the present case, however, no single relationship takes precedence in that way. What is more, the roles of specialists are often not confined to a single village, but encompass two or even all three. This chapter examines the prestations exchanged by members of different castes, both in connection with their normal caste-based occupations and at life-crisis rituals. These turn out to be conceptualized in the same way as prestational exchanges *within* castes (see 4.2, below). For this and other reasons I shall criticize conventional 'jajmani system' analyses, and argue that the relevant social unit locally is a micro-region composed of all three villages.

4.1 On the Threshing Floor

Most villages have communal threshing areas where the rice crop is threshed and winnowed. Before the grain is measured into sacks for storage or sale, the village servants and artisans who serve the farmer's family receive their respective shares. These usually contain two components, *varattusampaḷam* ('income-salary') and *māṉiyam* ('honour, respect').[1]

Example A
Palasuppiramaniya Konar gives 8 *marakkāls* of paddy each to the Blacksmith and Carpenter as *varattusampaḷam*, with a further 2 *pakkās* each as *māṉiyam* should they wish to collect it (they may not, for the extra amount is small); 2 *pakkās* each as *māṉiyam* to the Oduvar and Velar Priests; the same to Sanmukam the Barber, and

[1] Similar distinctions are mentioned by Benson (1977: 243) for Andhra Pradesh, and by Raheja (1988; 1989: 89) for Uttar Pradesh.

Candiran the Washerman;[2] and 4 *pakkās* to the Pallar channel-controller, Veyilmuttu.

Example B

Kurusami Konar gives nothing to the two Asaris, and only 1 *pakkā* to the second Washerman; otherwise things are as for Example A.

Example C

Cellaiya Tevar gives 4 *marakkāls* plus 2 *pakkās* to the Blacksmith and Carpenter, as *varattusampaḷam* and *māṉiyam*, respectively; 3 *pakkās* to the Velar; nothing to the Oduvar (unexplained); 3 *pakkās* to Candiran, his Washerman; 2 to the Barber; and 6 to the channel-controller.

Example D

Muttuccami and Sanmuka Tevar (brothers) each give 4 *marakkāls* plus 2 *pakkās* to both Blacksmith and Carpenter; 2 *pakkās* to each Priest, and to Candiran; 1 *pakkā* each to Raj, the other Washerman (who serves neither house), and the Barber; and 4 *pakkās* to the channel-controller.

The general pattern is clear. The grain received by most recipients is entirely *māṉiyam*, and their *varattusampaḷam* is given separately. However, the Carpenter and Blacksmith get their *varattusampaḷam* and *māṉiyam* payments both together at this time. The rate for the former is 4 *marakkāls* of paddy for each pair of bullocks owned: thus, household A has two pairs of animals, C has one pair, and B has none. This is because farmers normally have one plough and one cart for each pair of bullocks owned, and the prestation covers maintenance work on these.

Payments to specialists are regulated by convention and are independent of the amount of work actually done, within the limits of the specialist's normal duties. When these experts perform extra work, however, they are recompensed on a piece-work basis. Convention determines what is normal work and what is extra. If a farmer wants a new cart or plough, for example, he pays the Carpenter for this.

[2] He would give 2 *pakkās* to the other Washerman, Raj, too if the latter claimed it. The *marakkāl* and *pakkā* are both measures of volume, roughly equivalent to 4.5 kg. and 1 kg., respectively.

4.2 Gifts and Obligations

The distinction between *varattusampaḷam* and *māṉiyam* was explained to me in terms of a more general set of concepts. The *varattusampaḷam* is a kind of *sampaḷam* ('salary') given, as one man said in English, 'for labour'. As for the *māṉiyam*, it is said to be the *sāṣtiram* of the donor to make it and of the specialist to receive it. The dictionary meanings of *sāṣtiram* include 'science' and 'specialized knowledge', and this prestation recognizes the special qualities by virtue of which an expert is able to fulfil his or her function.

These qualities are inherited by members of a caste, whether or not they actually learn the technical skills of their hereditary calling. David (1977*b*: 183) says that the 'propensity to perform the caste occupation is held to be substantially transmitted from parents to children . . . caste occupations . . . relate directly to the caste's shared natural substance.' Reiniche makes a similar point when she contrasts purely technical 'savoir-faire' with the 'Savoir' characteristic of the caste concerned (1977: 89). Both formulations can be glossed by saying that anyone can *do* carpentry, but only persons of Taccan Asari caste can *be* Carpenters.

Not surprisingly then, there are two words for 'occupation': *vēlai* means 'job' in the normal sense of paid employment;[3] and *toḻil* refers to one's inherited caste specialization, which one may or may not follow in practice. One's *vēlai* is a contingent matter. It is something one 'knows how' to do. Expressions like '*inda vēlaiyai eṉakku seyya teriyum* (this work to-me to-do is-known)' are intransitive. Such work is external to oneself; it is known *to* one. By contrast, *toḻil* is ascribed by birth. Being, say, a Barber involves not merely 'knowing about' something, but 'Knowing' it. The 'Knowledge' associated with *toḻil* is *sāṣtiram*, and a man of Barber caste might say *adu en sāṣtiram irukkiṛadu* (that is my *sāṣtiram*)'. No matter what his *vēlai*, he *is* a Barber, and the *sāṣtiram* appropriate to the Barber *toḻil* is an essential quality of himself.

Clearly, the *māṉiyam* prestation is not given in exchange for work, but in recognition of the caste-specific *sāṣtiram* or Savoir associated

[3] The word *vēlai* is thus used locally in a quite different sense from that reported by David (1974) for Jaffna. This variability of concepts exemplifies the difficulties facing any would-be generalizing 'ethnosociology' of India (*pace* Marriott and Inden 1974; 1977; and 12.2, below).

with each *to<u>l</u>il*. Likewise, village artisans and servants receive their annual *sampaḷam* whether they actually do any work or not, so one must conclude that it too does not recognize their physical labour, but rather the technical knowledge which enables them to carry out their duties if required. In short, *sampaḷam* is given in respect of the *savoir-faire* which the performance of *vēlai* entails.

On the threshing floor, the appropriate volume of grain for the specialist is measured accurately, and a small extra amount is then casually added. By the same token, specialists should always be willing to provide slightly more of a service than convention demands. These are both ways of ensuring *sandōsam* ('mutual satisfaction'), so both parties can be confident that the other bears no grudge. Almost any transaction is likely to end with the donor asking: '*Sandōsamā* (Is it satisfactory)?' However rancorous the initial haggling, the recipient becomes wreathed in smiles, shakes his head in the South Indian gesture of assent, and confirms: '*Sandōsandāṉ* (It *is* satisfactory)'.

As the earlier examples (4.1, above) show, "economic" specialists are rewarded in the same ways as those whose tasks are "religious". Indeed, all such rewards might be said to contain "economic" and "ritual" components, the *sampaḷam* and *sāṣtiram* respectively, whether the recipient be a Carpenter or a Priest. In fact, it is helpful to regard "economic", "religious", etc., as *attributes* of most social relationships rather than as distinct *types* of relationship (Khare 1977: 107; cf. 4.3.4, below).

For a proper understanding of these concepts, it is crucial to add that *sāṣtiram* is also used to refer to exchanges *within* caste-groups, such as those at weddings and similar occasions. Even the obligations upon specific relatives to attend such events are described in this way. For example, it is said to be the *sāṣtiram* of a *tāymāmaṉ* (senior MB or equivalent) to participate in the life-crisis rites of his sister's child. Conversely, it is the *sāṣtiram* of his sister's family to invite him to do so, and make the appropriate prestations in return.[4] So when *any* qualified person fulfils a duty or obligation, and when s/he receives a return prestation for so doing, both are termed "*sāṣtiram*". At harvest-time, it is the *sāṣtiram* of the farmers to give *māṉiyam* prestations, and the *sāṣtiram* of the experts to claim them. Moreover, the actual items exchanged are themselves referred to as the *sāṣtirams* of donor and recipient. That is, "*sāṣtiram*" is used not only for the

[4] Obligations are not necessarily reciprocated directly: the ZS will one day make the same prestation to his own ZC.

rights, obligations, and qualities inherent in one's social identity, but also for the material or non-material prestations whereby such rights and obligations are discharged.[5]

Discussion of these prestational concepts has taken us well beyond consideration of the duties of service castes, priests, and artisans. In a sense the mother's brother (say) is an 'expert' rather like the Barber, although his 'clientele' lies purely within caste boundaries. For the rest of this chapter, however, the emphasis will be on prestational exchanges between members of different castes.

4.3 The Specialist Castes

This section describes the rights and obligations of the various local caste specialists, emphasizing their everyday routine work and rewards, and mentioning other special occasions on which they have roles to play. It also considers their geographical spheres of competence, showing how their clienteles are distributed among the three villages.

4.3.1 *Barbers*

The Barber shaves and cuts the hair of the men in his client households. He receives a *māṉiyam* on the threshing floor (see 4.1, above), and an annual or semi-annual *sampaḷam* in cash or grain. In addition, because he is regarded as a 'village son' (*kuḍimakaṉ*), he is entitled to cooked food twice daily from his 'mothers', the wives of his client households. Barbers are also funeral priests and doctors, and their wives are midwives.

Sanmukam shaves the entire non-Harijan Hindu populations of Terku Vandanam and Vadakku Vandanam. He receives daily cooked food from these households, plus Rs 5 per annum as *sampaḷam* (the Terku Vandanam Nayakkars give 3 *marakkāls* of grain instead). Asaris (TV 6, 8, 13) give no food or annual payment, but pay cash for shaves and haircuts. He is the usual ritual officiant in all three villages. Ramasuppu, the Kalinkapatti Barber, gets a *sampaḷam* of 3 *marakkāls* of grain per household per annum. He assists Sanmukam, his senior relative, in the latter's ritual duties in the three villages (cf. 10.7.1,

[5] The applicability of a Maussian analysis to Indian transactions is considered by Parry (1980: 105; 1986).

Example D, below). Suppaiya (VV 9) serves 10 Nadar households, who give him Rs 5 annually. Though a Hindu, he officiates at Nadar funerals and lives in their quarter. He does not shave Hindus or officiate at their rituals. A Barber from Kamanayakkanpatti serves the other Nadar households.

4.3.2 *Washermen*

The Washerman or his wife visits clients' houses daily, to collect washing. Only one's best clothes are given to the Washerman. Like Barbers, Washermen are 'village sons' and receive food from their clients twice daily (cf. 4.3.1, above).[6]

Candiran lives in a tiled house provided rent-free by Terku Vandanam village. He gets daily food plus Rs 10 annually (usually in instalments) from his 55 client families, who include members of most Terku Vandanam castes. Raj also has a rent-free house, and is rewarded in the same way as Candiran by his 30 client families. Asaris do not give them daily food, but supply them with raw rice at festivals, as well as Rs 15 per annum in cash.

There are more than eighty-five non-Harijan households in Terku Vandanam. A few may be attached to neither Washerman, but the discrepancy probably reflects the fact that their definition of "family" differs from mine of "household". Neither Washerman has any regular clients in the other villages, but they are sometimes involved in ritual activities there.

Sodalaimuttu receives daily food and 6 *marakkāls* of grain annually from his 10 client households in Kalinkapatti. He claims to perform ritual duties, but I never saw him do so. Velu also lives in Kalinkapatti, but washes for clients in Kadambur town, who pay him in cash. He is the *tampi* (terminological yB) of Candiran. Kadakkarai, Raj's father, gets Rs 10 a year from his Vadakku Vandanam clients, and three Koppampatti families give him 6 *marakkāls* annually. He claims to work only for Hindus, but actually serves Nadars too.

The Paraiyars have a Tinda Vannar ('impure Washerman') who serves them as both Washerman and Barber, as follows. Perumal gets a rent-free house in Terku Vandanam, and another in nearby Puduppatti, where he also works. He gets Rs 6 annually from every

[6] The *kuḍimakan̲* serve each other free, as a direct exchange.

household, plus food twice daily. At harvest-time, clients with land give him 2 small *pakkās* of grain as a *sāṣtiram*. He officiates at funerals.

4.3.3 *Temple Priests*

Temple priests (*kōvil pūsāri*) conduct regular and festive worship in local shrines, and do non-routine worship (*pūja*) whenever worshippers require this. If, for example, someone wants to make a vow, or offer *poṅkal*, Priests will officiate in return for *sāṣtirams* of coconuts, plantains, rice, etc. Priestly office usually passes from father to son.

A plot of *māṉiyam* land is attached to some temples. It is cultivated by or for the Priest, to whom its produce accrues. This use of *māṉiyam* is consistent with that discussed earlier (4.2, above). The land is *māṉiyam*, but its produce is the Priest's *sampaḷam*: the latter is the perquisite of the incumbent, while the former remains associated with the office.

Arumuka Oduvar is the Priest of the Amman and Pillaiyar temples in both Terku Vandanam and Kalinkapatti. Both Amman temples have *māṉiyam* land associated with them: 5 *marakkāls* of wet land in Terku Vandanam, and 4 acres of dry land in Kalinkapatti. Arunacala Velar officiates at the Aiyanar temple in Terku Vandanam, a smaller Aiyanar temple in Vadakku Vandanam, and the Turkkaiyamman temples in all three villages. The Aiyanar temple in Terku Vandanam has 0.3 acres of *māṉiyam* land. It contains the temple well, and is worked as garden land.

As usual (Dumont 1959: 79; 1970: 24), the Aiyanar priest is also a Potter. Arunacalam's family serves all three villages, making pots for secular and ritual purposes. At the 1977 Aiyanar festival he made clay figures (*uruvam*) of humans or animals, in return for cash *sampaḷams*. The blindfold statues were taken to the centre of the village for the 'eye-opening' (*kāṇ tiṟakkatal*). Customers offered *sāṣtirams* of paddy, a vesti, plantains, coconut, and a live rooster. The Velar cut one claw off the bird, dabbed blood on the forehead of the statue, and removed the cloth from its eyes. The statues were then taken in procession to the Aiyanar temple. Some said that this rite was to prevent the statues' glances causing smallpox among worshippers. Others, with typical pragmatism, said it was merely to increase the Velar's income.

Kurusami Kavundar officiates at the annual festival of the Perumal temple in Terku Vandanam. He receives a *sāṣtiram*—a share of the festival offerings—but no *sampaḷam*, nor is he treated like a fully fledged priest on other ritual occasions. Fr. Njanappirakasam is the parish priest of St Xavier's Church in Vadakku Vandanam. The villagers donated 10 acres of *māṉiyam* land for his upkeep. He also receives first-fruits at all harvests.

Harijan priests usually act only at their annual temple festival, but are nevertheless best seen as village priests because their temples belong to entire caste-groups and are not family-deity (*kuladeyvam*) shrines. Moreover, these festivals involve higher castes to some degree (Good 1985*a*). Such priests get no *sampaḷam*, however, and merely receive a share of the festival offerings as *sāṣtiram*. In every case, the officiant is a member of the caste concerned.

Mediums (*sāmi piḍikki*, 'god caught'; *sāmiyāḍi*, 'god dancer') incarnate the chief deities at festivals. The role is often hereditary. At family and Harijan festivals, mediums are drawn from the lineage or caste concerned, but at village festivals several castes may be represented. The Terku Vandanam goddess is incarnated by Teyva Pillai from Manditoppu village, whose family came originally from Terku Vandanam. The Amman's medium in Kalinkapatti is Ovammal, an Ayotti Reddiyar woman.

4.3.4 *Artisans*

The village Carpenter and Blacksmith receive their *sampaḷam* and *sāṣtiram* prestations on the threshing floor (see 4.1, above). Their *sampaḷam* covers maintenance work on clients' carts, ploughs, and houses, for which the clients provide the raw materials. Clients make these prestations even if the artisan has done no work for them in that particular year, but the amount does not increase however many repairs have been needed.

Ramasami Asari and Ponnuccami Asari serve all Kalinkapatti and Terku Vandanam houses as Carpenter and Blacksmith, respectively. They also build new carts, ploughs, and furniture if commissioned, but in that case the customer pays an agreed cash price, separate from the regular *sampaḷam*. Most other Asari households in Terku Vandanam follow their hereditary occupations, but are rewarded differently. Suppan Asari has a workshop in Vadakku Vandanam, but is not treated as a 'village Blacksmith', and is paid in cash for work actually done. Others work for cash in Pasuvandanai and Koppampatti.

Perumal Asari the Goldsmith makes wedding ornaments, including marriage tokens (*tālis*). He also pierces children's ears, and fits the ear-rings which they wear from the age of 1 upwards. He gets a cash *sampaḷam* for the labour involved, as well as a *sāṣtiram* comprising Rs 1, half a coconut, a plantain, and betel. The cash is called *teṭcaṇai* (from the Sanskrit *dakṣiṇā*, 'gift to a guru'). His clients do not reward him annually, but only when his services are required. He works for all castes, including Harijans.

Ritualized payment is very common where artisans are concerned. When a Carpenter builds a new house, for example, he not only receives a cash *sampaḷam* but also, when he officiates at the ceremonial raising of the doorposts (*nilai viḍutal*), gets a *sāṣtiram* comprising the *pūja* materials and a *teṭcaṇai*. Like the Potter case (4.3.3, above), this illustrates how occupational specialists are in a sense priests when engaged in their speciality. The carpentry itself is rewarded by a negotiated cash payment, but this is supplemented by prestations at the doorpost ritual, when the Carpenter acts as priest. One revealing detail is that whereas priests usually break coconuts using a curved sickle, a Carpenter always uses a chisel, the tool of his trade.

On Tamil New Year's Day in April, the village bullocks were gathered in a field, yoked to their ploughs. Every bullock-owner put down a plantain leaf holding paddy, a coconut, several plantains, and his bullock goad. The Carpenter split the nuts using his chisel, returning half to the donor. The goads were cursorily sharpened by the Blacksmith, and both artisans performed worship (*pūja*). The goads were returned to their owners, who drove their bullocks, ploughs and all, clockwise around the field. Finally they untied the excited animals, which raced off home. The paddy, plantains, coconuts, and money were shared by the artisans.

This rite involves a *sāṣtiram* prestation to the artisans from their clients. Typically, the transaction is reciprocal: in return for paddy, coconuts, etc., the artisans give half a coconut and do some work (sharpening goads). Simultaneously, the artisans worship their tools and the farmers worship Pillaiyar, god of beginnings. The rite is an annual, public renewal of the mutual obligations between artisan and client.

4.3.5 *The Channel-Controller*

Veyilmuttu, a Pallar, inherited this office from his father. He has to open and close the main sluice-gates of the tanks daily during the rice-growing season. On the threshing floor he receives paddy from owners of wet land, at the rate of 2 *pakkās* per acre. He gets no share of any other crop. The entire payment is classed as *sāṣtiram*, because there was originally a plot of 7 *marakkāls* of *māṉiyam* land, the produce of which formed his *sampaḷam*. He has sold this, however.

4.3.6 *Harijans*

Pallars and Paraiyars have always formed the main agricultural labour-force. Even now most of them work as labourers, and are paid in the same ways as other agricultural workers (see 3.1.1, above). Such transactions involve the usual need for *sandōsam*, but the *sampaḷam/sāṣtiram* distinction arises only in connection with some of their more specialized activities (cf. also 4.3.5, above). Thus, Cakkiliyars are winnowers and scavengers for all three villages. If an animal dies the carcass is their *sāṣtiram*, and they may eat the flesh if they wish. The skin of the animal is important because they are also leather-workers. They make sandals, and the leather tubes used in the *kavalai* (see 3.1, above). They call occasionally to see whether anyone has shoes to repair. Customers pay for raw materials, but do not specifically reward the work itself. Instead they give food whenever Cakkiliyars ask for it, in the same way as for 'village sons', although in practice this happens only on festival days.[7]

Harijans act as grave-diggers (*veṭṭiyāṉ*) at higher-caste funerals (see 10.7.1, below), and the Cakkiliyars are messengers (*tōṭṭi*) for the Pallars. Indeed, Totti is the name of their sub-caste. The musicians at funerals and temple festivals are Harijans too, but come from outside the area. Higher castes recognize responsibilities of a paternalistic kind[8] towards Harijans. For instance, they contribute towards Harijan temple festivals.

[7] Alone among specialist groups, they co-opted us into the local system by coming to our house to collect food.

[8] Inter-caste relationships are often expressed in kinship terms; cf. the Asari-Pallar relationship (10.7.1, below) and the 'village sons' (4.3.1, above).

4.4 Inter-Caste Prestations at Life-Crisis Rituals

The duties and rewards of specialist castes at temple festivals have been described elsewhere (Good 1982*b*: 30–1; 1985*a*: 149). This section considers instead their roles at life-crisis rituals in clients' households. These are discussed in detail later (Chapters 7–10), and the following general remarks are merely intended to set these roles into the context of the general prestational categories established earlier (see 4.2, above).

It is the duty (*sāṣtiram*) of village specialists to attend life-crisis rituals in client households, and perform certain specified tasks. These are often related to their hereditary calling, and to that extent are covered by the annual *sampaḷam*. They often make little practical contribution to accomplishing the rite, however, and their prime purpose seems to be to mark the host household's continuing link with the specialist concerned, despite the changes and realignments which are occurring in its internal relationships. This is done by means of a reciprocal *sāṣtiram*: the specialist attends and performs his task, and gets an honorific material prestation in return.[9] For purposes of illustration it is enough to consider one context, marriage in Terku Vandanam, and contrast two of the specialized participants in that rite, the Velar temple priest and the Brahman domestic priest (cf. also 8.6, below).

The Velar's duty is to bring ash from the Aiyanar temple to the groom's house, and anoint the foreheads of participants and guests. In return the hosts give him 1 *paḍi* (about 1.5 kg.) of paddy, as well as the materials for temple worship (vegetable oil, betel, incense). This is not payment for his work (*sampaḷam illai*, 'salary not'), but a *sāṣtiram* due to him in his capacity as incumbent of a village temple. To underline this point, the Oduvar Priest gets two such *sāṣtirams*, one for the Goddess temple and one for the Pillaiyar shrine.

Brahman priests are not essential officiants at weddings, but their presence makes the ceremonies more prestigious. No priestly Brahmans live locally, so one is hired from a nearby town. He has no enduring link with the groom's household or sub-caste. His reward therefore contains two components, in addition to his travelling expenses. There is a *sampaḷam*, usually in cash, and a *sāṣtiram* which depends

[9] Their form resembles the *suruḷ tĕṅkāy muṟi paḻam* ('rolled-up betel coconut-half plantain') prestation made to honoured guests at most types of ritual.

upon the caste of his client but contains the items used in the wedding—rice, paddy, coconuts, betel, camphor, incense—together with raw vegetables, new clothes, and Rs 1.25 as *teṭcaṇai*. The vegetables replace the cooked meal at the host's house, which the Brahman cannot compromise his purity by accepting.

For Velars and other local specialists, the prestations given and received at their clients' life-crises are entirely *sāṣtiram*. The Brahman is not enmeshed in the annual cycle of *sampaḷam* prestations, however. Local specialists merely fulfil *sāṣtiram* obligations by attending and carrying out their ritual duties, and are rewarded in accordance with the *sāṣtiram* of the host. On the other hand, while it is of course the *sāṣtiram* of a Brahman domestic priest to officiate at weddings, a fact recognized in the prestations made to him, he is not a member of the local community and the work is outwith his routine obligations. He therefore gets a *sampaḷam* 'for labour'. At life-crisis rituals, then, local specialists receive only *sāṣtiram* prestations from the host household. Specialists who are outsiders, and whose relationships with their clients are merely transitory, receive both *sāṣtiram* and *sampaḷam*.

4.5 The 'Jajmani System'

This chapter has described what is usually known in the social anthropology of India as the 'jajmani system', namely 'the system corresponding to the prestations and counter-prestations by which the castes as a whole are bound together in the village, and which is more or less universal in India' (Dumont 1980: 97).

In many parts of India the word *jajmāni* occurs in local vocabulary, yet many writers—even Dumont, who opposes the use of "caste" as a sociological rather than an ethnographic concept (1980: App. A; cf. Leach 1960*b*: 1–2)—also use it as an analytical term, even with reference to localities where the word is unknown. The term 'jajmani system' (Wiser 1936) is still more problematic, for even where the word *jajmāni* is in use, the notion of a *system* is an analytical imposition. No such 'system' is likely to be apparent to a villager allegedly living under its sway. People know how their own caste-group interacts with each specialist, but usually not how other castes do so, nor how specialists arrange things among themselves. Moreover, the exchanges conventionally subsumed under this 'system' do not constitute a discrete class. In the present case, the categories *sampaḷam*, *sāṣtiram*, and *sandōsam* also apply to relationships within the caste and family, which no 'jajmani system' analyses take into account.

Even in the distant past, dyadic 'jajmani' relationships between farmers and specialists were by no means universal. Under the 'baluta system' of western India, for example, specialists were rewarded by the village as a whole (Fukuzawa 1972). Nowadays, at least, many villages display idiosyncratic mixtures of 'jajmani-type' and 'baluta-type' relationships. Thus, some Terku Vandanam specialists have jajmani-like dyadic links with their patrons, whereas the rewards of others, especially the priests, Barbers, and Washermen, can be seen as 'approximating to the baluta model' (Fuller 1989: 40). Whatever their precise form, the phenomena normally lumped together as the 'jajmani system' and depicted as a survival of traditional village India, are in fact merely the local remnants of a pyramidal system of economic expropriation which formerly focused on the sovereign (Fuller 1977: 111).

Though one of the few to make this last point, Dumont, like many other analysts,[10] portrays the 'jajmani system' as centred on the 'dominant caste'. This seems at odds with his claim that status transcends power, but he justifies his position as follows. In reality, members of the 'dominant' caste merely allow 'dependent' castes 'access to the means of subsistence through personal relationships with [them]' (1980: 106), but as both groups share an ideology in which power is 'encompassed' by ritual status (p. 107), the system appears religiously ordained, and oriented towards the whole (p. 108).[11] But in Terku Vandanam no such dominant caste is found, so either there is by definition no jajmani system, in which case the system is *not* a universal Indian fact; or Dumont is wrong to link it so closely to the dominant caste, a non-universal phenomenon. Either way, his analysis is inapplicable to the present case.

Dumont uses the word "system" in two senses. The "jajmani system" is firstly an institutionalized entity, made up of 'prestations and counter-prestations' (1980: 97). It is also an ideological system, namely, 'the religious expression of interdependence' (p. 108). But it

[10] The different analytical positions are discussed in Good (1982*b*: 31–2), which presents some of the arguments of this section in more detail.

[11] The hint of false consciousness is necessitated by the role played in his argument by the 'dominant caste'.

was argued above that the institutional system is an imposition by the analyst. Moreover, ideas regarding prestational exchanges apply within, as well as between, castes, and so cannot easily be seen as deriving from the relationship between householder and chaplain (p. 98), or as straightforward expressions of 'the language of hierarchy . . . a matter of pure and impure' (p. 108).

As an analytical term, 'jajmani system' is deficient because it arbitrarily extends the geographical and semantic scope of one particular indigenous notion, while failing to pay proper attention to those concepts which *are* current in the region being studied. Its abandonment need not lead, as Miller (1986: 537) seems to fear, to a hopeless relativism whereby every local situation is analysed in isolation. A different kind of generalization is needed, which does not distort indigenous categories by converting them into analytical labels, but interprets them on their own terms and then translates that interpretation wholesale into the vocabulary of comparative social science (cf. Comaroff 1980: 33). I have tried to do this for prestational concepts in Terku Vandanam (see 4.2, above).

4.6 The Micro-Region

What kind of picture emerges if we avoid viewing these three villages in terms of 'jajmani' and 'dominance'? Beck (1972) treats Coimbatore villages as segments of larger territorial units (*nāḍu*). Such nadus existed in medieval Tirunelveli too (Ludden 1985: 35). They are not evident there in modern times, but my data clearly show the need to treat all three villages as one sociological unit. I shall call this a *micro-region*, though not in the historically specific sense of Stein (1980).

Table 4.1 lists the roles and functions of each local caste-group, and the composition of its clientele. Many of these roles extend over two or three villages. Caste-groups are not equally important in these respects, however, and the character of their involvement varies. Those castes enjoying the alleged prerequisites of dominance, namely the Nadars (VV), Maravars (TV), Nayakkars (TV), and Ayotti Reddiyars (KP), contribute relatively little to this integration. The evidence suggests that neither village political economy, nor the solidarity of economically powerful caste groups, are of prime importance. Instead, the micro-region is delimited by the clienteles of those engaged in caste-specific specialized occupations. The activities of

TABLE 4.1. The Nature and Extent of Inter-Caste Relationships

Caste	Office, Role, or Function	Spatial extent[a]
Terku Vandanam		
1. Maravar	Panchayat President	TV, KP
	2 Panchayat members	TV, KP
	2 Talaiyaris	TV, KP
2. Paraiyar	Vettiyan	TV*, KP*
	Priest of Mariyamman Temple	TV
	Panchayat member	TV, KP
	'Sons' of TV Cettiyar	TV*
3. Nayakkar	Munsip	TV
4. Konar	Temple Dues Collector	TV
	2 Panchayat members	TV, KP
5. Pillaimar	Amman temple Priest	TV, KP
	Karnam	TV, KP
	Panchayat member	TV, KP
	Medium at Amman Festival	TV
6. Taccan Asari	Village Carpenter	TV, KP
	Jobbing Carpenter	VV
	'Fathers' of Pallar	VV*
7. Cettiyar	'Fathers' of Paraiyar	TV*
8. Kollan Asari	Village Blacksmith	TV, KP
	Jobbing Blacksmith	VV
	'Fathers' of Pallar	VV*
9. Velar	Aiyanar temple Priest	TV, VV, KP
	Potters	TV, VV, KP
10. Kavundar	Perumal temple Preist	TV
11. Vannar	Village Washermen	TV
	Ritual Roles	TV, KP, VV*
12. Panditar	Village Barber	TV, VV*
	Midwife, Doctor	TV, VV*, KP
	Funeral Priest	TV, VV*, KP
13. Tattan Asari	Goldsmith	TV, KP, VV
14. Tinda Vannar	Barber/Washerman	TV*
	Funeral Priest	TV*
Vadakku Vandanam		
1. Nadar	Panchayat President	VV
	4 Panchayat members	VV
2. Pallar	Channel-Controller	TV, VV, KP
	Vettiyan	TV* [VV*?]
	'Sons' of Asari	TV*
	Muniyasami temple Priest	VV*
	Panchayat member	VV

TABLE 4.1. *cont.*

Caste	Office, Role, or Function	Spatial extent[a]
3. Kampalattar	Panchayat member	VV
4. Cakkiliyar	Winnowers	TV, VV, KP
	Scavengers	TV, VV, KP
	Leather-workers, Cobblers	TV, VV, KP
	Vettiyan	TV*, VV*
	Totti	VV*
5. Konar	—	
6. Vannar	Village Washerman	VV
7. Maniyakkarar	Talaiyari	VV
8. Paraiyar	Vettiyan	VV*
9. Maruttuvar	Barber	VV*
	Funeral Officiant	VV*
Kalinkapatti		
1. Ayotti Reddiyar	2 Panchayat members	TV, KP
	Ampalam Headman	KP
	Medium in Amman Festival	KP
	(Former Munsip)	KP
2. Maravar	—	
3. Saiva Cettiyar	—	
4. Kottu Reddiyar	Munsip	KP
5. Pulavar	Funeral Drummers	TV*, KP*
6. Vannar	2 Washermen	KP
7. Telunku Asari	—	
9. Panditar	Barber	KP
10. Brahman	—	

[a] The notation is as follows: TV (Terku Vandanam), VV (Vadakku Vandanam), KP (Kalinkapatti): entire village (possibly excluding Harijans); * indicates some castes.

Oduvar and Velar priests embrace the entire micro-region. Harijans too, especially Cakkiliyars, fulfil functions like winnowing, scavenging, and grave-digging for all three villages. Others heavily involved throughout the micro-region are the artisans, Barbers, and Washermen. Most of these key caste-groups are found in Terku Vandanam, the largest village and geographical centre of the micro-region.

It seems generally true that neither Priests nor specialized Harijan groups are found in every settlement, suggesting that units like this may be widespread. Beck's data on 'sub-regions' (1972) are suggestive here, as is Benson's study of a group of villages in Andhra Pradesh. She attributes social cohesion to a single powerful family in one village (1977: 240), but it seems equally plausible to emphasize the role of service castes. Of the residents of Benson's central village, the Tailor serves five other villages, the Carpenter and Barbers four each, and the Blacksmith and Potters one each (1977: 244–6). Only the Washerman, among active specialists, does not serve clients in other villages. Benson does not discuss the ritual activities of these people, or of specialist Priests, but her data show how several settlements may be united in a network of prestations centred on a single caste specialist.

As the complicating factor of dominance is absent in the present case, it is even less problematic to claim that groups at the extremes of the caste hierarchy play the major integrating role. At the top of the status hierarchy, the Pillai and Velar Priests conform only partly to canons of Brahmanic behaviour, but it is their relative position not their substantive character which is important. For their part, Harijans have duties in which the 'religious' is inextricably mingled with the 'economic' (cf. Reiniche 1979: 12). This is consistent with Dumont's view that Indian society acquires its specificity from the way religion, *dharma*, and status encompass political economy, *artha*, and power.

I have defined the local social unit in terms of the geographical extensions of inter-caste relationships. Similar analyses might apply elsewhere, but my approach is not intended to replace a 'dominant caste'-centred analysis when the latter is clearly appropriate, or to supersede Beck's sophisticated blending of the principles of dominance and territory (1972). Moreover, the micro-region is an analytical construct. It is therefore merely heuristic and provisional, and in no way inimical to such striking analyses of local emic categories as Daniel's discussion of Tamil notions of place (1984: 79–95). The point is that in order to make sense of social relationships in Terku Vandanam—my primary intention—it is essential to take Vadakku Vandanam and Kalinkapatti into consideration too. The three villages are linked in many ways, but most of these links take the form of inter-caste *prestational exchanges*, in the widest sense of that term.

5
Relationship Terminologies

5.1 Categories, Rules, and Behaviour

In this chapter the relationship terminologies of local castes are described and analysed, with special emphasis on the consequences of eZDy marriage. The next chapter will describe the preferential marriage rules of local caste-groups, showing how these relate to marriage practices on one hand, and the prescriptive terminology on the other.

The starting-point is Dumont's crucial observation that 'kinship terminologies have not as their function to register groups' (1964: 78). Such lack of homology between terminological structure and descent group structure is amply demonstrated by his own South Indian data (1983 [1957*a*]: 52–68), but not all disjunctions between different levels of the kinship system can be explained in this way. Needham has shown that '(1) symmetric prescriptive terminologies can govern asymmetric affinal alliances; (2) asymmetric affinal alliances can be accompanied by a non-prescriptive terminology' (1967: 43).

Here the disjunction lies between sets of categories (terminologies) and sets of jural rules (systems of alliance). For heuristic purposes, it therefore seems necessary to distinguish three levels of data (cf. Needham 1973: 171):

(1) the *statistical-behavioural* level[1] consists of the aggregate consequences of the behaviour of members of the society or group in question. In the case of kinship, this level is exemplified by demographic data on residential, marital, and other observed patterns.

(2) the *jural* level comprises the normative, legal, moral, religious, and analytical statements of the group's members. Like Leach's 'as–if' descriptions (1954: 285), jural data consist of ideals and justifica-

[1] *Individual* behaviour raises different analytical problems, not addressed directly here. Briefly, it requires consideration of the strategic use which individuals make of the jural rules which ostensibly direct their behaviour (Bourdieu 1977: 58–71).

tions made explicit by group members themselves, though not always verbally. For example, statements of marriage preference belong to this level.

(3) the *categorical* level comprises modes of classification and systems of nomenclature. The relationship terminology is the archetype of data at this level. Categorical data generally differ from jural phenomena by being implicit. That is, members of society take them for granted and do not subject them to the explanation, justification, and idealization commonly associated with jural statements.

The interconnections among these levels are problematic, and it will not be possible to resolve such questions fully here. Briefly, though, the situation seems to be as follows. It cannot ever be assumed that the content of any one level is determined by or *congruent* with the content of any other (Needham 1967; 1973). On the other hand, the various levels must be *consistent* enough for contradiction to be avoided. They are best seen as different aspects of the same social facts, rather than as distinct types of such facts. Incongruences and inconsistencies are none the less present, as we shall see, so that a complete analysis requires us to take all three levels into account. This will be done at the conclusion of the following chapter.

5.2 Terminological Prescription among the Maravars

Unlike other local caste groups, Maravars and Nadars do not practise eZDy marriage. Dumont's seminal analysis of the so-called 'Dravidian' terminology (1983 [1953*a*]: 3–17) concerns just such a system, so this case is dealt with first. We shall then confront the more complex case of marriage with the eZDy.

Table 5.1 displays the Maravar terminology, collected by a combination of the 'hypothetical question' and 'genealogical' methods (cf. Barnard and Good 1984: 41–2). The terms are glossed by a list of the close genealogical positions to which they apply. It must be emphasized, however, that one or other of terms 1–28 applies, in principle, to every member of the sub-caste, whether their exact genealogical connection to Ego is known or not. It should most definitely *not* be concluded that the listed denotata are in any sense the 'real' or most basic meanings of the corresponding terms. They

TABLE 5.1. Terminology of the Kondaiyankottai Maravar

Relationship term	Genealogical referents	Level
1. *tāttā*	FF, MF, FFB, MFB, FMB, MMB	+ 2
2. *pāṭṭi, ācci*	FM, MM, FFZ, MFZ, FMZ, MMZ	+ 2
3. *appā, ayyā*	F	+ 1
4. *periyappā, periyayyā*	FeB, MZH (older than F)	+ 1
5. *sittappā, siṉṉayyā*	FyB, MZH (younger than F)	+ 1
6. *ammāḷ, attā*	M	+ 1
7. *periyammāḷ, periyattā*	MeZ, FeBW	+ 1
8. *siṉṉammāḷ, sitti*	MyZ, FyBW	+ 1
9. *māmaṉ*	MB, FZH, WF, HF	+ 1
10. *attai*	FZ, MBW, WM, HM	+ 1
11. *māmiyār*	HM	+ 1
12. *aṇṇaṉ*	Be, FBSe, MZSe	+ 0
13. *akkāḷ*	Ze, FBDe, MZDe	+ 0
14. *tampi*	By, FBSy, MZSy	− 0
15. *taṅkacci, taṅkai*	Zy, FBDy, MZDy	− 0
16. *attāṉ*	MBSe, FZSe, WeBe, HeB, eZH	+ 0
17. *madiṉi*	MBDe, FZDe, WeZe, HeZ, eBW	+ 0
18. *maittuṉār, macciṉaṉ māppiḷḷai*	MBSy$_{ms}$, FZSy$_{ms}$, WeBy, WyB, yZH$_{ms}$	− 0
9. *koḻundaṉ*	MBSy$_{ws}$, FZSy$_{ws}$, HyB, yZHy$_{ws}$	− 0
20. *koḻundiyāl*	MBDy$_{ms}$, FZDy$_{ms}$, WeZy, WyZ, yBW$_{ms}$	− 0
21. *sammandi, nāttiṉār*	MBDy$_{ws}$, FZDy$_{ws}$, HyZ, yBW$_{ws}$	− 0
22. *sammandakkāraṉ*	DHF, DHM, SWF, SWM	± 0
23. *makaṉ*	S, BS$_{ms}$, ZS$_{ws}$, HBS, WZS	− 1
24. *makaḷ*	D, BD$_{ms}$, ZD$_{ws}$, HBD, WZD	− 1
25. *marumakaṉ*	BS$_{ws}$, ZS$_{ms}$, WBS, HZS, DH	− 1
26. *marumakaḷ*	BD$_{ws}$, ZD$_{ms}$, WBD, HZD, SW	− 1
27. *pēraṉ*	SS, DS, BSS, ZSS, BDS, ZDS	− 2
28. *pētti*	SD, DD, BSD, ZSD, BDD, ZDD	− 2

are included only because they allow non-Tamil speakers to grasp what is really a self-contained categorical system with its own internal structure, independent of any *particular* genealogical usage.

For example, terms stand in fixed structural relationships to one another, independently of the particular genealogical uses to which they are put. The simplest such relationship is *reciprocity*. In general, kin terms may be arranged in sets, such that one set contains all possible reciprocals of one, and only one, other specified set, and vice versa. If it is known which term Ego uses to a given alter, it is therefore also known which term will be used in return. These formal relationships apply to all genealogical contexts in which the component terms of the sets are used, and while it is true that these relationships are detected in the first instance through behaviour, they exist independently of the particular behavioural context in which they are observed. The reciprocal sets found in Table 5.1 are as follows:

1, 2	↔	27, 28
3, 4, 5, 6, 7, 8	↔	23, 24
9, 10	↔	25, 26
12, 13	↔	14, 15
16	↔	18, 20
17	↔	19, 21
22	↔	22

The ‘principle of reciprocal sets’ is said to be a universal feature of kin terminologies (Scheffler and Lounsbury 1971: 77). Empirical evidence does not support such a generalization (Good 1978*b*), but in this case, with the partial exception of term 11, an honorific modification of term 9, there *is* full adherence to the principle. This reflects the perfect symmetry of the Maravar terminology, and the same is not true for those local caste-groups which practise eZDy marriage.

Villagers work out terminological usages, if these are not already known, by means of simple mnemonics. If you know what term to use for person A, and also what term A uses for person B, you can easily work out what term you yourself should use for B. For example, a woman[2] might say: ‘*taṅkacci makaḷ, makaḷ*’. This means, less cryptically, ‘my *taṅkacci* calls this person ‘*makaḷ*’, so I too should call her *makaḷ*’. To translate this as ‘my yZ calls her D, therefore I call her yZD_{ws}’ would miss the point. If it really was her yZD who was involved, she would not need a tautologous *aide-mémoire* to work it out. The point is that the mnemonic is true of *all* behavioural contexts, because the relationship it expresses is a formal one inherent in the logic of the system of categories.

So there are formal, structural relationships in the terminology

[2] It was generally women who reasoned in this way. This may be because the terminology is harder for them to apply abstractly, given the ambiguity and transience of the parallel-cross distinction in their case (see 14.4, below).

which do not derive from particular, behavioural uses to which that terminology may be put. It is therefore necessary to portray this structure in a way which does not appear to tie it to any particular genealogical situation.

5.3 The 'Dravidian' Terminology according to Dumont

The 'Dravidian' kinship system has received immense amounts of analysis,[3] but the most satisfactory account of the terminology *per se* remains that by Dumont (1953*a*). I shall summarize his analysis, and then go on to criticize some aspects of it.

A 'classificatory' terminology is a structured set of zones which together make up the entire semantic space around Ego. Every zone is labelled with a distinctive kin term, and every member of Ego's sub-caste is classifiable into one or other of these zones. Dumont identifies four organizing principles upon which this division of semantic space is based (1983: 3).

First, sub-caste members are divided into *parallel* and *cross*-relatives. Dumont rejects these particular terms because the distinction is not conceptualized in this way by the people themselves. He prefers to speak of 'consanguines' (or 'kin') and 'affines', respectively. In my view, however, it is precisely the neutral character of "parallel" and "cross" which makes their use desirable. The term "consanguine" should only be used to express *indigenous* theories of blood relationship (cf. 5.4, below). In either event, there are two classes of male relative: the F belongs to one and the MB to the other.[4] These classes are opposed by the structural principle of 'alliance', and persons standing in opposite classes are 'affines' (1983: 6).

Secondly, Ego's relatives are divided according to *relative age*, into senior and junior. Thirdly, there is classification by *generation*. This term is unfortunate because of the complications introduced, for most local groups, by eZDy marriage. I shall speak instead of *terminological levels*. The terminology distinguishes six such levels:

[3] Analyses of the 'Dravidian' kinship system have been published by, among others, Beck (n.d.; 1972; 1974), Carter (1973), Dumont (1950; 1953*a*; 1953*b*; 1957*a*; 1957*b*; 1961*b*; 1964; 1983), Emeneau (1967), Gough (1956; 1979), Hocart (1927), Leach (1960*c*; 1971), Morgan (1871), Rivers (1907), Tambiah (1965), Trautmann (1981), and Yalman (1962; 1969).

[4] Throughout this book, I use such abbreviations *only* to specify precise genealogical positions (see p. xiv).

three senior to Ego, and three junior. One complication is that relative age also subdivides parts of the +1 level, though it is age relative to Ego's parents which is taken into account here. Fourthly, there is classification according to the *gender* of alter.

Affines and kin are structurally opposed categories, says Dumont (1961*b*: 81), each implying the absence of the other. Thus, the F and MB are alike in generation but differ in being respectively kin and affine to Ego. Similarly, the MB's child, the cross-cousin, is Ego's affine. Alliance therefore has a diachronic dimension as well as a synchronic one. Clearly it must transcend generation in this way if it is to be opposed to descent. The diachronic preservation of this alliance relationship is achieved by means of the cross-cousin marriage rule (1983: 14). Only one marriage of this type need take place in each generation, in order to maintain the alliance between the entire group of Ego's kin and the entire group of the cross-cousin's kin.

Dumont sees the kin/affine distinction as less fundamental in the −1 level, because "nephews" are distinguished from "sons" only by the prefix *maru-* (1983: 15; Table 5.1, terms 23 and 25). It is not clear why such linguistic factors should have any bearing upon the intensity of the kin/affine opposition, however. One surely cannot argue that "son" and "nephew" are only slightly differentiated while basing one's entire analysis upon the opposition between their reciprocals "father" and "mother's brother". This inconsistency draws attention to the fact that Dumont invariably treats kinship terms in isolation from their reciprocals, a strange procedure given his emphasis upon structural relationships.

Two levels removed from Ego, Dumont sees no distinction between kin and affines. Cross-cousin marriage implies

> an affinal link between Ego's two grandfathers, and this is . . . why there is normally only one term for both of them, for both are kin in one way, and affines in another: mother as well as father is kin to Ego, and so are their fathers, who have at the same time an alliance relationship. (1983: 14–15)

This is not convincing however. Granted, the mother may be kin to Ego, because some Jaffna Tamils say that during her wedding a woman changes to become 'physically identical with her husband' (David 1973: 521). The corollary of this, however, is that she ceases to be of the same substance as her father. This lends ethnographic support to a point which can be made on purely logical grounds.

Dumont himself argues against bringing the mother into the relationship between Ego and his "mother's brother", whom he sees as 'essentially' Ego's father's affine (1983:14)[5]. But if so, it follows that the MF—Ego's father's MB or equivalent—is 'essentially' the FF's affine. If 'affinity' has a diachronic dimension, then any affine of Ego's F and FF must also be an affine of Ego himself.

Dumont seems uneasy about this part of the original argument, because the recent reprint contains a justificatory footnote (1983: 15, n. 8). Unfortunately, it too uses the notion of "consanguinity" in a Eurocentric way. Moreover, there are not necessarily, as Dumont supposes, only two kinship terms for the +2 level (cf. Beck 1972: 228, 287). Although Table 5.1 contains only two, so that FF = MF and FM = MM, some older Maravars use four terms.[6] It is not clear which situation is more common, although considerations of overall symmetry have led some to suggest that the equation of FF with MF may well be more basic (Allen 1975: 89–90).

Be that as it may, the Maravar terminology is clearly of symmetric prescriptive type. Such a structure is congruent with repeated bilateral cross-cousin marriage—or putting it another way, with a series of sister-exchanges—as in Figure 5.1. All the genealogical identities depicted there correspond to terminological identities found in Table 5.1.

An important caveat must be stated here, however. Such diagrams are often used not only to depict real or fictive *genealogies*, as here, but also to portray the structures of prescriptive *terminologies*. This is undesirable, as it gives primacy to genealogically close denotata, or at least encourages the visualizing of terminologies in that way. Such figures have also been used to represent structured *alliance relations* between groups. Each triangle then represents all the male members of a single unilineal group in a given generation. This practice has been cogently criticized by Leach (1961*a*:61–3). Of these— respectively— behavioural, categorical, and jural uses of such diagrams, only the first is legitimate.

In fact, Figure 5.1 is by no means the only kind of genealogy which would be consistent with the terminology. The fit would be just as

[5] As Dumont says, to translate *māmaṉ* as "mother's brother" is as misleading as to render it "uncle". His example is ill-chosen, however, because Tamil-speakers *do* bring the M into the relation between Ego and his MB. Thus, the latter is referred to by the special term *tāymāmaṉ* (*tāy* = "mother").

[6] These are: *pōtti* (FF), *pōttiyayyā* (MF), *appāttāḷ* (FM), *ponnattāḷ* (MM). There are no similar terms for the −2 level.

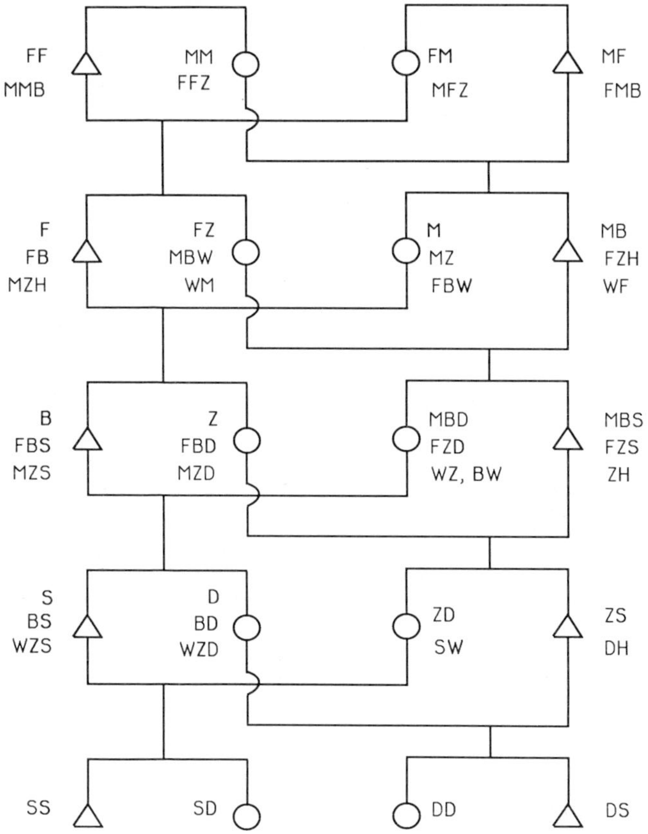

FIG. 5.1 Repeated Bilateral Cross-Cousin Marriage

good in situations of universal and repeated marriage with either the patrilateral or matrilateral first cross-cousin, even though the terminology, being symmetric, does not distinguish 'wife-givers' from 'wife-takers'. It is always possible for rules to make further fine discriminations not inherent in the categories, so long as these rules operate within the framework of categorical boundaries (cf. 6.9, below).

Figure 5.2 displays the terminological structure in the non-genealogical format chosen by Dumont to avoid such problems. My diagram differs slightly from his, however. Firstly, *four* boxes appear in the ±2 generations, though these are often labelled by a total of only two relationship terms. Secondly, Dumont's figure placed the "mother", senior and junior "sisters", and "daughter" in one column, and the "father's sister", senior and junior "female cross-cousins", and "daughter-in-law" in the other. The double vertical line in his figure thus separated potential spouses at the ±0 and −1 levels, while uniting actual spouses at the +1 level. Yet if alliance is a diachronic phenomenon it seems illogical to distinguish present and future spouses in this way. I follow Allen (1975: 83) in grouping 'terms for categories of relatives who may not intermarry' on one side of the central line and 'terms for those who have, could have, will or may do so' on the other. The positions of "mothers" and "father's sisters" are therefore reversed in comparison with Dumont's figure.

Level	△	○	○	△
+2	*tāttā*	*pāṭṭi*	*pāṭṭi*	*tāttā*
+1	*periyappā* *appā* *sittappā*	*attai*	*periyammāḷ* *ammāḷ* *sitti*	*māmaṉ*
+0	*aṇṇaṉ*	*akkāḷ*	*madiṉi*	*attāṉ*
−0	*tampi*	*taṅkacci*	*koḻundiyāl* *[sammandi]*	*maccinaṉ* *[koḻundaṉ]*
−1	*makaṉ*	*makaḷ*	*marumakaḷ*	*marumakaṉ*
−2	*pēraṉ*	*pētti*	*pētti*	*pēraṉ*

FIG. 5.2 The Structure of the Maravar Relationship Terminology (Terms in square brackets are used by female Egos only)

There need not be only one indigenous kinship term for each box. Each might well contain a number of individuating terms, as elaborations of the basic structure. This would not of course invalidate it. If, however, terms were to overflow the bounds of Figure 5.2's boxes, these *would* threaten the basic structure, and would have to be examined with great care. This happens in the case of eZDy marriage, as we shall see (5.6).

The central point to emerge from this discussion is that the terminologically-prescribed category is *koḻundiyāl* (Table 5.1, term 20) for a male Ego, and *attāṉ* (term 16) for a female Ego. That is, a man marries a cross-relative of the −0 terminological level, and a woman marries a cross-relative of the +0 terminological level.

5.4 Substance or Structure?

Dumont's analysis is avowedly concerned only with the structural interrelationships of terminological categories. It therefore seems misguided of him to use the cultural distinction between 'consanguines' and 'affines' to label one of the most basic of those interrelationships. This criticism would apply even if such a distinction were made in exactly this way by all actual users of the terminology. In fact, there is no evidence that it is made by *any* of them.

Some Tamils—not all (McGilvray 1982*a*: 54)—do have notions of common blood, but these do not conform to Dumont's. For instance, *all* sub-caste members in Jaffna are said to share the same blood. *Some* of those whom Dumont calls consanguines are said to share common bodily substance too, making them concorporals (David 1973: 522). This, however, must be seen as merely a local expression of the basic structural fact that, by definition, the F is a parallel relative and the MB a cross-relative. A given genealogical position is always either cross- or parallel, and such distinctions can always be made analytically even when local people do not recognize them.

Dumont's retention of cultural categories leaves him open to attack. In a long critique, Scheffler translates 'consanguine' and 'affine' into Tamil (with, at best, only local validity) as *paṅkāḷi* and *māmaṉ-maccinaṉ*, respectively (1977: 870), and thereafter proceeds to argue as though the central issue is the origin, meaning, and spread of these two terms. In fact they are mentioned only in passing by

Dumont (1950: 6; 1957*b*: 274) with, in the case of *paṅkāḷi*, several restrictions and qualifications (1957*b*: 277). It is at the analytical level that Dumont's distinction is to be understood, of course, even though he insists on expressing it in pseudo-cultural terms. Such confusions can be avoided if one adopts the neutral labels 'parallel' and 'cross-', respectively.

Scheffler assumes a priori that certain genealogical usages, usually the 'closest', are primary (Scheffler and Lounsbury 1971). He argues that the kin–affine opposition is based upon the opposition between brothers (*paṅkāḷi*) and brothers-in-law (*maccin̠an̠*), and that Dravidian kinship terms are characterized by 'polysemy by extension'. In short, 'the broader "affine" class . . . is based on the narrowly defined class which includes the brother-in-law relationship alone' (1977: 871). This conclusion stems from his translation into Tamil of Dumont's terms 'consanguine' and 'affine'. Even if these translations were not highly suspect, it would still be most unclear what the quoted statement could possibly mean, as either synchronic analysis or hypothetical linguistic history. In what sense is the term *māman̠* say, 'based on' the term *maccin̠an̠*?

In Dumont's argument, affines are defined *analytically*. Terms such as *paṅkāḷi* illustrate that some Tamils have reached conclusions similar to his own, but in no way does his analysis derive from or depend upon this. Local linguistic forms are irrelevant, because the terminological structure in question is found in several languages, including some which do not even belong to the Dravidian language family. That is why no actual terms appear anywhere in Dumont's paper (1983: 7).[7]

David makes the more cogent point that there are actually *three* broad categories of relative, although two of them share the same relationship terms. Parallel relatives are of two sorts: (1) agnates of Ego, whom he calls 'sharers' of bodily substance (*sakōtarar*);[8] and (2) the cross-relatives of Ego's cross-relatives. Though genealogically distant, the latter are unmarriageable on terminological grounds, so David calls them 'non-uniters' (*sakaḷar*). Marriages occur with the

[7] Dumont published (1983: 30–4) a rejoinder to Scheffler, who responded by restating his arguments in virtually unmodified form (1984; see also Good 1985*b*; Scheffler 1985). The local meaning of *paṅkāḷi* is explained later (see 6.3): it clearly cannot be used in the sense claimed by Scheffler.

[8] This term was not in spoken use in Terku Vandanam, though it did figure in printed wedding invitations.

third category of persons, the cross-relatives, whom he calls 'uniters' (*sampantikkārar*; 1973: 525).

Logically, cross-relatives could also be divided into close and distant, the latter being cross-relatives of Ego's cross-relatives' cross-relatives. Moreover, the Tamil terms given by David are not widely used in these specific senses (McGilvray 1982*a*: 54, n. 23).[9] His analytical point, that there are parallel relatives whose only connection with Ego is through a multiplicity of affinal links, still stands, however. If Dumont's use of "consanguine" is meant literally, it ignores these non-uniters entirely. Such a focus on close relatives would be contrary to the essential spirit of his entire analysis, as we have seen. If, therefore, it is *not* to be taken at face value, it merely confuses the issue and is best avoided. By contrast, an analysis in terms of cross- and parallel relationships can accommodate all David's broad types, and would be unaffected by any other cultural subdivisions which future fieldwork might uncover.

Dumont's formula, *kinship equals consanguinity plus affinity* (1961*b*: 81), uses ideas which are not universal and fails to account for all usages of either the cross- or parallel kinship terms. But my criticism is directed at his labels rather than his conclusions, and Figure 5.2 remains the best available way of portraying the structure of the 'Maravar-type' terminology.

5.5 Sister's Daughter Marriage

Most local caste-groups also practise marriage with the eZDy, however, and we now face the complex task of unravelling the terminological concomitants of this. I have presented elsewhere (Good 1980*b*) a detailed critique of earlier attempts to treat ZD marriage theoretically, and confine myself here to summarizing points relevant for the present argument.

Lévi-Strauss's analysis of ZD marriage foundered upon his failure to comprehend 'Dravidian' kinship. This was partly because he misinterpreted his sources (Rivers 1907; Thurston and Rangachari 1909; Hocart 1927; Aiyappan 1934), but mainly because he systematically played down the *symmetry* of the system in order to support the grandiose claim that 'India thus verifies the surprising correlation

[9] Among the Maravar, for example, *sammandakkārar*, the local dialect form of *sampandikkārar*, has a much narrower meaning (see Table 5.1, term 22).

. . . between generalized exchange and the role of "creditor" played by the bride's matrilineage' (1969: 437). This assumes, gratuitously and for the most part wrongly, that South Indians are matrilineal, and—more importantly—ignores the fact that *no* South Indians practise generalized exchange. The terminology is quite clearly symmetric, and I know of no case where one cross-cousin is actually prohibited as a spouse, although there *are* asymmetric preferences (see 6.4, below).

The confusion stems from the way Lévi-Strauss distinguishes preference from prescription. Terminologies and rules are both prescriptive, he claims, because both say 'what must be done' (1969: p. xxxiii). 'Preferences' appear only in behaviour, and so are associated with 'statistical models', whereas prescriptions can be represented by 'mechanical models' (p. xxxv). Such views lead him to a false conclusion. In fact the existence of, say, a MBD preference is no evidence for the occurrence of prescriptive or compulsory matrilateral cross-cousin marriage, as Table 6.2 illustrates. Such preferences therefore have no connection with asymmetric generalized exchange, which is nowhere found in the area under discussion.

Matrilateral marriage, he claims, is 'the most lucid and fruitful of the simple forms of reciprocity', whereas ZD marriage is 'its poorest and most elementary application' (p. 451). This ignores the fact that MBD and ZD are identical under the conditions of Figure 5.3. The most fundamental error is, however, to propose a single, genealogically based cause for two quite distinct phenomena, preferential alliance on the one hand, and terminological prescription on the other. To portray either phenomenon in genealogical terms is seriously misleading (see 5.3, above). It is not the genealogical MBD or ZD who is the preferred or prescribed spouse, but someone from the preferred *group* in the first case, and someone of the prescribed *category* in the second.

Such criticisms do not apply to the other main analysts of ZD marriage, Lave (1966) and Rivière, although the latter does take the Lévi-Straussian view that FZD and ZD marriages are similar because the direction of exchange reverses at 'each genealogical level' (1966*b*: 554–5). There do indeed seem to be such reversals when one uses a genealogical diagram to depict the terminology, but even in Figure 5.3 we can see that there are no clear-cut genealogical levels. Every position can be defined as belonging to at least two levels: MM is also FZ, MB is also ZH, MBD is also ZD, and so on. To talk of the

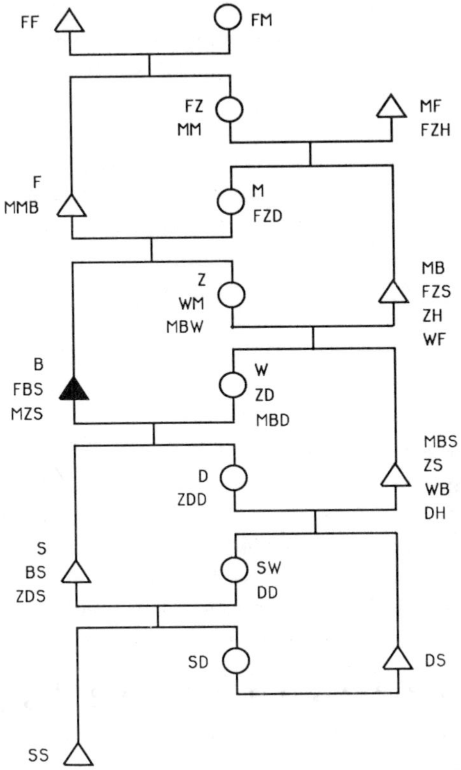

FIG. 5.3 The Results of Repeated Sister's Daughter Marriage

direction of exchange reversing at each 'genealogical level' is therefore somewhat confusing. Moreover, relationship terms (for they are what we are considering when discussing prescriptive systems) do not practise 'exchange', directional or otherwise! This is yet another argument against using such diagrams for other than genuinely genealogical purposes (see 5.3, above).

Lave assumes that ZD marriages usually involve 'nearly a physiological generation's difference between spouses' (1966: 191). This is a common delusion (cf. also Shapiro 1966: 85): the idea is that when an "uncle" marries his "niece" he must be much older than his bride. In Terku Vandanam, however, although the seniority of the husband is slightly above average in eZDy marriages (7 years as against 5.7), there is by no means a generation between them (Good 1980*b*: 485).

In any case, Lave's and Rivière's analyses are only partially relevant to the present context. They both deal with *prescriptive* ZD marriage, and although this necessarily involves matrilateral cross-cousin marriage too (cf. Aiyappan 1934; Leach 1961*a*: 60) it does not automatically entail the patrilateral form. The present case differs in two ways. First, the terminology is *symmetric* prescriptive in type. Second, not every ZD is a potential spouse, only the *elder* sister's daughter. Given that a husband must be older than his wife, the possible spouse is in fact the eZDy. These latter requirements are built directly into the terminological prescriptions.

5.6 The Terminology Associated with eZDy Marriage

In considering eZDy marriage, it is necessary to distinguish between *terminological identity* and *genealogical identity*. For example, when Rivière (1966*a*: 739) writes MBD = ZD and FZD = M, these are terminological identifications which are, as he says, diagnostic of prescriptive ZD marriage. This does not mean, however, that a person living under such a regime has only one actual relative in each terminological category. Ego's FZD and M *may* be the same person, but need not be. In the latter eventuality, though, Ego applies the same relationship term to both. This is thus an example of terminological identity.

In South India, however, a symmetric prescriptive terminology is coupled with a preference for eZDy marriage. As a result, certain relatives who would otherwise be terminologically distinct may become genealogically identical. Reference to Figure 5.3 shows, for example, that Ego's FZ (*attai*) may also be his MM (*pāṭṭi*). The local convention is to call her *attai*, but this does not indicate any terminological identification of FZ with MM, because whenever these two relatives are *not* one and the same, Ego addresses them by means of different terms. The situation is one of genealogical identity.

However, eZDy marriage involves some unusual terminological identifications too. Table 5.2 reproduces the terminology used by most local castes practising such unions. Alternative usages are sometimes found, reflecting individual variations even within each caste group. One man may refer to his MBDy as *koḻundiyāl* (term 20 in Table 5.2), while another uses *marumakaḷ* (term 26). The latter usage seems more logical since the FZSe is referred to as *māmaṉ* (term 9), but the former follows the practice of castes prohibiting eZDy marriage.

TABLE 5.2. Terminology Associated with eZDy Marriage

Relationship term	Genealogical referents
1. *tāttā*	FF, MF, FFB, MFB, FMB, MMB
2. *pāṭṭi, ācci*	FM, MM, FFZ, MFZ, FMZ, MMZ
3. *ayyā, appā*	F
4. *periyappā*	FeB, MZH (older than F)
5. *sittappā*	FyB, MZH (younger than F)
6. *attā, ammāḷ*	M
7. *periyammāḷ*	MeZ, FeBW
8. *siṉṉammāḷ, sitti*	MyZ, FyBW
9. *māmaṉ*	MBe, FZH, WF, HF, FZSe, MBSe, BSe_{ws}, ZSe_{ms}, eZH, HeB, WeBe
10. *attai*	FZ, MBW, WM, HM
11. *māmiyār*	HM
12. *aṇṇaṉ*	Be, FBSe, MZSe, ZSe_{ws}
13. *akkāḷ*	Ze, FBDe, MZDe, ZDe_{ws}
14. *tampi*	By, FBSy, MZSy
15. *taṅkacci, taṅkai*	Zy, FBDy, MZDy
16. *attāṉ*	HeB, ZHe
17. *madiṉi*	ZDe_{ms}, MBDe, FZDe, BDe_{ws}, WeZe, HeZ, eBW
18. *maittuṉār, macciṉaṉ, māppiḷḷai*	MBy_{ms}, WBy, HeB, $yZHy_{ms}$
19. *koḻundaṉ*	MBy_{ws}, $MBSy_{ws}$, $FZSy_{ws}$, HyB, ZHy_{ws}
20. *koḻundiyāl*	ZDy_{ms}, $MBDy_{ms}$, $FZDy_{ms}$, WZy, yBW_{ms}, MZy_{ms}
21. *sammandi, nāttiṉār*	BDy_{ws}, $MBDy_{ws}$, $FZDy_{ws}$, HyZ, yBW_{ws}
22. *sammandakkāraṉ*	DHF, DHM, SWF, SWM
23. *makaṉ*	S, BS_{ms}, ZS_{ws}, HBS, WZS
24. *makaḷ*	D, BD_{ms}, ZD_{ws}, HBD, WZD
25. *marumakaṉ*	BSy_{ws}, ZSy_{ms}, WBS, HZS, DH, $MBSy_{ms}$, $FZSy_{ms}$, WBy
26. *marumakaḷ*	ZDy_{ms}, WBD, HZD, SW, $MBDy_{ms}$, $FZDy_{ms}$
27. *pēraṉ*	SS, DS, BSS, ZSS, BDS, ZDS
28. *pētti*	SD, DD, BSD, ZSD, BDD, ZDD

Table 5.2 was obtained using the 'hypothetical question' method.[10] Tamils often specify relationships in stepwise terms (Dumont 1957*b*: 273), so there is no problem of comprehension. This method deals only with terminological identities. For instance, the use of *attai* to refer to the MM, mentioned above, does not appear in Table 5.2, and could not have been elicited by the method employed. In analysing the terminology one is interested solely in terminological identities, however, so the limitations of the method become a positive advantage.

Table 5.2 reveals a strong tendency for cross-relative terms to reflect relative age rather than genealogical position. Thus *māmaṉ* (term 9) is applied not only to MBe (+1 level in Figure 5.2), but to MBSe and FZSe (level +0), and even to ZSms and BSws (level −1), should they be older than Ego.

Marriages between relatives are almost always regarded 'as if' they were MyBe-eZDy unions, and the terminology employed by potential spouses reflects this, whether they actually lie in this genealogical relationship (or a more distant equivalent), or whether they are genealogical cross-cousins (or equivalent). For some reason, previously unrelated spouses sometimes address one another's relatives as if they themselves had been cross-cousins. Only in such cases does one find terms like *attāṉ* (term 16) or *maittuṉār* (term 18) in practical use.

The prescribed spouse for a male Maravar is a *koḻundiyāl* (term 20 in Table 5.1). From the male viewpoint, the system is one of symmetric prescriptive marriage with the terminological equivalent of a junior cross-cousin. The Maravar terminology makes no distinctions between types of ZD, but in most other groups a male Ego can refer to his eZDe as *madiṉi* (term 17 in Table 5.2); his eZDy as *koḻundiyāl* (term 20); and his yZD as *marumakaḷ* (term 26). In practice, *marumakaḷ* is often used for both the eZDy and the yZD even though only the former is marriageable, but it is clearly possible to make all necessary discriminations should one wish to do so. The ban on marriage with the yZD may reflect the strong feeling against too wide an age discrepancy between H and W, at least in a first marriage.

[10] That is, by asking questions in the form: 'What term do you use for your mother's brother's wife?' For a more complete discussion of these issues, see Barnard and Good 1984: 41–7.

From the male viewpoint, there is symmetric prescriptive marriage with a *junior cross-relative*; the category of 'potential spouse' is genealogically broader than among Maravars. The basic equation is

$$\text{FZDy} = \text{MBDy} = \text{eZDy} \neq \text{FZDe} = \text{MBDe} = \text{eZDe}$$

This situation cannot be represented by a 'mechanical' model like Figure 5.1, which introduces a factor—generation—irrelevant in the present context. Even if questions of relative age are left aside, no more than two of these three possible spouses can be represented in a diagram of that type. This is no great drawback, for as explained earlier, such models perpetuate the confusion whereby purely categorical distinctions are visualized in genealogical terms.

However, it *is* possible to construct a diagram of the more satisfactory type favoured by Dumont. In Figure 5.4 the parallel relative terms are structured exactly as in Figure 5.2, but the cross-relative terms differ. The Maravar terminology involved different cross-relative terms for male and female speakers, but the structure was the same for both. In Figure 5.4, on the other hand, the surface structure of the cross-relative terminology depends on the gender of the speaker. The underlying structure is still constant, however: there is one term in Figure 5.4 for a younger cross-relative of the same sex as Ego, and two terms for younger cross-relatives of the opposite sex to Ego.

Maravar-type terminologies are usually taken to exemplify the Dravidian system. This may be partly due to a historical accident: Rivers, Hocart, Emeneau, Dumont, Leach, Tambiah, and Carter all worked among groups which, for one reason or other, prohibited eZDy marriage (Beck n.d.). Given this immense body of work by so distinguished a collection of anthropologists, it is hardly surprising that ethnographers who met actual cases of eZDy marriage should have taken it as a variant of this basic form. Yet, logically, one could just as plausibly see the Maravar type as a simplified derivative of that incorporating eZDy marriage.

Beck (n.d.) showed that eZDy marriages occur among at least some of the population of every district in the four southern states of India (Andhra Pradesh, Karnataka, Kerala, and Tamil Nadu). Moreover, although it is not found among the Sinhalese (Robinson 1968:

Level	△	○	○	△
+2	*tāttā*	*pāṭṭi*	*pāṭṭi*	*tāttā*
+1	*periyappā* - - - *appā* - - - *sittappā*	*attai*	*periyammāḷ* - - - *ammāḷ* - - - *sitti*	*māmaṉ*
+0	*aṇṇaṉ*	*akkāḷ*	*madini*	
-0	*tampi*	*taṅkacci*	*koḻundiyāḷ*	*marumakaṉ*
-1	*makaṉ*	*makaḷ*	*marumakaḷ*	
-2	*pēraṉ*	*pētti*	*pētti*	*pēraṉ*

FIG. 5.4 Structure of the Relationship Terminology Associated with eZDy Marriage
(a) Terms Used by a Male Ego

405; Yalman 1971: 213), it *has* been reported from Jaffna,[11] and one would also expect it among 'Indian Tamil' plantation workers in central Sri Lanka. The geographical distribution of eZDy marriage is therefore very wide, and where permitted it occurs at least as frequently as first cross-cousin marriage (Beck 1972: Table 5.9). Although terminology, behaviour, and mode of alliance need not be congruent, it seems reasonable to assume that terminologies should often reflect the local occurrence of eZDy marriage. It is therefore possible that many other caste-groups possess terminologies like that in Table 5.2 and Figure 5.4.

[11] See the discussion of Banks 1957 in Tambiah 1973*b*: 124, where 'own cross-cousin's daughter' can only refer to a genealogical or terminological "sister's daughter".

<table>
<tr><th>Level</th><th>△</th><th>○</th><th>○</th><th>△</th></tr>
<tr><td>+2</td><td>tāttā</td><td>pāṭṭi</td><td>pāṭṭi</td><td>tāttā</td></tr>
<tr><td>+1</td><td>periyappā
- - - appā - - -
sittappā</td><td>attai</td><td>periyammāḷ
- - - ammāḷ - - -
sitti</td><td rowspan="2">māmaṉ</td></tr>
<tr><td>+0</td><td>aṇṇaṉ</td><td>akkāḷ</td><td>madiṉi</td></tr>
<tr><td>-0</td><td>tampi</td><td>taṅkacci</td><td rowspan="2">sammandi</td><td>koḻundaṉ
- - - - - - - - -</td></tr>
<tr><td>-1</td><td>makaṉ</td><td>makaḷ</td><td>marumakaṉ</td></tr>
<tr><td>-2</td><td>pēraṉ</td><td>pētti</td><td>pētti</td><td>pēraṉ</td></tr>
</table>

(b) Terms Used by a Female Ego

5.7 Summary

At the start of this chapter, three levels of ethnographic data were distinguished: conceptual categories, jural rules, and statistical behaviour patterns. The question of the degree of incongruence or inconsistency which may exist among them was introduced. The relationship terminologies of local castes were then examined, comparing those who forbid eZDy marriage with the majority who permit it, and introducing the theoretically and practically important distinction between terminological identity and genealogical identity.

Dumont's classic analysis of the 'Dravidian' kinship system was summarized critically. In particular, the analytical labels 'parallel' and 'cross-' relatives were preferred to his terms 'consanguines' and 'affines', which do not reflect local notions regarding blood relationships, and have allowed the status of his argument to be misrepresented.

It was shown that local Maravars prescribe marriage only between cross-relatives of the same terminological level—that is, cross-cousins or their terminological equivalents—with the additional proviso that a man must be senior to his bride. Those groups who favour eZDy marriage prescribe marriage with a genealogically much broader category: a man can marry *any* junior cross-relative, whatever her genealogical position relative to him.

6
Marriage Rules and Behaviour

6.1 Local Marriage Rules

The previous chapter showed that whereas the Maravars' ideal-type 'Dravidian' terminology is predicated on an absolute distinction of terminological levels, most local caste-groups permit marriage with the eZDy and make relative age the main criterion for classifying cross-relatives within the ±1 and ±0 levels. In both cases, however, the terminology is of symmetric prescriptive type. This chapter deals with preferential rules and practical behaviour with regard to marriage, and considers discrepancies between the *symmetric* prescription on the one hand, and the partly *asymmetric* preferences and practices on the other. The theoretical problems which such discrepancies entail are discussed at the end.

South Indian kinship systems are conventionally said to involve 'cross-cousin marriage', because the MBC and FZC are permitted spouses whereas the FBC and MZC are forbidden. This description is rather misleading, however. First, not all cross-cousins are marriageable: a woman must marry her terminological senior, and a man his junior. Second, the prescribed spouse is not necessarily a first, second, or Nth cross-cousin in any genealogical sense, but rather someone standing in the same terminological category, relative to Ego, as these cousins. Thirdly, all local caste-groups except the Maravars and Christian Nadars permit eZDy marriage. The Maravar case is discussed in the next section. As for the Nadars, Hindu groups *do* allow such marriages (Beck 1972: 254), and even the Catholic church permits them by special dispensation if one partner is otherwise unmarriageable because of some disability. Several Nadars told me that if they wished to make an eZDy marriage under other circumstances, they would simply not hold the wedding at church. No one in Vadakku Vandanam had actually done so, however. For Catholic Nadars, even marriages between first cousins involve each family paying a small fine to the church: this should be borne in mind when assessing Table 6.1.

6.2 Exogamous Groups

6.2.1 Kondaiyankottai Maravars

Maravars are said to have eighteen matrilineal, exogamous branches (*kiḷai*) grouped three by three into six exogamous clusters (*kottu*; Fawcett 1903; Thurston and Rangachari 1909: v. 33). Local information partly bears out Fawcett's account, although, as we shall see, only a minority of the branches named by him are actually present locally, and the correlation of branches and clusters is much less clear than he suggests.

These matrilineal branches are 'descent groups' only in the restricted sense proposed by Dumont (1983: 108 n.), where 'descent' refers solely to transmission of membership in an *exogamous* group, not to succession or inheritance (cf. also 1.2, above). For Maravars,[1] both succession and inheritance are regulated by *paramparai*, that is, transfer from F to S or the nearest agnatic equivalent. Residence after marriage is viri-patrilocal, so the branches are widely dispersed. The branch system is incompatible with ZD marriage because the MB and ZD belong to the same exogamous group, as Maravars themselves pointed out to me (see also Aiyappan 1934; Lévi-Strauss 1969: 432–3). Marriage with a classificatory "sister's daughter" is not thereby ruled out, but no cases were observed.

All local Maravars know their branch, and most also know their F's branch. Few people can name their cluster, however, although almost everyone knows that such units exist. People tended to agree with the overall system described by Fawcett if confronted with it, but only one man mentioned it spontaneously. He had read about it in a book called the *Kiḷaivakaikottu*, at the palace of the (Maravar) ex-Zamindar of Kadambur. He also said that the clusters were paired into three *pavaḷams* ('coral'). His own *pavaḷam* is *Sēyavaṉ* (an epithet of the god Murukan), but he did not know the others. No one else mentioned this, but it supports Fawcett's suggestion that clusters are grouped into exogamous pairs. In some places married Maravar women wear coral necklaces called *pavaḷams* (Kadhirvel 1977: 9), but this is not done locally.

[1] Succession and inheritance always occur, ideally, from F to S. Post-marital residence is virilocal for most groups.

Seven branches and four clusters are represented in Terku Vandanam and Kalinkapatti. No one could name any others, so presumably none are found among their relatives elsewhere. Dumont was told that there were only eleven branches altogether (1983: 41), and despite the discrepancy in absolute numbers my findings support his view that Fawcett's is a purely theoretical list. It was drawn from a song praising the caste, and the reality seems much less systematic. Dumont was also told that the cluster was not a higher-order unit than the branch, but an 'honorific grouping' of *lower* order, and one Terku Vandanam man also claimed that there were two clusters per branch. The full list of branches is as follows: (i) *maruvīḍu*, 'affinal house'; (ii) *vīramaṉattaṉ*(or *vīramuḍitāṅki*) 'royal crown-bearer'; (iii) *sētar* (or *sēturai*), 'king of Ramnad'; (iv) *Akattīsvar*, a Tamil sage; (v) *seyaṅkoṇḍar*, 'conqueror'; (vi) *nāṭṭumaṉṉar*, 'king of the country'; and (vii) *Aḻakarpāṇḍiyaṉ*, a medieval king. These correspond to numbers 5, 1, 2, 4, 3, 9, and 6, respectively, in Fawcett's list. The clusters are called: (a) *miḷakāy*, 'pepper'; (b) *veṟṟilai*, 'betel leaf'; (c) *mundiri*, 'grape-vine'; (d) *sīrakka*, 'cumin, fennel'. Of these, (c) and (d) are not on Fawcett's list.

As so few informants knew their cluster, data on the correlation between cluster and branch membership are meagre. Moreover, replies conflicted. Most correlations are based on the unsupported testimony of single individuals. My few respondents all linked branch (i) with cluster (a), but branch (ii) was variously linked with both clusters (b) and (c). Different members of branch (iii) claimed affiliation with clusters (a) and (d); of branch (iv) with (b), (c), and (d); of branch (v) with (a), (b), and (c); of branch (vi) with (c); I have no evidence for branch (vii).

These links show no discernible pattern. They do not confirm either Dumont's suggestion that 2 clusters = 1 branch, or the statements of Fawcett and many of my local informants, that 1 cluster = 3 branches. People agree[2] that one should marry into a different cluster as well as a different branch, but the point is academic because so few of them know to which cluster they belong. The entire structure may be the rationalization of a process of *ad hoc* fission (Dumont 1983: 42).

[2] The one exception was the Terku Vandanam President, who said that spouses could be from the same *kottu* as long as their *kiḷais* were different. But this was after he had just read Fawcett's list, according to which he and his wife belonged to the same *kottu*!

All Maravars have family deities (*kuladeyvam*) inherited from their fathers. These are specified by both name and place: for instance, the family deity of the Terku Vandanam and Kalinkapatti Talaiyaris is Terku Vandanam Kalasami, i.e., Kalasami whose temple lies in Terku Vandanam. In all, 17 family deities are named by Maravar men and women[3] living in Terku Vandanam. Their shrines are dispersed throughout Tirunelveli and Ramanathapuram Districts (the geographical spread of the sub-caste). The statuses of these deities befit the status and hereditary occupations of Maravars themselves. For instance, Terku Vandanam Kalasami is the assistant of Lord Aiyanar, the guardian of village territory, just as the Maravar Talaiyaris assist the local law-enforcement officer, the Munsip.

Couples sharing the same localized family deity cannot marry. Maravars therefore have both matrilineal *and* patrilineal exogamous descent groups, and the cultural stress placed on the former should not blind us to this fact.

6.2.2 *Other Castes*

The Maravar *kiḷai* is not the only type of exogamous grouping found locally. There is some confusion over details, but this section summarizes points on which there is general agreement.

Thurston reports 'totemistic septs' among Reddiyars (cf. 'Kapu', Thurston and Rangachari 1909: iii. 230–1), and mentions a moiety organization among them. Sure enough, the Ayotti Reddiyars of Kalinkapatti have patrilineal groups called *vāḍars* or *vāḍais* ('street, village'). There are twenty-four of these, divided equally into two exogamous moieties which represent, for a male Ego, his 'affines' (*sammandakkārar*),[4] who are marriageable, and his 'heirs' (*sokkāraṉ*; cf. 6.3, below), who are not. Every *vāḍai* is associated with one particular family deity, and vice versa. I have insufficient data to assign *vāḍais* to specific moieties.

Totti Cakkiliyars, too, have patrilineal moieties, but these are not subdivided. Their names were given to me as *sāṉa* and *dāsari*. The Cakkiliyars' mother-tongue is Telugu, and it seems likely that these names are dialect forms of *sāṅkam* and *dāsari*, the names of Saivite

[3] A wife worships her husband's *kuladeyvam* after marriage, so strictly speaking it is the H's and WF's family deities which are in question.

[4] *Sammandakkārar* is also an affinal relationship term (see Tables 5.1 and 5.3).

and Vaisnavite sects, respectively (Thurston and Rangachari 1909: ii. 112, 450). Many Telugu castes are divided on sectarian lines, though inter-sect marriage is frequent (Mudiraj 1970: 287). Madigas, the Andhra equivalents of Cakkiliyars, have sectarian priests called Jangams and Dasaris (Mudiraj 1970: 283). The Vadakku Vandanam situation is thus an extreme variant of that pattern, in which moiety exogamy is compulsory rather than merely preferred. I found no case of Cakkiliyars violating this rule, though their marriages are irregular in other ways, and rather unstable.

Kammavar Nayakkars (TV 3) have three types of patrilineal grouping, the family name (*kuḍumpa pēr*), clan (*kōttiram*, Sanskrit *gotra*), and family deity. There is a direct correlation between family name and family deity, and all agree that the family names of husband and wife have to be different. However, although the majority describe the clans as exogamous in normal fashion, several families say they are endogamous. As with most castes, there is no correspondence whatever with the list of 'septs' reported by Thurston and Rangachari (1909: iii. 98).

The Vaniya Cettiyars (TV 7) all belong to a single clan, the same one as my research assistant Palanimurugan. His father confirmed that the group was endogamous, adding that there were also exogamous groups called *kulams* ('family, descent').

Asaris (TV 6, 8, 13) are divided among five trades (*vēlai*): namely Carpenter (*taccan̲*), Goldsmith (*taṭṭān̲*), Blacksmith (*kollan̲*), Brazier (*kannan̲*), and Stonemason (*kallan̲*). These groups are normally endogamous. One Carpenter had married a Blacksmith girl, but his father said that this would not have been allowed in the old days. One informant mentioned five endogamous sub-castes (*jāti*) cutting across this occupational division, according to region of origin. There was vague awareness of endogamous *kulams* too.

Some people in other caste-groups mentioned that they belonged to a clan or *kulam*, but none of them could even state their own affiliations. Paraiyars, Konars, Pallars, and Pulavars have no such subdivisions. All except Christian Nadars have patrilineally inherited family deities, although women adopt their H's deity after marriage. Most people must marry someone with a different family deity, but Konars, whose deity is usually a local form of Aiyanar, have no such rule.

6.3 Subdivisions of the Exogamous Group

There are two other types of subdivision of the exogamous group, both of which have exclusively male membership. First, a man's *paṅkāḷis* are simply his full and half brothers. The word means 'partner, share-holder, co-heir', and clearly refers to the fact that the father's property will be divided up among this particular group.[5]

The *paṅkāḷis* are included in the *sokkāraṉs*, who comprise the children and children's children of *paṅkāḷis* for two to three gener-

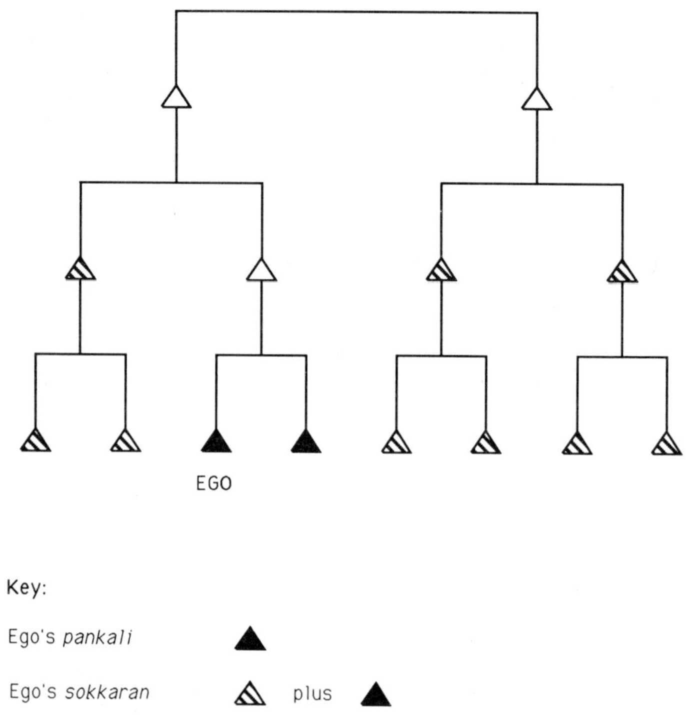

FIG. 6.1 Pankali and Sokkaran

[5] The work *paṅkāḷi* is often found in similar contexts in South India (Dumont 1957*b*: 274–5; Beck 1972: 305) and Sri Lanka (David 1973: 524). The Terku Vandanam usage is more restricted than any of these, however.

ations, depending on residence, genealogical knowledge, and so on.[6] As F and S are neither *paṅkāḷis* nor *sokkāraṉs* to each other, the *sokkāraṉs* are more like a kindred than a lineage. Membership differs slightly for each set of male siblings. Figure 6.1 displays the *paṅkāḷis* and *sokkāraṉs* of a given Ego in a hypothetical lineage of three generations depth. Such ties are gradually forgotten as genealogical distance increases. It is not clear what purpose the *sokkāraṉ* relationship serves.[7] It is certainly not an expression of common 'blood', for several men had *sokkāraṉs* to whom they were related only through a second marriage or unofficial liaison.

Example A
Konar: Suppaiya and Madasami named each other as *sokkāraṉ*. I could see no genealogical reason for this, but they explained that Madasami had had 'two fathers'. After his own F died, his M had lived with Suppaiya's yB, a bachelor. The latter had also died, but the liaison was perpetuated in the *sokkāraṉ* relationship.

Example B
Konar: Suppaiya (not the same man as in Example A) said that N was his *sokkāraṉ*. Apparently Suppaiya's widowed mother had been the mistress of N's father.

6.4 The Urimai Relationship

Most South Indians regard one genealogically defined relative as the preferred marriage partner. Such ideal potential spouses are said to have an *urimai* ('claim') over each other. The woman is referred to as the *urimaippeṇ*, where *peṇ* means 'girl' and, in this context, 'bride'. In some places one must make a gift to the *urimai* partner if one marries someone else (Srinivas 1952: 147; Dumont 1983: 68; Beck 1972: 243; Yalman 1963: 27). This happens in parts of Tirunelveli (Dumont 1963: 303), but there is no such expectation in Terku Vandanam.

[6] This meaning of *sokkāraṉ* is more genealogically precise than the Ayotti Reddiyar usage (see 6.2.2, above).

[7] There is a clear parallel with the Piramalai Kallar's *uḍanpaṅkāḷi* or *uḍandaikkārar*, who are parallel cousins to the second or third degree (Dumont 1957*b*: 173).

The three possible choices for *urimaippeṇ* are the FZDy, MBDy and eZDy, although many informants could see no distinction between MBDy and eZDy marriage. These two relatives become identical under conditions of repeated eZDy marriage, of course (cf. Figure 5.3). Of the larger caste-groups, only the Maravars, Pallars, and Asaris (TV 6 and 8) were unanimous about their *urimai* partner. In other cases I report the majority view. For smaller groups the situation is sometimes unclear (Table 6.1). Many people were vague, or could not state any preference. Furthermore, people often named a specific cross-cousin as *urimaippeṇ* only to add that eZDy marriage was 'better'.

6.5 The Selection of Marriage Partners

No caste-group has significant or enduring alliances with particular villages, or lineages. Assuming terminological and age requirements are met, the most important characteristics of an ideal spouse are, in no particular order: personality; the character of their family and ancestors; overall wealth; size of dowry; and horoscope. Ideally the spouse should already be related (*sondam*): character and wealth are then known, marriage prestations are reduced, and horoscopes are not needed. Artisans and village servants stress the desirability of a son-in-law interested in their traditional calling (*sondatoḻil*).

Isogamy is the norm. The class (*vakuppu*) and status (*takuti*) of bride and groom should normally be the same, but an educated bridegroom of lower status is acceptable. It is unclear what is meant by "status" in this context though, and the last point is purely theoretical for most local people. They may be voicing urban preferences gleaned from the cinema.[8]

Views on sister exchange (*sakōtari parimāṟṟam*) vary from person to person, but no caste-group formally prohibits such marriages. Some say that such close interrelationships are good because serious disputes are rendered less likely, while others argue that a dispute affecting one couple would probably cause trouble for the others too. In any case, the fact that such marriages are allowed is further evidence for isogamy.

[8] Education may lead to demands for a high dowry (Tambiah 1973*b*: 63).

The general attitude during marriage negotiations between non-relatives is one of mutual suspicion. The other family's claims to wealth and land are carefully verified, and the pros and cons of the union are discussed interminably by the main protagonists, their friends, and neighbours. Once the match is agreed, though, things move rapidly and the wedding usually takes place within a month. The prestations involved, and the wedding itself, are discussed in Chapter 8.

Women never receive landed property (*sottu*, *nilam*) from their parents, at marriage or subsequently, unless the family has no sons. A newly married couple normally settles in the husband's native village, particularly if he expects to inherit land from his father.[9] Barbers and Washermen have a preference for neolocal residence after marriage. This reflects the universal but limited nature of demand for their services: they must clearly settle somewhere where they can get employment.

6.6 Second Marriages

Only Maravars admit allowing widows to marry again, although several other groups condone this in practice. All allow widowers to remarry however, and the practice is quite common. No caste-groups practise polyandry, but all local Hindu castes allow men[10] to take second wives, subject to the first wife's consent, if their first marriage is childless. Sororal polygyny is the most common form under such circumstances. Very little ceremony is associated with such a second marriage. Polygyny occurs for other reasons too:

Example C

Maravar: Kurusami had married his FZDD Malaiyammal (see 6.8.1, Ex. C, below). They had a daughter and three sons. His WM was a widow, for whom the cost of marrying her other D would be a great burden. Kurusami and his W were very hard-working, and were occupied on his land or carting business from dawn until dusk.

[9] Normally, every son receives an equally yielding share of landed property, preferably once they are all married and have sons of their own. Their father may retain a small plot for his own subsistence, or be supported by his sons on a monthly rota.

[10] This 'customary' right is illegal according to the Hindu Marriage Act.

Malaiyammal had been ill, and as the children were not old enough to work an extra pair of hands was needed. All these factors decided Kurusami to take Malaiyammal's yZ as a second wife.

He left one evening in new clothes, returning after midnight with his bride and some of her male relatives. There was no ceremony or feast: a few children were smeared with sandal-paste, and the relatives left later that day. The new wife wore her eZ's *tāli*, and the latter continued to wear the beads normally tied next to it. Everyone ate from one hearth (contrast Beck 1972: 203), and the wives shared all the work. The children still addressed the new wife as *sitti* (MyZ). No elaborate prestations (cf. 8.5, below) were involved. Kurusami had bought his new wife some saris, including that in which she arrived, but these were sometimes worn by her sister thereafter.

The contrast between this vestigial rite and those described in Chapter 8 is very marked. One possible reason for the truncated nature of the ceremony is that it involved the same two families as the groom's previous marriage, but events are perhaps best understood in relation to Dumont's distinction between 'principal' and 'subsidiary' marriages (see 12.3, below).

6.7 Divorce

Divorce (*tīrttal*, 'causing to be finished') is permitted by Maravars, Nayakkars, Panditars, Asaris, Vannars, Paraiyars, Pallars, and Cakkiliyars. It often results from a personal or financial dispute involving the two families rather than the couple themselves. Another common cause is that one partner had all along preferred someone else, but had submitted formally to their parents' wishes.

Example D
Maravar: Sanmuka Tevar's daughter was divorced in February 1977. Her entire dowry was returned to her F, and her saris and other garments were given back to the donors. Her family returned the Rs 101 *parisam* (see 8.5, below), and the *tāli* was handed back to the groom's F.

This returning of the marriage prestations is the most important aspect of divorce proceedings. It is not simply a matter of the divorcing couple drawing up an overall 'balance- sheet' and making a single payment from one side to the other. Instead, all wedding gifts from close relatives must be returned exactly and individually. This demonstrates that a whole framework of relationships hinges on each marriage, and shows yet again that the study of prestations is crucial to an understanding of South Indian society.

A surprising number of cases came to my attention in which people had changed marital partners. By no means all of them involved formal divorce and remarriage. Even among caste-groups which do not officially allow divorce, many men resident in Terku Vandanam have previous marriages, or prolonged extra- or pre-marital liaisons.

Many men also have concubines (*vaippāṭṭi*) from other castes. The circumstances range from virtual prostitution to *de facto* marriage. For example, one Terku Vandanam Pillai man has a second family in Kalinkapatti with a Reddiyar woman. Her family is wealthy, but she is slightly disabled and hence perhaps unmarriageable. He spends more time with her than with his wife, and when her eldest daughter reached puberty he openly took the role of father and was accepted as such by her relatives. This is an extreme case, though. Such relationships are usually much less open, so I cannot be sure of knowing every case even in Terku Vandanam. Most important men are reputed, however, to have at least one extra-marital liaison with a woman of different caste.

6.8 Marriage Practice

Every adult in the three villages was interviewed. His or her genealogy was obtained, together with information on place and date of birth, and—where relevant—the family deity, clan, *vāḍai*, branch, and cluster affiliations of themselves and their parents. All the local members of every caste-group can be linked together on a single genealogical diagram, some five generations deep but with an extremely wide horizontal spread.

Marriage is set within a firm framework of caste endogamy. Only four of the 380 marriages in the sample cut across caste boundaries: (i) the Vadakku Vandanam headmaster, probably a member of a Scheduled Caste, has a Nayar wife; (ii) a Pulavar man had married a Nayakkar woman in Madras; (iii) a Nayakkar man has a Maravar wife—ironically, this repeats a marriage in the previous generation and so is terminologically correct; (iv) one Konar man has a Nayakkar wife. The Christian couple in case (i) voiced moral objections to caste itself. In cases (ii)–(iv), the children belong to their father's caste. When asked about the daughter of couple (iv), Suppaiya Konar, a very distant relative with no particular motive for wishing to make the best of things, waved my questions aside: 'Any one of us would marry her.'

All other local marriages are isogamous unions between spouses of the same sub-caste. Table 6.1 records the proportions of marriages with the key genealogical relatives: MBDy, FZDy, and eZDy. The samples used comprise every marriage for which at least one spouse is alive and resident locally; the marriages of full and half siblings of both spouses; and the marriages of the children, children's children, etc., of all these people. The aim is to include all and only those for whom reliable genealogical data are available. Even so there are loose ends at the fringes of the consolidated genealogies, and the percentages in the Table are therefore minimum values, especially for smaller caste-groups.

One consequence of repeated eZDy marriage is that Ego's wife is not only his ZD but also his MBD (Figure 5.3). There were a few such cases in practice, which are listed in Table 6.1 as being with the eZDy because that is how local people view them. Most eZDy marriages display no such ambiguity, however.

6.8.1 The Maravar Case

The Maravars of Terku Vandanam and Kalinkapatti can be linked together on a single genealogical diagram. The sample in this case comprises 58 local marriages, and a further 86 for which enough is known about the couple and their parents for it to be certain whether or not the spouses were first cousins.

Of the 58 local unions, 5 (8.6 per cent) are MBDy marriages and 6 (10.3 per cent) are FZDy marriages. The full sample of 144 contains 18 (12.5 per cent) of each type. There is, then, no bias in practice towards the relative specified by the *urimai* rules. The overall figure of 25 per cent for first cross-cousin marriages is high, both relatively in comparison with other South Indian data (Beck 1972: Table 5.9), and absolutely when demographic factors are taken into account. A groom must be terminologically senior to his bride, but there is also a strong feeling against too large an age discrepancy, so by no means everyone has a marriageable cross-cousin in the first place. It is impossible to give exact figures in the absence of precise marriage dates, but it would appear that in most cases where a cross-cousin of appropriate age had been available, that person had indeed been married.

Table 6.2 presents in matrix form the distribution of marriage alliances among the various branches. Here the sample size is 119, made up of the 58 local marriages and the marriages of the parents of these people.[11] There is no evidence of any directional bias (between 'wife-givers' and 'wife-takers'), nor of any exogamous groupings involving more than one branch. The rules of branch exogamy are scrupulously adhered to, however, with one exception (Ex. F, below).

Interestingly, however, an 'elementary structure' of marriage exchange is much more evident at branch level than in purely genealogical terms. Only 12.5 per cent of marriages conform to the stated *urimai* preference for the FZDy (Table 6.1), yet in 34 (59 per cent) of the 58 extant local marriages the wife belonged to her HF's branch. Fawcett (1903) noted this practice, and local people themselves drew my attention to it. It is formally equivalent to 'short-cycle' generalized exchange (Lévi-Strauss 1969), because there is a reversal—in the branch affiliations of the couple—in each generation of the patriline.

Beck noted (n.d.: 11) that the more Tamil castes stress unilineal descent, the less important become other criteria of marital correctness, like terminological category. The Maravar data bear this out, for terminologically incorrect unions are tolerated provided the rule of branch exogamy is satisfied.

Example C

Kurusami married his FZDD Malaiyammal, his "daughter" (*makaḷ*), i.e., a parallel relative of the wrong terminological level. Moreover, his eB Suppaiya had previously married his FZDy, so that Suppaiya's W is Kurusami's WMZ. Kurusami's marriage is agreed (even by him) to have been wrong on all these counts. Everyone emphasized, however, that the rule of branch exogamy had not been broken, and drew attention to the fact that both men had married into their F's branch in the approved way.

[11] Each couple was of course counted only once, however many married children they had.

TABLE 6.1. Frequencies of First Cross-Cousin and eZDy Marriage

			Identity of wife (%)			
Sub-caste	Urimai	Sample size	MBDy	FZDy	eZDy	Total
Maravar (TV, KP)	FZDy	144	12.5	12.5	—	25.0
Paraiyar (TV)	FZDy/MBDy	77	9.1	11.7	10.4	31.2
Nayakkar	MBDy	67	11.9	9.0	9.0	29.9
Konar (TV, VV)	MBDy	86	14.0	3.5	9.3	26.8
Pillaimar	?	75	2.7	1.3	8.0	12.0
Taccan Asari	FZDy	46	—	15.2	10.9	26.1
Cettiyar	MBDy	48	2.1	2.1	6.3	10.5
Kollan Asari	FZDy	34	11.8	11.8	23.5	47.1
Velar	?	16	6.2	—	6.2	12.4
Kavundar	FZDy/MBDy	5	—	20.0	—	20.0
Vannar (TV, VV, KP)	MBDy	34	8.8	8.8	11.8	29.4

Panditar (TV, KP)	eZDy	14	—	—	14.3	14.3
Tattan Asari	FZDy	3	—	—	—	—
Tinda Vannar	?	3	—	—	—	—
Nadar	FZDy/MBDy	291	9.5	7.6	0.3	17.4
Pallar	FZDy	126	4.0	4.8	0.1	8.9
Kampalattar	?	54	1.9	5.6	1.9	9.4
Cakkiliyar	FZDy	43	—	9.3	2.3	11.6
Maniyakkarar	?	17	—	—	11.8	11.8
Maruttuvar	MBDy	14	7.1	14.3	7.1	28.5
Ayotti Rediyar	eZDy	131	5.3	6.9	11.5	23.7
Saiva Cettiyar	eZDy	27	7.4	—	3.7	11.1
Kottu Reddiyar	?	20	—	—	20.0	20.0
Pulavar	?	21	—	9.5	9.5	19.0
Telunku Asari	FZDy	8	—	—	—	—
		1404	7.1	7.2	5.7	20.0

Note: Second marriages have been included. In some cases, caste members did not agree over the identity of their *urimaippeṇ*.

TABLE 6.2. Pattern of Inter-Kilai Marriage in Terku Vandanam

Husband's Kilai		Wife's Kilai (i)	(ii)	(iii)	(iv)	(v)	(vi)	(vii)
(i)	*maruvīḍu*	—	16	8	2	10	1	0
(ii)	*vīramuḍitāṅki*	12	—	7	6	1	0	0
(iii)	*sētār*	8	1	—	1	6	0	1
(iv)	*akattiṣvar*	3	3	1	—	0	0	1
(v)	*sēyaṅkoṇḍar*	7	2	7	1	—	5	0
(vi)	*naṭṭumannār*	0	0	0	0	7	—	0
(vii)	*aḻakarpāṇḍiyan*	0	0	0	0	1	1	—

Example E
Cellaiya married his MBWZ (*attai*). This was agreed to be wrong strictly speaking, but was again justified with reference to the different branch affiliations of the pair. Dumont reports unions with terminological "father's sisters" among other Maravars (1983: 99).

Example F
There was just one case in which branch exogamy had *not* been observed, although terminologically the marriage was quite acceptable. It came to my notice when those most directly involved gave fictitious branch affiliations for themselves and their parents, making their accounts inconsistent. Evidence from distant relatives revealed what had happened.

So terminologically wrong marriages are openly acknowledged, whereas breaches of branch exogamy are concealed. This is precisely what Beck's argument predicts. The sequel to Example C confirms her other observation that relationships created by a new marriage take priority over those created by earlier marriages, if the two do not coincide (1972: 226). When Kurusami married again (6.6, above), I saw this as a repetition of his 'wrong' marriage with his FZDD. Everyone disagreed however, pointing out that the WyZ is a prescribed spouse.

Lest the above examples create a false impression, it should be made clear that all other Maravar unions *do* conform to the terminological prescription. In the three villages as a whole, over 95 per cent of all marriages conformed—even at the time (cf. 6.9, below)—to prescriptive requirements.

Family deity exogamy is also fully observed. In one case H and W share the same deity, but there are none where deity *and* location are the same for both. The genealogy confirms that there are no systematic affinal connections with other villages, but Sillankulam, three miles to the south, has an important agnatic link with Terku Vandanam. About half those having Terku Vandanam Kalasami as family deity reside there.

The requirement that a husband be his wife's senior is built into the terminological prescription. Senior cross-cousins are distinguished from juniors, and only the latter are marriageable for a male Ego. For the fifty-eight Maravar marriages, the mean age difference between H and W is 5.6 years for all marriages and a little less for MBDy and FZDy unions. The H is indeed older than his W in all cases but one.

Example G

Even the solitary exception proves the rule, as the man is senior terminologically, though chronologically junior. This case provides yet another example of how the relationships created by a recent marriage supersede those existing previously, for it is the second marriage in a 'sister exchange'. As a result of the prior marriage of his eZ, the man became the eBWB of his eventual bride. Such vicarious seniority was enough to cancel out a small age difference of less than a year.

The separate examination of categories (5.3) and rules (6.4) gives rise to contrasting sets of expectations regarding Maravar marriage behaviour. To which set does the empirically observed marriage pattern conform more closely? As we saw, marriage behaviour in so far as it affects first cousins[12] is almost perfectly symmetrical overall. The Maravar data clearly suggest, therefore, that the symmetric prescription plays a greater part in regulating behaviour than the asymmetric preference.[13] But the correspondence is not necessarily the same among other local sub-castes, and in any case it is misleading to look only at the overall group. All *individual* Maravar marriages

[12] It is only truly meaningful to speak of symmetry or asymmetry in connection with *first* cross-cousins. Given the convoluted nature of the genealogy, more distant relatives are almost inevitably related both matri- and patrilaterally, though not necessarily equally closely.

[13] If this is so, one might justifiably ask, why bother having the rule in the first place? A partial answer emerges below.

are asymmetric, except in those comparatively rare cases where the spouse is both their MBC and FZC.

6.8.2 Other Local Castes

Among the local population as a whole, there are 100 (7.1 per cent) MBDy marriages, 101 (7.2 per cent) with an FZDy, and 80 (5.7 per cent) with an eZDy, out of a total sample of 1,404 (Table 6.1). In other words, marriages with these closest possible relatives make up 20.0 per cent of the total. The Maravars are therefore far from unique in having such a densely intertwined genealogy. If Maravars and Nadars are excluded, the totals become 54 (5.6 per cent), 61 (6.3 per cent) and 79 (8.2 per cent), respectively, out of a sample of 969, so that eZDy marriage is the commonest form among groups which permit it.

The Terku Vandanam Asari sub-castes both state a quite unambiguous FZDy preference, but differ from the Maravars in also allowing eZDy marriage. The Taccan Asari (TV 6) genealogy reveals high percentages of marriages with the FZDy and eZDy, but none at all with the MBDy. In contrast to the Maravars, these Asaris observe the asymmetric rule to something like the maximum extent permitted by the exigencies of demography.

Kollan Asaris (TV 8) state their *urimai* preference even more vehemently if anything, and some even assert that MBDy marriage is not merely less preferable but positively to be avoided. Yet in practice their sample involves *equal* numbers of marriages with the FZDy and MBDy, as well as many with the eZDy. The proportion of close marriages (47.1 per cent) is remarkably high; more to the present point, their behaviour appears to give the lie to a jural preference upon which they insist with greater passion than any of their neighbours.

Overall, Table 6.1 shows that group behaviour may be perfectly symmetrical, totally asymmetrical, or anywhere in between. This lack of correspondence between the *urimai* preference and the empirical marriage pattern, together with the vagueness of many informants on such matters, suggest that such rules have little influence on behaviour locally. In fact most people were at a loss when asked to explain marriage preferences. One Kollan Asari argued that the MBD had the same blood (*irattam*) as Ego—hence the avoidance of MBD marriage—whereas the FZD and eZDy did not until they acquired it at their wedding. His argument cannot logically be sustained, however, for MBD is identical to ZD under the conditions of Figure 5.3. To complicate matters further, a visiting relative disagreed and offered an explanation based on the terminology. It too contained logical inconsistencies.

6.9 The Overall Pattern

Needham (1973) was the first to show how the confusion between prescription and preference, which had bedevilled kinship theory for many years, could be resolved by differentiating the 'categorical' level, at which one finds terminological prescription, from the level of 'jural' marriage preferences. In those terms, Table 6.1 shows that neither the symmetry of the prescriptive terminology nor the asymmetry of the *urimai* preference necessarily determine empirical marriage patterns.

This state of affairs could arise purely from demographic contingency, with the *urimai* partner always being married whenever one exists (P. G. Rivière, pers. com.). In the present case wilful nonconformity to the *urimai* rule does occur, although in the absence of accurate data on marriage dates it is impossible to be precise about its extent. But Rivière's point remains important, for it draws attention to the absolute, demographic *necessity* of inter-level incongruence. The three levels of data are indeed autonomous.

So far my discussion has emphasized the distinctions between these levels, but all three must combine into a system which actually works for those living by it. People do succeed in marrying in ways which are agreed to be correct, and manage to apply kin terms to one another in logical, consistent ways. Neither the terminology nor the marriage rules can therefore be *contradictory* with respect to each other or to behaviour. There are indeed logical lacunae, but these are not serious enough to cause the collapse of the system.

The terminology—with or without eZDy marriage—is a symmetric-prescriptive one, and as a result the terminological structure is perfectly congruent with repeated bilateral cross-cousin marriage. All the genealogical identities depicted in Figure 6.1 correspond to terminological identities included in Table 5.1. Moreover, such a system would be in perfect accord with the requirements of branch and family deity exogamy. But Figure 6.1 is by no means the only genealogy which would be consistent with the terminology. The fit would be just as good if there was universal and repeated marriage with the patri- or matrilateral first cross-cousin, even though the terminology, being symmetric, does not distinguish 'wife-givers' from 'wife-takers'. It is always possible to have rules which make further fine discriminations not inherent in the categories, so long as these rules operate within the framework of categorical boundaries.

As depicted by Fawcett (1903), the Maravars' branch system seems to represent a second classificatory framework, as all-embracing as the relationship terminology but, like Australian section systems, group- rather than ego-centred. In practice though, it proves to be merely an *ad hoc* system of fissionable exogamous groups. Although the division into branches and clusters—and for that matter into *kulams*, clans, and family deity congregations—does involve use of categorical labels, these are merely names applied to empirically-existing groups. There is no element of prescription here, nor, in practice, any consistent, formal logic.

The most widespread and explicit rules among local caste groups are those concerning exogamy and *urimai* relationships. Considerations of symmetry and asymmetry simply do not enter into the formulation of the negative, exogamic rules, but the positive rules are usually quite explicitly asymmetric.

Most local sub-castes combine a symmetric prescription with an asymmetric *urimai* preference, raising contrary expectations about empirical practice. The terminology suggests that MBDy and FZDy marriages ought to be equally frequent, as these genealogical positions are not distinguished categorically, whereas the *urimai* rule suggests that one such relative will be married in preference to the other. It subdivides the category to which both belong, so that a genealogically defined member of the prescribed terminological class is singled out and made the subject of a preferential rule. This rule does not conflict with the prescription, but merely makes a further distinction which retains the categorical boundaries intact in their precise, original forms.

Contradiction *would* arise though if, say, a rule were to link FZDy with FBDy, while excluding MBDy and MZDy. Categorical boundaries would then be broken down and there could not be full conformity to both prescription and preference. So preferential rules which further restrict marriages *within* a given prescribed category are acceptable: rules which transgress prescriptive categorical boundaries are not. Thus the terminology sets limits beyond which the rules cannot go, but within these limits the rules enjoy full autonomy.

Marriages contravening branch rules are more reprehensible than those violating prescriptions. This seems paradoxical, as terminological prescriptions are valid *by definition* whereas preferences are merely rules which 'should' or 'could' be followed but need not be. Yet the situation is quite logical. When a marriage involves two 'strangers', between whom no previous relationship is known, their respective families begin addressing one another 'as if' the marriage had involved cross-cousins. That is only to be expected of a prescriptive system. But things go further, as Beck's generalizations and the above examples (6.8.1) show. Marriages which were 'wrong' at the time become 'right' in retrospect, because the relationships they create supersede those existing beforehand. No marriage can be 'wrong'—in the prescriptive sense—in the long term.

No opportunity for redefinition arises in the case of rules. When they are broken the breach is permanent and cannot be healed retrospectively. For comparatively weak rules like those concerning the *urimai* partner, disobedience does not matter much, particularly when justified in terms of other values such as those favouring marriage into a wealthy and respectable family. When a rule carries strong moral sanctions it will tend not to be broken, however, and if it *is* broken this will if possible be concealed. The exogamic rules *vis-à-vis* branches and family deities are of this type. Only one breach had occurred, and this was hidden from me by those involved. Rules, then, differ quantitatively: they become more or less coercive. Not so with prescription. A system is either prescriptive or not: there are no degrees (cf. Maybury-Lewis 1965: 226).

Inter-level inconsistency is not just inevitable in practice but necessary in principle. Thus, rules do not correspond exactly to behaviour but regulate and set limits upon it. These limits may or may not be observed in particular cases. A rule which was entirely congruent with behaviour would lose its very essence. It would no longer *direct* or *justify* behaviour and would instead merely *describe* it.

Similarly, rules are not inevitable entailments of the categorical system, though they are of course phrased in terms of concepts furnished by that system. Again discrepancies must exist; a rule which merely stated what was already given by the system of classification would be pure tautology. For instance, a rule stating that 'a man must marry his *kolundiyāl*' would be in effect saying 'a man must marry a marriageable woman'. It would convey nothing that was not already true *by definition*.

The position regarding marriageability may be summed up as follows. The empirical state of affairs at one level is never determined by what happens at another, yet there is not complete autonomy either. For example, certain rules, or forms of behaviour, do not occur because they would directly violate the logic of the system of categories.

6.10 Summary

This chapter dealt first with the preferential marriage rules of local caste-groups. On the negative side, various exogamous descent groups were described, including the matrilineal clans of the Maravars. The positive preference for a genealogically defined *urimai* relative was explained, and non-kinship factors like reputation and economic wealth were briefly discussed.

Statistical behaviour was then considered. The relative proportions of MBDy and FZDy marriages vary empirically from 50 : 50 to 0 : 100, and do not necessarily reflect either the symmetric prescription or the asymmetric *urimai* preference.

The concluding sections of the chapter related the marriage preferences of local caste-groups to their practices on the one hand, and their prescriptive terminologies on the other. It was argued the system can only work as long as the terminology and marriage rules do not contradict each other, although certain types of inconsistency and incongruity are perfectly possible. Prescriptions and rules differ in character, however. All marriages are terminologically correct in retrospect, because the relationships they create supersede those existing beforehand, whereas rule-breaking cannot be redefined out of existence in this way. Breaches of a rule which carries strong moral sanctions are therefore concealed if possible.

Finally, inter-level inconsistency was shown to be inevitable, even in principle. Rules are not mere descriptions of behaviour, but performative statements (see 12.5, below) intended to direct, justify or rationalize it. Similarly, they must convey something more than the system of classification to which they refer, if they are not to be mere tautological definitions.

7
Puberty Rites in the Three Villages

7.1 Introduction

This and the three following chapters deal in turn with local rites of passage, beginning with a consideration of the rituals marking female puberty. The rite discussed here is practised by all local groups except the Nadars, who are of course Catholics.[1] It is known in everyday speech as *saḍaṅku*. Other, more formal, titles are *irudu maṅkalaṣnāṉam* ('puberty auspicious-bath') and *pūppuppuṉita nīrāttu viḻā* ('menstruation purity bathing festival'). Both names emphasize the bathing of the pubescent girl, but there is more to the ritual than that.

The most elaborate Sadanku during my stay is described in the next section. It was, however, rather atypical as regards the social identities of participants (cf. 13.1, below). Moreover, many details differ from case to case. The description is therefore followed by a summary of the main features of Sadankus in general, referring where appropriate to other examples.

7.2 The Sadanku Ceremony: An Example

Example A
Maravar: Karuppaiya Tevar's eldest daughter, Sanmukattay, was secluded in a hut on the veranda. She wore old saris, and the Washerwoman came every two days to collect her dirty clothes for washing. The ceremony was held seven weeks after her first menstruation, on 16 March 1977 (Indian General Election Day). The

[1] I witnessed no Sadankus in Vadakku Vandanam. The only one to be held in Kalinkapatti during my stay coincided with a Terku Vandanam wedding, and although I attended the feast I did not see the ritual. The geographical spread of this particular ceremony is not clear. Penny Logan (pers. com.) has observed it among non-Brahmans in Madurai city, but it is not universal in the Madurai region (Reynolds 1980; Dumont 1957*b*; cf. 11.3, below).

printed invitations gave the exact time of the ceremony, and relevant astrological details.[2] The hosts were named as her parents, Karuppasami (her MB), and Sanmuka (MF ['deceased']). There was a list of relatives from whom 'gifts are expected', namely, her FFB, FMB, two FyBs, and her two MBs.[3] The auspicious period was 9 a.m. until 10.30 a.m., and for once events kept more or less to time. The bamboo pavilion (*pandal*) outside the house was decorated with white cloths by the Washerman. The Brahman officiant tied strings of margosa leaves (*vēppilai*) over the house doors as a protective amulet (*kāppu*), and arranged the items shown in Figure 7.1 on the platform (*maṇavaṛai*) inside the pavilion. In front (east) of the platform was a small fire of sticks and ghee.[4] The Brahman broke a coconut, and laid half before the images of Lord Pillaiyar (see Fig. 7.1).

A *kumpam* (see Fig. 7.1) is a brass pot wrapped with white string in a criss-cross pattern, and filled with water. A coconut stands in the neck, on a pad of margosa or mango leaves. Such pots are used in Hindu temples to prepare water for the ritual of divine unction (Good 1987*a*: 17).

Several women carried gifts to the Pillaiyar temple,[5] led by Tamilarasi (FFBDDy, *sammandi*) and Parvati (MBW, *attai*), who had the 'bridal' sari. The gifts were laid on the temple steps and worshipped. The Oduvar priest gave out holy ash. The women completed a clockwise circuit of the settlement on their way back. The trays were displayed in the pavilion.

To the sound of *kuruvais*, the ululating cries with which Tamil women mark all auspicious transitions, Sanmukattay was led clockwise round the benches by Tamilarasi, then seated facing east. The Brahman garlanded her, put ash and kumkum on her forehead, and poured milk into her right hand for her to drink. He sprinkled dilute cow's urine over her head, then over the crowd and house too.

[2] All such rituals are arranged for auspicious days and times. Weddings never occur in Adi (July–Aug.), Purattasi (Sept.–Oct.), and Markali (Dec.–Jan.), but this is not true of Sadankus (see 7.3, Ex. C, below).

[3] Genealogical positions and relationship terms refer to the 'bride' as Ego in the case of Sadankus, and the groom in the case of Kaliyanams.

[4] The twigs are of *arasamaram* wood (*Ficus religiosa*).

[5] The police would not let them go to the village goddess temple, which was near the polling-booth. The police also ordered that the 'radio' at the house be turned off. 'Radio' systems broadcasting highly amplified film music are hired for most Sadankus and weddings, but loudspeakers are banned within earshot of polling-stations.

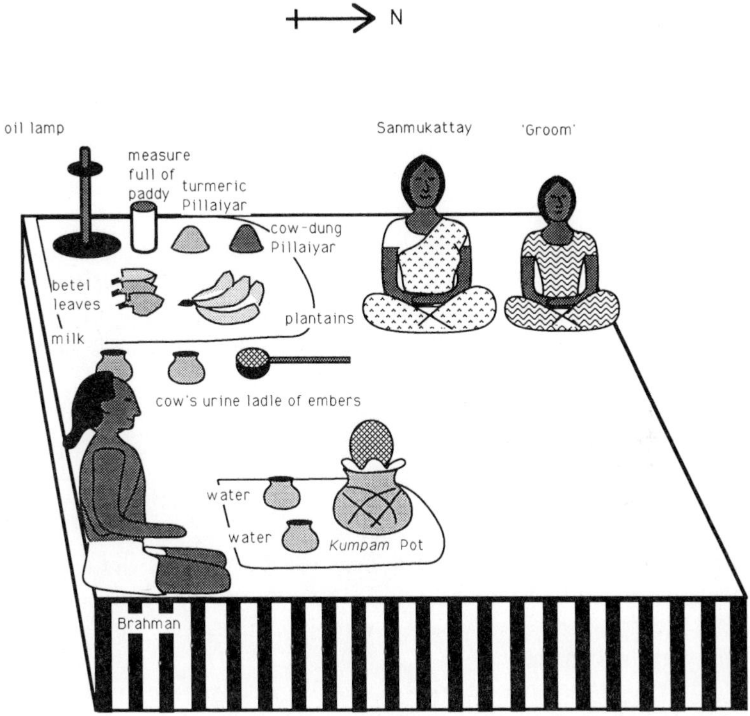

FIG. 7.1 Ritual Arrangements at a Maravar Sadanku

She was led outside by Parvati, and sat on a stool facing east. Tamilarasi poured water over her. Turmeric paste was rubbed on her face and hands. The Brahman poured milk and cow's urine over her, then poured the big pot over her head. The Washerwoman produced dry clothes to wrap round her, and she was led into the house by Tamilarasi. The sari tray was worshipped by the audience,[6] then carried inside.

Tamilarasi, now in the role of 'bridegroom' (*māppiḷḷai*), was led out by Tayammal (FFBD, *attai*), and seated facing east. Sanmukattay,

[6] At a wedding, the *tāli* would also be on the tray.

in her new sari, was led out by Parvati. She went clockwise round the bench and sat at the right of her 'groom'. The Brahman gave rice, ash, and red kumkum to the 'bride' and 'groom'. They drank milk from their right hands.

Parvati smashed three poppadums over Sanmukattay's head. She picked up a half-coconut and the plantains, and passed these over the benches, one on each side of the couple. Tayammal, standing behind, immediately passed them back. This exchange was carried out three times (*kuruvais* each time).

This ritual is called *ālatti*: it forms a regular part of Sadankus, weddings, and other rites. It may involve any suitable (auspicious, cooling, purifying) objects which come to hand. In general, it protects against evil eye and is a ritual of welcome for an important guest (cf. Marglin 1985*b*: 69).[7]

Important guests were called out one by one, to put holy ash on Sanmukattay's forehead and give her a small sum of money. They then did likewise to the 'groom', giving a smaller sum. The order of precedence among these donors reflected their status in the community rather than their genealogical relationship (if any) to the hosts. On this occasion the Karnam's eB was first. The Karnam himself followed, then myself, and my wife Alison. Next came Ponnaiya Tevar and his son, the President. Two vessels given by relatives were displayed in front of the bench.

The two *attais* circled a bowl of sandal-paste over the couple, then anointed them with it (*kuruvais*). Tamilarasi, Sanmukattay, and Parvati processed back to the house, in that order. Each grasped in her right hand the left wrist of the woman following.

Sandal-paste and betel were distributed to guests, and the feast began almost at once. Most people in the village were fed. After eating, each household head made a cash contribution which was recorded on a *moy* ('list') kept by members of the hosts' family.

Note that the *māppiḷḷai* was a girl. This term, normally applied by male speakers to junior male cross-relatives (Table 5.1, term 18), refers to the bridegroom in the context of weddings, just as *peṇ* normally means 'girl', but also 'bride'. The Sadanku 'groom' is always a close cross-relative of the mature girl who is unmarriage-

[7] The *ālatti* rite in Terku Vandanam seems to incorporate the viewing of auspicious objects, which occurs separately in Batticaloa (see 11.7, below; McGilvray 1982*b*). Marglin's comments refer to the *bandāpanā* rite, an Orissan equivalent of the *ālatti*.

able for reasons of sex or relative age. Sanmukattay's 'groom' was her second cousin—she has no female first cross-cousins.

7.3 Main Stages of the Sadanku Rite

Every case is unique with regard to its details, and the exact identities of key participants. This section summarizes the features common to all Sadankus, and also mentions significant variations. The following examples will be cited where appropriate, for purposes of illustration:

Example B
Maravar: The Sadanku of Muttulaksmi, D of Pappa Tevar, was much less elaborate than example A, because the family are very poor. There was no 'radio', Brahman priest, procession, or pavilion, and hardly anyone attended except the immediate relatives. None the less, the bathing and the wedding episode were performed. Both are clearly essential, however attenuated the Sadanku may be otherwise.

Example C
Velar: Karuppayi now lives in Tuticorin and her menstruation began there. A Washerwoman there had dealt with her laundry during the 16-day seclusion, but the rite was held at her natal house in Terku Vandanam. The ceremony was more than a month after her first menstruation, but I was told it could be at any convenient time between 16 days and 3 months after puberty. Paraiyar musicians led the procession and played at the ceremony. The Brahman officiant laid out the pavilion as shown in Figure 7.2.

Example D
Maravar: Ramalaksmi was secluded in a hut for 16 days. The invitation named her father Sanmuka and his surviving elder brothers as hosts. The 'expected' donors included Nayakkars, Pillais, and others. The family were hoping to entice large gifts from the ex-employers and merchants named, few of whom actually attended. There was a radio system, a procession, and a pavilion, but no Brahman. Most villagers were fed.

Seclusion: When a girl first menstruates, she is excluded from social life because of her impurity (*tīṭṭu*), and confined in a temporary

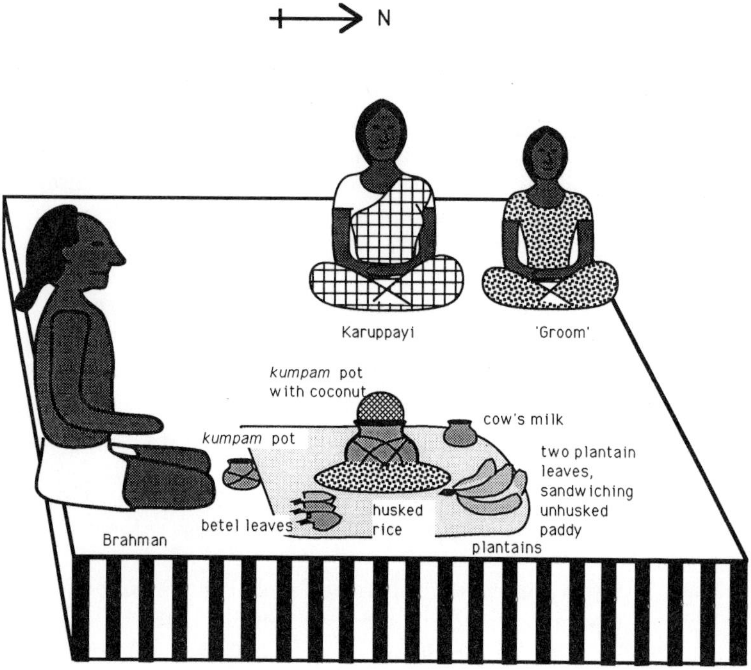

FIG. 7.2 Ritual Arrangements at a Velar Sadanku

hut outside the house. She wears old saris and a Washerwoman deals with her dirty laundry. Seclusion lasts for a notional 16 days.[8] The Sadanku should follow immediately, but may be delayed for astrological reasons or to suit relatives. There may be printed invitations similar to wedding invitations, though the name of the 'groom' does not appear.

[8] The period of seclusion is often, though not in Terku Vandanam, shorter for higher castes and longer in south Tamil Nadu than north (Ferro-Luzzi 1974: 126, 122). Similar trends are often found to apply to subsequent menstrual periods too (p. 129), but again not in Terku Vandanam (see 9.6, below).

Example C

I asked Arunacalam and Kurusami Velar, the girl's FF and F respectively, why the ceremony was in Purattasi, a month inauspicious for weddings. They said this applied only to true weddings: for other kinds of ceremony it was auspicious (cf. Beck 1972: 283).

Preparations: A ceremonial pavilion is built outside the house. Inside is a platform, consisting of two wooden benches placed side-by-side in a N–S direction. A 'radio' system is usually hired to blast out Tamil film music for 24 hours.

Procession: Women—the donors or their wives—process to a temple carrying the gifts the girl has received, including the sari to be worn in the wedding episode. The Priest anoints the women with ash. They process clockwise around the temple, and complete a clockwise circuit of the village streets.

Bath: The girl is led from the house by the woman I shall call the Main Officiant, and seated on the bench. The Brahman purifies the ritual arena, and cools her. He then bathes her with cow's milk and urine, as well as consecrated water. If no Brahman is present, the girl is taken straight outside from the house and bathed by the Main Officiant.

Example B

Muttulaksmi was bathed inside the house. It should have been done by her *attai* (FZ) but in her absence other married women did this.

Example C

Karuppayi was led east into the street by Uccimali (FyBW, *sitti*). The Brahman poured the two *kumpam* pots (Fig. 7.2) over her head as she sat on the ground (*kuruvais* each time). The music rose in crescendo.

Example D

Ramalaksmi was led out south of the *pandal*. Malaiyalaku (related as both FZDe and FBSW, *madini*) dipped margosa leaves in water, and circled the girl three times clockwise, sprinkling her, before pouring the whole pot over the girl. She rubbed turmeric on to the girl's face, removed her ornaments, and loosened her hair, then poured two more pots of water.

The purification on the platform can only be done by Brahmans because only they know the necessary mantras. I asked Arunacalam, FF of the girl in Example C, why she had been bathed. 'Because she was impure (*tīṭṭu*).' Why had a Brahman bathed her? 'Only a Brahman can remove *tīṭṭu*.' This orthodox response, from a conservative, elderly Priest, is of course at variance with the empirical facts, as the other examples show.

Wedding Episode: The 'bridegroom' is led out by the Main Officiant or an assistant. She may wear a turban or jacket, as well as the costume of blouse and long skirt worn by all little girls. The 'bride' is led out by the Main Officiant, garlanded and resplendent, and sits at the right of the 'groom'. The Brahman makes offerings to the couple. The 'bride' is always the first recipient, a reversal of the order at weddings. In the absence of a Brahman, the Main Officiant does this, and she now takes over in any case. She cools the couple with sandal-paste and/or cow's urine, and smashes poppadums over their heads: this also happens at weddings and its sexual connotations provoke much amusement among the onlookers.

Example C
The girl's *periyammāḷ* (FeBW) officiated. It could equally well, people said, have been her *sitti* (FyBW or MyZ). In either event, this woman is necessarily also the *attai* (FZ, MBW) of the 'bridegroom'.

An *ālatti* rite is done by the two women officiants, using auspicious, cooling or purifying objects. The couple may exchange garlands, as at a wedding. Sandal-paste, ash, or turmeric are applied to them by the female officiants. The audience, too, cool themselves with sandal-paste and ash.

Example D
The 'groom' and 'bride' exchanged garlands twice. Each exchange was marked by *kuruvai* shouts, as was the binding of the couple's right hands by Sodalaimuttu (FeB).

Important relatives and guests are invited to smear ash on the foreheads of the couple, and give them money. The 'bride' is anointed first and given the larger amount (Rs 3–5, say, as compared to Rs 1 for the 'groom'). Afterwards, a procession made up of: (1) the Main Officiant; (2) the 'bride'; (3) the 'groom'; and, sometimes, (4) the Minor Officiant, circles the platform once clockwise, and goes into the house.

The Feast: For the rest of the day, small groups of guests are fed, in no set order of priority. The food is vegetarian (*saiva sāppāḍu*, 'Saivite meal'), comprising boiled rice, vegetables, and a dessert, all served on plantain leaves. After eating, household heads make cash gifts to the hosts, who record them on a list (*moy*) and give betel in return. Hosts draw up *moys* at all rites of passage with a view to reciprocating in the future. The procedure exactly parallels that at a wedding, except that gifts are smaller at a Sadanku (Rs 3, say, rather than Rs 5). The entire village is fed in this way, except the Barbers and Washermen, who receive food to take home. Any Harijans who present themselves are fed the remnants of the meal out in the street. None of these contributes towards the *moy*.

7.4 Intra-caste Prestations

This section analyses some prestational exchanges involving relatives, in order to elicit the general principles which operate. For convenience *moy* gifts are also dealt with here, although they are made across caste boundaries too.

Example A
At Sanmukattay's Sadanku (7.2, above) the expenses totalled Rs 600 in cash and Rs 240 in kind—mainly their own rice, of which 1 *kōṭṭai* was used.[9] Cash received during the ceremony totalled Rs 190. The major contributors were: (i) the President, her FFBS (*sittappā*), Rs 21; (ii) her FZH (*māmaṉ*), Rs 21; (iii) MB (*tāymāmaṉ*), Rs 11; (iv) FFB (*tāttā*), Rs 10. Cash gifts at the feast totalled Rs 581 from over a hundred donors[10] of various castes. None of the 14 donors in this group who gave Rs 10 or more were close relatives. The total cash income was thus Rs 771, showing that even a large-scale function need not cost the hosts very much.

Gifts to Sanmukattay came from: (i) and (ii) her FyBs (*sittappā*); (iii) FFMBDD (*attai*), a widowed neighbour; (iv) MB (*tāymāmaṉ*), the husband of Parvati, the Main Officiant; (v) FZ and FZH (*attai*, *māmaṉ*); (vi) MZ and MZH (*sitti*, *sittappā*); (vii) FBWMZS (*māmaṉ*); (viii) FFBWZD and FFBWZDH (*attai*, *māmaṉ*).[11] Other donors

[9] They expressed this as 1.5 'quintals', or 150 kg.
[10] The *moy* was written up next day by my research assistant.
[11] They were also her MBWMZDH and MBWMZD, for whom the appropriate kinship terms are the same.

were: two Cettiyars from Tuticorin (natives of Terku Vandanam), a Nadar from Talaiyuttu, and the local Goldsmith. She thus received gifts from all her parents' siblings except her unmarried MB, who gave money during the ceremony.

Example B

The main contributors to the *moy* were relatives: (i) her FZD (*madiṉi*), a duty inherited from her deceased parents, Muttulaksmi's FZ (*attai*) and FZH (*māmaṉ*); (ii) her FZH's second W (*attai*); (iii) FMZSW (*sitti*); (iv) FeB (*periyappā*); (v) FFBS (*sittappā*); (vi) her M's deceased B's DH (*aṇṇaṉ*), who had inherited his WF's obligations in the absence of an adult male in his WM's household.[12] The *moy* realized Rs 120 altogether. The four surviving MBs (*tāymāmaṉ*), including the F of the 'groom', jointly provided Muttulaksmi's new sari, and some brass vessels. After her next menstruation, important relatives brought gifts of cooked food.

Example D

The family did not know the total cost, but had borrowed Rs 600 from the Kalinkapatti Talaiyari, at 10 per cent per month. Sixty *pakkās* of rice were consumed. The pavilion and radio each cost Rs 30; the plantain trees and electricity (an extension cord from Suppaiya Tevar's house) cost Rs 12.

The *moy* collection realized Rs 363, the main donors being the FeB and MZH. Six others gave Rs 10 or more, including Suppaiya Tevar and Alakarsami Nayakkar. Saris were given by the girl's MB (*tāymāmaṉ*) and FFZS (*māmaṉ*); brass vessels by her FeB and his W, her MeZ (*periyappā* and *periyammāḷ*); and, oddly, a vessel from Madan, a Pallar from Vadakku Vandanam.

The emphasis given to reciprocity means that one gives only as much as one has received in the past or expects to receive in future. This limits all aspects of the ceremony for poor families. Cross-relatives will not give large presents, nor can the hosts expect to recoup much through the *moy*, because few people attend and give only small donations. Prestations are influenced by local residence, not just genealogical relationship. Thus in Example B, Karuppaiya Tevar, a distant relative living in Terku Vandanam itself, was one of

[12] His WF would have been MB to Muttulaksmi, and he or his son could have been expected to contribute with the other MBs to her sari, etc. Dumont (1983: 87–9; 1957*b*: 259–61) discusses the inheriting of a MB's obligations.

the biggest donors to the *moy*, whereas some of Pappa Tevar's own brothers from elsewhere neither attended nor contributed.[13]

Whereas the responsibilities of parallel relatives are thus modified by contingencies of residence and ability to attend, a more formal obligation devolves upon certain cross-relatives. The girl's MBs (*tāymāmaṉs*), FZs (*attais*), and FZHs (*māmaṉs*) are all expected to give brass vessels, jewellery, or clothing. More distant relatives of these categories may be involved too, particularly if they live locally. The obligation falls mainly upon married affines. Providing he has at least one married brother, an unmarried MB need do little more than provide a small cash gift. This is reasonable, given that sons acquire their shares of the patrimony only after they have married. In Muttulaksmi's case, the largest cash gifts, too, came from the family of her deceased FZH, her terminological *māmaṉ*.

It is important to distinguish between gifts in kind and in cash, because the recipient varies. The sari and vessels go to the girl herself; like those she will receive at her wedding, they are her property and cannot be disposed of by her father, father-in-law, or husband without her permission. The money, whether given during the ceremony or after the meal, is used by the girl's F to defray the expenses of the function.

Though individually small, *moy* donations are significant overall. Even in the comparatively elaborate Example A, they met most of the cost of the ceremony. Gift-giving is less complex and ostentatious than at a wedding, however, because that complete nexus of gifts centring on the groom is absent. The prestations involving the community as a whole are identical in form to those at a wedding. Villagers attend the Sadanku, eat, give money which is recorded in a *moy*, and get betel in return. The expenses of a Sadanku are less, and *moy* gifts are typically smaller too.

7.5 Inter-Caste Prestations

Every household is served by a number of specialists from other castes (4.3, 4.4, above), who are also involved in Sadankus at their

[13] His eB Ramasuppu, a resident of Terku Vandanam, did not contribute either, but whether this was due to his extreme poverty or to some dispute, I am unsure. Karuppaiya and Pappa are *sokkāraṉ* (see 6.3, above), which implies a certain obligation.

clients' households. The following detailed examples show how some of the specialists are rewarded.

Example A

The Brahman officiant received a cash *sampaḷam* of Rs 5, and a *sāṣtiram* of 4 coconuts, 1 *paḍi* of rice, 1 *paḍi* of paddy, and a *teṭcaṇai* of Rs 1. The Washerman (Candiran) got Rs 25 in all: Rs 10 as cash payment for his duties, and Rs 15 in lieu of a vesti. The Priests got 1 *paḍi* of paddy, a coconut, plantain, camphor, incense, and betel. The Oduvar received two such prestations, for the Amman and Pillaiyar temples, and the Velar got one, for the Aiyanar temple. These were not payments for work done, but recognitions of the recipients' offices, i.e., they were *sāṣtiram* (4.2, above).

Example B

Muttulaksmi's clothes were washed by Candiran every 2 days. At the ceremony he got Rs 1, the girl's sari, some vegetable oil, and jaggery. No temple was visited during the rite, and I do not know whether *sāṣtiram* gifts were made to the Priests.

Example C

The Paraiyar band received Rs 30 cash. The Brahman got a Rs 5 *sampaḷam*. His *sāṣtiram* included 2 *paḍis* each of paddy and rice, a coconut, etc. He was also given his bus-fare. The Washerman in Tuticorin had been given Rs 10. A local Washerman would have received foodstuffs, not money. The Oduvar was rewarded as in *Example A*.

The Barber, Carpenter, Blacksmith, and Priests are recipients at all their clients' Sadankus. They do not always provide any significant services, and the prestations from the hosts are in any case explicitly *not* rewards for work done in the rite: they are *sāṣtiram*, not *sampaḷam*. Priests receive a *sāṣtiram* gift for each temple in their charge. The *sāṣtirams* of the Barber and Artisans are less elaborate. All these prestations serve to indicate that the link between specialist and client will survive the structural changes which the client household is undergoing as a result of the rite.

Two inter-caste prestations merit special attention. The Washerman launders the clothes polluted by menstrual blood and loans the cloths used in the pavilion. In return he gets a cash payment and a vesti. The cash seems to be a *sampaḷam*, making him the only local specialist so rewarded at a Sadanku. This implies that his work is felt to be beyond the call of duty, and so not covered by his annual *sampaḷam*. The Brahman's reward also contains both components, because he is an outsider with no enduring link to the host family. He gets travelling expenses, a cash *sampaḷam*, and a *sāṣtiram* consisting mainly of the items used during the rite.

7.6 Discussion

Sadankus, especially elaborate ones, display many overt resemblances to weddings, such as the binding of hands, exchanges of garlands, and breaking of poppadums (cf. 8.3.1, below). There is also, of course, a 'bridegroom'. The identity of this personage is considered in more detail later (14.1). For the moment we need only add that according to Arunacalam Velar, the Sadanku 'groom' is a female in order to prevent the ceremony being a real wedding. Only the father's *maccin̲an̲*'s (cross-cousin's) daughter could play the part, he said.

Example B
Muttulaksmi's 'bridegroom' was her MBDy. Remember that the preferred (*urimai*) partner for a Maravar girl is her MBS.

Example C
Karuppayi was FZDe to her 'groom'. According to her grandfather Arunacalam the FZD is the *urimaippeṇ*.[14]

Example D
Ramalaksmi was MBD to her 'groom', rather than FZD in line with the *urimai* preference. She herself has no MBD, however. Her case is unusual because her father and his four brothers had married five sisters.

In several ways, the emphasis at a Sadanku is the reverse of that at a wedding. It takes place entirely at the 'bridal' house, whereas weddings are at the groom's; ash is put first on the forehead of the 'bride' at a Sadanku; she gets more money; and she precedes the 'groom' round the bench at the end. The exact form of the

[14] On another occasion, her father Kurusami said that the MBD was the *urimai* girl.

ceremony is not constant even within a single caste. Example D involves actions (for example, an exchange of garlands) omitted from the generally more elaborate Example A. The presence of a Brahman seems to lead to greater emphasis on purification—the bath and what precedes it—while in his absence the 'wedding' becomes more prominent. There is a core to the ceremony, of certain key stages which cannot be omitted. How they are to be accomplished is often decided during the rite itself, however, as protagonists debate alternative courses of action, often with great vehemence. This does not mean that the details are arbitrary (cf. 12.5, below). The arguments arise because each caste, even each family, has its own, idiosyncratic practices. The Brahman does not have sufficiently detailed knowledge of his clients to be able to conduct the ceremony without their aid.

8
The Local Wedding Ceremony

8.1 The Significance of the Wedding

If "marriage" cannot be defined in any universal sense (see 1.3, above) then clearly the same is true of "wedding". I use the word here simply to translate the Tamil word *kaliyāṇam*, the associations of which—'happiness, prosperity, marriage, wedding, festivity, gold, good character, virtue' (Fabricius 1972: 208)—are strongly positive and auspicious. Marriage is the only Hindu rite of passage which does not entail impurity: quite the reverse, for the couple (especially the bridegroom) are temporarily treated as deities (Dumont 1980: 53).

Marriage is an occasion for elaborate inter-caste prestations (see 8.6, below). It also initiates a complex and protracted series of intra-caste exchanges (see 8.5, below) which continues through the birth of children to the couple, until the marriages of those children complete that particular cycle one generation further on. Moreover, the regulation of female sexuality, through marriage and other means, is crucial to preservation of caste identity and family purity. With all this in mind, it is easy to see how marriage provides 'the link between the domain of caste and that of kinship' (Dumont 1980: 110).

8.2 The Mukurttakkal Ceremony

Wealthy or orthodox households perform the *mukūrttakkal ūṉṟutal* ('auspicious-post erecting') at an auspicious time before the Kaliyanam, to inaugurate the building of the marriage platform.

Example A

Pillai: The ceremony was performed three days before Murukan married his FZSD Tankarajammal in September 1976. The groom's F and B had to be present and the bride's M attended, but the bride and groom did not. Village artisans officiated, the Carpenter Ramasami among them.[1]

The ritual items were arranged on the house veranda (Fig. 8.1). The six-foot-long post was held upright in front of them. It should be of bamboo, but none was available so palmyrah wood was used instead. Mango leaves and flowers were tied round the upper end. A *kāppu* amulet (cf. 7.2, above) was tied round it, and another placed on a tray.

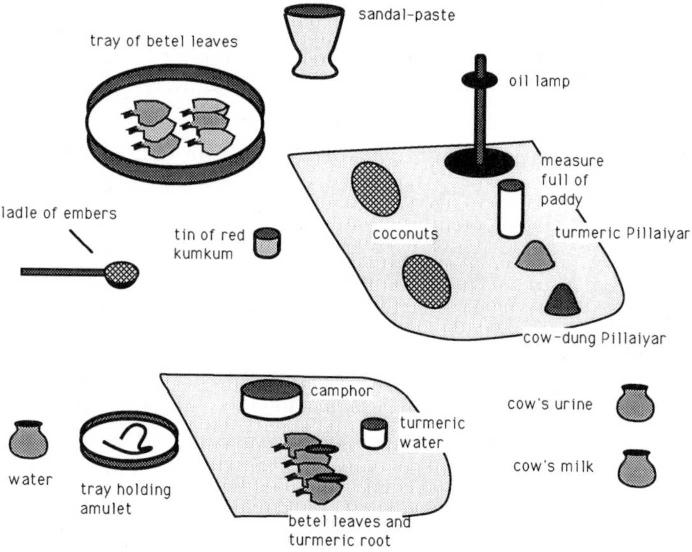

FIG. 8.1 Ritual Arrangements at a Pillai Mukurttakal Ceremony

A hole was dug at the south-western corner of the courtyard, and the Artisan measured out the marriage platform with this as a reference point. The Oduvar Priest sprinkled coconut water over everything, and waved incense and burning camphor over all the items on the leaves. Important guests took turns to pour cow's milk into the hole. The post was lowered in, to *kuruvai* cries from the

[1] I was new to the village, and could not identify everyone.

women present. These women tied the remaining *kāppu* amulet around a wooden rice-pounder. They took the turmeric root and pounded it in a mortar, while the Artisan began laying bricks and mortar for the marriage platform. Sandal-paste, betel, and kumkum were distributed, and the guests dispersed.

The post stands at the corner of the platform, but is not an integral part of it. There are clear similarities between this ceremony and the doorpost-raising rite in a new house (4.3.4, above). Again the Carpenter performed priestly duties, in association with the Oduvar. Dumont (1957*b*: 222) says the marriage post should be made from wood with white sap, and Beck (1969: 564–5) relates this to the general colour symbolism of South Indian ritual. Here the milk presumably has similar significance. The ceremony is said to bring good health and long life to the couple—a vague pronouncement typical of local exegeses. Beck sees it as a 'cooling' process prior to the wedding (1969: 564–5).

Being so auspicious, weddings are particularly susceptible to evil eye, hence the use of *kāppu* amulets. The disposition of these, as well as the similarity in shape, leads to an identification of the marriage post with the rice-pounder. It is used to grind turmeric root into the paste used to make the Pillaiyar figure (Fig. 8.1). The grinding of turmeric thus marks the fact that this ceremony inaugurates the wedding.[2]

8.3 The Kaliyanam Ceremony: Two Examples

No two weddings are exactly alike, so the descriptions of two actual examples are followed (8.4) by a summary of the key features of all ceremonies.[3] To make the accounts as comparable as possible, the main examples chosen are two weddings in Maravar families of above-average wealth. One took place at the groom's house, the other at a large temple in a nearby town.

[2] In auspicious rituals, Pillaiyar is 'a point of reference or a beginning to whatever else occurs' (Beck 1972: 140–1).

[3] Complete descriptions of the weddings referred to in this chapter are given in Good (1978*a*: Ch. 9).

8.3.1 Household Wedding (vīṭṭu kaliyāṇam)

Example B
Muniyasami married his MBD Viralaksmi on 6 April 1977. The invitations were signed by their fathers, Sanmuka and Kurusami, respectively. Special guests named were the bride's MB (*tāymāmaṉ*), and the groom's MB (*tāymāmaṉ*) and yZH. The bride's F is of course a *tāymāmaṉ* of the groom, but another MB played this role at the wedding.

Preparations: The pavilion (*pandal*) was in the courtyard of the groom's house, with the marriage platform (*maṇavaṟai* at the western end, facing east. It had a ceiling of red cloth, and plantain trees were tied to the corner-posts. The Brahman officiant put amulet strings (see 7.2, above) over the house door and platform roof. He performed other preparatory rites, and set out the ritual arena as shown in Figure 8.2. The Velar Priest distributed ash from the Aiyanar Temple among the guests.

The Ceremony: The bridegroom was led out by his *tāymāmaṉ* and seated on the platform beside piles of vestis and towels. He gave clothes to his MB and F, then took a set for himself[4] and withdrew to dress. The President sat down and was garlanded.[5] The Brahman gave him a set of clothes, and received in return Rs 1 on a tray of betel leaves. The bride was led out by Vellattay and Minatci (her HyZs; *madiṉi*), to the sound of *kuruvais*, and sat at the President's left. He put ash on her forehead, and she was led back to the house.

The bride's sari and *tāli* (a gold ornament on a turmeric-stained string) were taken round and worshipped. The groom reappeared in his new clothes, led by Ayyatturai (*maittuṉār*, yZH; cf. 14.1, below) and followed by two boys. After circling the platform clockwise, the groom sat down. Ash and kumkum were put on his forehead and the Velar Priest asperged him with water.

The bride was led out in her new sari (*kuruvais*) by Minatci and Komati (her FZDy; *nāttiṉār*) and seated at the groom's right. Her *tāli* was tied by Minatci with perfunctory help from the groom, to *kuruvai* shouts by all the women present. The bride gave two

[4] For a full list of the clothes given, see 8.5, below.

[5] The President is a *māmaṉ* (MFBS) of the bride, but was singled out from among many equally distant relatives because of his political status.

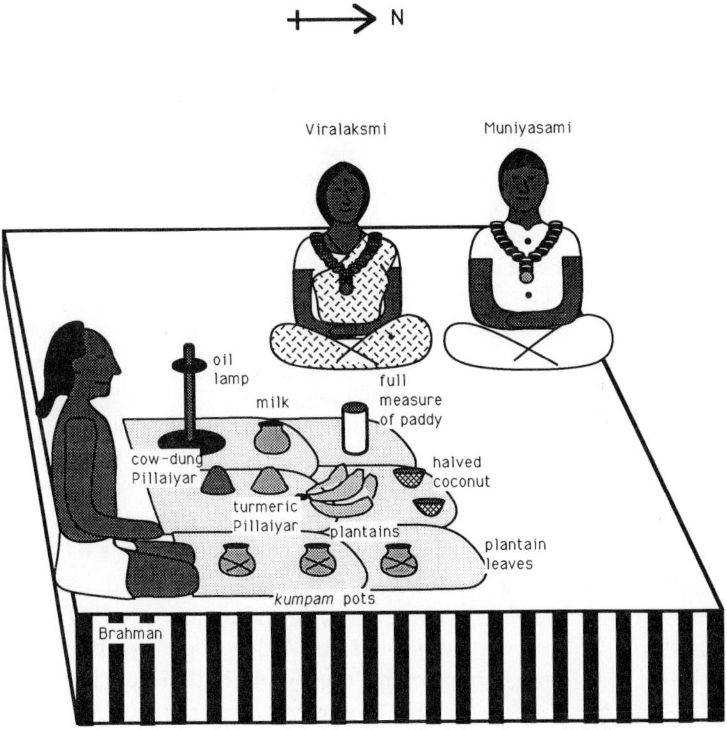

FIG. 8.2 Ritual Arrangements at a Maravar Household Wedding

coconuts to Minatci and one to her other HyZ, Vellattay. These two then performed the *ālatti*. The bride and groom exchanged garlands, helped by the two Officiants. The same garland was passed twice from bride to groom and back.[6] The Brahman put pieces of plantain into their right hands, and poured milk on top. Both of them ate.[7] Minatci smashed three poppadums over their heads.

[6] The second exchange should, I think, be initiated by the groom, though there is much variation in practice.

[7] The food is eaten inside the house at Nayakkar weddings. The bride is served first, a reversal of the normal order.

Several relatives presented them with framed pictures of gods, film stars, or politicians. The bride's father tied their right hands together with a scarf. The President was the first to be invited to give ash and money to the groom and bride. Afterwards there was a procession three times clockwise round the platform, involving: (i) Ayyatturai (yZH); (ii) the groom; (iii) the bride; (iv) Minatci (married yZ; bride's *madiṉi*). The feast began at once. In the afternoon the bride fetched water from the well, and the couple later left for her natal village.

8.3.2 Temple Wedding (kōvil kaliyāṇam)

Kailasanadar Temple in Pasuvandanai, eight miles from Terku Vandanam, is a typical large Siva temple. Its precinct is roofed over, and the important deities have separate shrines inside. Resident Brahman Priests perform worship there several times daily.

Example C

On 12 December 1976, in Pasuvandanai temple, Muttupandi Tevar of Terku Vandanam married his MFBSD Komati, from Kila Mankalam. No pavilion was built, as the temple itself served this purpose. A blanket was used as a marriage platform, and far fewer ritual items were deployed than in Example B. Instead, the couple visited different parts of the temple, reinforcing the point that the pavilion and platform in a 'house wedding' represent a temporary temple (cf. 13.1, below).

The officiating Brahman[8] collected a Rs 10 fee, and filled out the temple marriage register, which was signed by the groom and witnessed by the Presidents of Kila Mankalam (a Nayudu) and Pudupatti (a Maravar).[9] The Brahman took a tray of coconuts, plantains, betel and kumkum from the groom's side, and added the *tāli* given by the bride's party. The groom's family produced the couple's garlands and clothes on another tray. The Brahman handed the groom the shirt and vesti, which had been sprinkled with turmeric.[10] The garlands were offered in the main shrine, then the

[8] This same Braham officiated at the Velar Sadanku (see 7.3, Ex. C, above).

[9] The marriage is recorded in the temple register, but *not* with the civil authorities. Few marriages are registered in this latter sense.

[10] Donning new clothes is always essentially a ritual act, for they are normally bought by villagers only at festival times.

Brahman handed over the sari and blouse. The couple retired to dress.

The temple musicians started playing. The wedding party entered the main shrine, where the Brahman performed worship and gave ash to the bride and groom. The groom was garlanded by the Brahman (*kuruvais*), and then placed a garland around his bride's shoulders (more *kuruvais*). The couple went round the temple, the groom carrying the *tāli* tray. They worshipped in all the shrines, then sat on the blanket facing east. On the groom's right was his bride, and on his left Suppaiya, his yZH (*maccin̲an̲*).

The *tāli* was worshipped by the guests. The Brahman unwrapped it and the groom tied it round the bride's neck (*kuruvai*), helped by Komati (his eZ), the Main Officiant, and Kuruvammal (yZ; W of Suppaiya). Komati put ash on the couple's foreheads. The Brahman gave half a string of flowers to her and the rest to the bride. The groom garlanded his bride, and she returned it. She put a garland round his neck, and he returned it. Each transfer was marked by *kuruvais*. The groom's father put ash on their foreheads, then sat down in front of them. The bride's father did likewise, and they held their children's right wrists together while the Brahman bound them with a new towel.

The Pudupatti President gave ash and money to the couple, and other men followed suit. Each donor received betel from the Pudupatti President. Finally the couple rose. A procession, comprising: (i) Suppaiya (yZH); (ii) the groom; (iii) the bride; and (iv) Komati (eZ), went thrice clockwise round the images of the nine planets. The couple sat down on the blanket and the groom presented clothes to Komati. The couple were led off to the bride's party, and were greeted with *kuruvais*. After a few minutes, the groom and his yZH sat down again. The bride's father put Rs 151 on a tray of betel in front of them,[11] and then the yZH gave Rs 101.

Meals were served in the temple hall. Most of the Terku Vandanam guests were Maravars.[12] The couple left at noon to spend some days in the bride's natal village. They returned to Terku Vandanam before the start of Markali (December–January), a month inauspicious for weddings.

[11] The money was not actually from him (see below).

[12] Temple weddings are said to appeal to poorer people, partly because fewer guests attend, but in this case the family and many guests were quite well off.

8.4 The Main Stages of the Kaliyanam Rite

This section summarizes the main general features of Kaliyanams. The emphasis is on 'house' rather than 'temple' weddings, partly because they are more common and partly to facilitate comparison with Sadankus, which are never held in temples.[13]

A pavilion and platform are erected just as for a Sadanku, but at the groom's house. This task may be inaugurated a few days earlier, when the marriage post is raised. On the wedding day, the Brahman—more likely to be hired than at a Sadanku—sets out the necessary ritual artefacts. The resemblances between Figures 7.2 and 8.2 scarcely need comment. Again three pots of water are used, although no one is bathed. This reference back to the Sadanku, which the bride must, of course, have undergone before she can marry, shows that it is not merely a matter of the Sadanku mimicking a Kaliyanam. The two rites refer to each other in reciprocal fashion.

The groom is led out to the platform by his *tāymāmaṉ* (MB) or *macciṉaṉ* (yZH, WyB). He makes gifts of clothes to certain relatives before retiring to dress. The bride is led out by the Main Female Officiant or her assistant. The *tāli* and wedding sari are worshipped by the guests. The bride retires.

The groom and bride are led out and seated on the platform. The Brahman performs purificatory and cooling rites like those at a Sadanku but with the groom taking priority. The Main Officiant then takes over. She helps tie the *tāli*, and then she and her assistant perform *ālatti*. Before or after this the couple exchange garlands and their wrists are bound together by their fathers. This part of the ceremony varies greatly from case to case, and a variety of cooling, purifying, and honorific practices are usually added, but the events just described represent the bare minimum.

Important guests give ash and money, but whereas at Sadankus the 'bride' receives first and gets a larger sum, both the order and the size of these gifts are reversed at a Kaliyanam. The couple then circle the platform three times clockwise, in a procession which comprises: (1) the *macciṉaṉ*; (2) the groom; (3) the bride; (4) the groom's sister—who participates here even if unmarried, and so unable to be

[13] In towns, girls are sometimes taken to worship in a temple during their Sadanku—after their bath, of course. The rites themselves take place elsewhere, however.

Main Officiant. The *maccinan̲* is sometimes referred to as the *māppiḷḷai tōḷi* or groom's supporter (*tōḷi* means 'a carrying litter').

The couple often take a joint meal, in the presence of only their closest relatives. The meal for the guests, the social identities of those fed, and the *moy* prestations, are structured just as for a Sadanku but larger in scale. Later on, the newly-weds set off to the bride's natal home.

Example A

Both families were Terku Vandanam residents. The wedding was at the groom's house in the morning and the couple processed to the bride's natal home in late afternoon. At the threshold the groom's married eZ (the Main Officiant) washed their feet, and was given money in return. The couple received sweets from the bride's M. They stayed only a few minutes.

This visit assumes greater importance when it takes place in another village. Moreover, the Pillai are unique locally in allowing the bride's M to attend the actual Kaliyanam at the groom's house.[14] Usually she stays away even when it is in her own village, because she is 'shy' of her new son-in-law. This conflicts with David's statement that a certain rite performed by the bride's M is 'essential' to a Tamil wedding (1973: 523).

After spending two or three days with the bride's family, the couple return to take up residence in the groom's village, eventually getting a separate house of their own. In the early years of marriage a wife often visits her parents, however, and her first child is nearly always delivered there (see 9.2, below).

8.5 Intra-Caste Prestations

Intra-caste prestations at a Kaliyanam are much more complex than those at a Sadanku. The local pattern accords broadly with data from other areas (Dumont 1957*a*; 1957*b*; Tambiah 1973*b*).

The prestational cycle begins with a gift from the groom to his prospective bride, called the *parisam* ('touch, contact'). Its purpose is to obtain the girl's consent, and her acceptance of it indicates that the couple are betrothed. Other suitors should not approach her parents

[14] The couple's mothers even participated in the Kaliyanam rite, helping bind the couple's hands. It is more orthodox for mothers to attend (see 11.8, below).

thereafter. The *parisam* is handed over at the bride's house and becomes her personal property. It includes at least Rs 101 in cash, a sari, and the usual accessories like plantains, betel, and flowers. A previously agreed sum is also given at this time to buy the gold for the bride's *tāli*. The groom's family pay for this, but the bride's father arranges for its manufacture.

The agreed dowry (*sīdaṉam* or *varateṭcaṇai*) is ideally given by the bride's father during the actual Kaliyanam. It includes a gold chain worth twice as much as the *parisam*. This doubling of the return gift occurs among Piramalai Kallar too (Dumont 1957*b*: 231). The bride also receives jewellery, brass or bronze vessels, etc., depending on the wealth of the family and the earlier negotiations. The 2:1 ratio is generally observed though, especially when the two families are closely related. Items given as *sīdaṉam* are the property of the bride and cannot be disposed of without her consent.

The groom's family provides the wedding clothes and bears the cost of the Kaliyanam (partly offset by the *moy* collection), including the meal and the prestations to village specialists (see 8.6, below). In the long term, their contribution also includes the groom's share of their landed property.

'Dowry' is the local English translation for *sīdaṉam* and my use of it merely reflects that. Tambiah (1973*b*: 92) also finds it useful to describe the *parisam* as 'bride-price', and so he concludes that South Indian marriages contain payments of both types. This has the effect of converting "bride-price" and "dowry" into analytical terms used to refer to aspects of more complex transactions, rather than descriptive terms denoting distinct *types* of transaction. This does not seem a helpful way of proceeding, particularly as the two prestations are not in fact independent. The *sīdaṉam* amount is agreed at the same time as the *parisam*, and the overall balance sheet is not only known in advance, but more or less fixed by custom. In such circumstances it seems preferable to treat both transactions together, as part of a single reciprocal exchange.

In the following examples, the informant is the groom in each case:

Example C

Muttupandi Tevar gave a *parisam* of Rs 101, a sari, and other gifts to a total value of Rs 150. I do not know how much was given for the *tāli*, which is not elaborate in the Maravar case. The *sīdaṉam* comprised vessels and 10 *pavaṉs* (80g) of gold, worth Rs 4,300.

The overall expenditure was as follows: *parisam* and sari for bride's consent, Rs 261; printed invitations, Rs 36; radio, Rs 17; cooking vessel rent, Rs 50; cooks, Rs 20; building kitchen, Rs 10; rice, Rs 300; vegetables and spices, Rs 30; sandalwood, Rs 1; flowers and betel, Rs 26; bullock carts, Rs 160; clothes for bride and groom, Rs 236. Adding in new clothes for his family, he estimated the total expenses as Rs 1,500.

Most of the 114 donors to the *moy* gave Rs 5. It realized Rs 867.50 in all. The main contributions were the above-mentioned gifts from his MZ and yZH, and Rs 21 from the bride's MZ.[15] These were listed separately, along with Rs 10 from his yZH/FZS, and Rs 5 from a woman (relationship unknown). The biggest contributors to the main *moy* were Kurusami Tevar (relationship unknown), and Suppa Nayakkar, the ex-Munsip of Terku Vandanam, a neighbour.

Example D

The joint weddings of two Konar brothers contained the bare minimum of ritual. The family is landless and both grooms are day-labourers. Neither bride received any cash or gold dowry, and one was given only some old vessels worth about Rs 100. Double weddings are cheaper than two separate ceremonies, and so are quite common. Nevertheless, the grooms' family's expenses came to about Rs 1,100, mainly on food, clothes, and the two *tālis*. Only about Rs 200 was recouped through the *moy*.

Example E

Sankarapandi Konar gave Vijaya, to whom he was unrelated, a *parisam* of Rs 201 and a sari, as well as an agreed sum of Rs 1,000 for the *tāli*. Her *sīdaṉam* included many good-quality vessels, a gold chain worth Rs 2,000, and three buffaloes. When her husband and father-in-law wished to sell a buffalo in order to buy a radio, they had to get her consent, which she withheld for some time.

Example F

Ramakrisna Nayakkar gave Mariyammal (his FMZHZSD) a *parisam* of Rs 101 and a sari. Rs 200 was given for the *tāli*, ostensibly by the

[15] Gifts were thus received from all surviving siblings of the couple's mothers, neither of whom had a MB, or any living descendants of a MB.

groom but actually by his eZ. His family did not give precise figures for the *sīdanam*, saying it was 'only four or five pots and a chain'. This disparaging attitude is doubtless customary, but the small *sīdanam* certainly contrasted sharply with the wealth of the groom's family, perhaps because he was the youngest son, and his bride a widow's daughter.

Not all castes practise these *parisam-sīdanam* exchanges. Barbers, Washermen, and Harijans lack the landed property which provides the context for such gifts. Dowries are not customary among these castes and the girl is normally given only vessels and ear- and nose-rings (*tōḍu* and *mūkkutti*, respectively).

Wedding invitations are given out straightforwardly to non-relatives, and to the groom's *paṅkāḷis* or *sokkārans* (see 6.3, above), but affines (*sammandar*) such as *māmans* or *maccinans* will not attend unless Rs 1 is enclosed with the invitation as an *alaippu suruḷ* ('invitation rolled-up betel'). *Suruḷ* is a widely used name for reversible marriage prestations (Dumont 1957*b*: 231). Rolling up implies reciprocity, while betel leaves, wrapped round areca nuts, are indispensable components of most ritual exchanges. The affine gives a return *suruḷ* of Rs 2 on the wedding day. The *moy* records half as coming from him and half from his wife, and lists it separately from the money given after eating. Once again, then, there is a doubling of the reverse prestation. The groom's 'affines' are of course, by definition, parallel relatives of the bride.

In addition to the clothes for himself and his bride, the groom must give garments to certain others—a vesti and shirt (or towel) for men, and a sari and blouse for women. Recipients include his Z and ZH; MB and MBW; the bride's parents, siblings and siblings' spouses; and sometimes her parents' siblings too. All recipients contribute to the *moy* a sum equal to the value of the clothes plus Rs 5. This return payment is also called *suruḷ*. The groom may choose to give vestis to other friends and relatives, and these are eventually reciprocated, too.

Example B

Muniyasami Tevar gave saris to his two yZs, and vestis to his three MBs—one of whom was also his bride's F. He also gave vestis to the President (his WMFBS) and a Velar friend.

Example E
Sankarapandi Konar had to give saris equal in value to the bride's to his sisters, and vestis to their husbands; likewise to his wife's parents; his MB and MBW; the bride's unmarried yB; and the bride's MyZ and MyZH. He also gave vestis to Nallaiya Konar, the then President of Terku Vandanam, and a Konar friend.

Example F
Ramakrisna Nayakkar gave clothes to his and his bride's MBs; his eB and his bride's *aṇṇaṉ* (her FBS/MZS); his eZ and eZH.

The gift to the bride's M cannot usually be made at the wedding itself. She does not normally attend, even at another house in her own village, because she is 'shy' of her new son-in-law.[16] She receives her sari a month later, when she first visits the groom's house.

Dumont (1983 [1957*a*]: 29–30) distinguishes 'external' prestations between the two families, including the *parisam* and *sīdaṉam*, from 'internal' prestations within each family, such as the *moy* collection. This dichotomy does not apply here. The Kaliyanam is at the groom's house, with none of the Kallar's toing and froing (see 11.3, below), so there is only one *moy* to which both sides contribute. In any case, since marriage with a close relative is so common, and pronounced unilineality is lacking, it is hard to separate the two 'families' analytically.

8.6 Inter-Caste Prestations

The inter-caste prestations associated with a Kaliyanam are more elaborate than for a Sadanku. All village specialists have definite roles to play. Obviously, these duties fall only upon the specialists and officiants of the groom's village.

The Blacksmith presents the couple with a blade for slicing vegetables. The Carpenter gives a ladle made from coconut shell, and a tool for mashing lentils. The Barber shaves the groom. The Washerman provides cloths to decorate the platform. The Oduvar Priest anoints the bride's sari and *tāli* at the Pillaiyar Kovil before the main ceremony. A Brahman may supervise the ceremony, but the key

[16] Some women will never speak their son-in-law's name.

role belongs to a female relative of the groom. These duties are standard for marriages in most non-Harijan castes. The counter-prestations from the hosts show variations in detail, but not in general principles.

Example F

At the wedding of Ramacandiran and Mariyammal, the Brahman officiant received Rs 8 as *sampaḷam*, and a *sāṣtiram* of 9 coconuts, 2 *pakkās* of husked rice, 2 *paḍis* of paddy, some uncooked vegetables, a vesti, and a *teṭcaṇai* of Rs 1.25 (cf. 4.3.4, above). The Velar and Oduvar Priests each got a coconut and 1 *paḍi* of paddy. Each Artisan received 1 *paḍi* of paddy, a coconut, etc. The Washerman got 6 measures of millet, a coconut, and some plantains. The Barber received a vesti.

Most specialists are merely fulfilling their *sāṣtiram* obligations, and are rewarded in accordance with the *sāṣtiram* of the family concerned. The Brahman is not a member of the local community, however, so his work falls outwith his routine obligations and he therefore also receives a *sampaḷam* payment. Such prestations to Brahmans are nominally gifts, not payments for services rendered (Subramaniam 1974: 87), and doubtless they prefer to view the *sampaḷam* differently from my informants.

When the Kaliyanam takes place in a temple, the Brahman priests and temple servants must also be rewarded. The Pasuvandanai temple (Ex. C) is by no means the largest in the region. In Kalugumalai temple (see 16.2, below), for example, many more people have to be recompensed.

Finally, as at a Sadanku, all fellow-villagers are invited to the wedding and the subsequent feast. Every household head then makes a contribution which is recorded in the *moy* list. The hosts can recoup Rs 500–1,000 in this way, thereby accounting for up to half the expenses of a typical wedding.

The Barber and Washerman are given cooked food to take home by everyone except the Artisans, who give only the raw materials. Paraiyars (in Terku Vandanam) and Cakkiliyars (in all three villages) are fed outside at the end, although usually only a few of them turn up. The higher castes do not attend Harijan weddings, though, nor do Harijans contribute to the *moy* of the higher castes.

8.7 Discussion

In a Hindu marriage the couple are exalted and treated like Brahmans, or even gods (Dumont 1980: 53). They are cooled, purified and anointed, dressed in rich clothes, worshipped by the *ālatti*, and honoured by the gifts. The marriage platform is a temporary temple and their circumambulation of it is a *piradakṣiṇam*, or journey around the cosmic axis.[17]

All local weddings are unorthodox, compared even to accounts purporting to describe marriage behaviour for the castes concerned (Kearns 1868; Thurston 1906; Thurston and Rangachari 1909), to say nothing of ideal ceremonies in texts. One point of difference from almost every source is that local marriages are always held at the *groom's* natal house. Moreover, they exclude the rite said to be binding by the *Hindu Marriage Act*, namely the Saptapadam ('seven steps'; cf. 11.8, below).[18] In this, though, they are far from unique.

There is clearly a close resemblance in form and content between Sadanku and Kaliyanam rites. Sometimes there is exact correspondence, as in the arrangement of the platform (Figs. 7.2 and 8.2) and the *ālatti* rite (7.3, 8.4, above). Sometimes there are reversals, notably in location and in the order of precedence of female and consort. There is also a reversal in the final circumambulation. At a Sadanku the Main Officiant leads, followed by the 'bride' and 'groom'. At a Kaliyanam the order is reversed, and all three are led by the *maccinaṉ*, who does not figure in the Sadanku (cf. 14.4, below).

The overriding impression is one of complementarity. A Kaliyanam cannot occur until the female has undergone her Sadanku: conversely, the latter anticipates many features of the former. Both bride and groom are in turn the main centres of attention; each family in turn hosts a ritual. In most cases the couple are already closely related, so the two rites are attended by virtually the same group of their caste-fellows. Caste specialists from both villages take part in turn. Finally, *both* rites are necessary to transform the immature girl into a mature, married woman.

[17] Cf. 13.2. This interpretation is supported by the fact that at 'temple weddings' the couple circle the main shrine of the temple at the start, and the procession at the end goes around the Nine Planets.

[18] The Act prohibits marriage with a first cousin or ZD (*Hindu Marriage Act 1955 (amended 1976)*: sect. 3 (g) (iv)), unless such marriages are customary for both families (sect. 5 (iv)).

9
Rituals of Birth and Infancy

9.1 Pregnancy

Pregnancy lasts 'ten months' by Tamil reckoning, which takes the first and last calendar months fully into account. I heard no distinctive local ethno-biological views about conception. Pregnancy is little ritualized, but sometimes, when a woman is 'five months' pregnant (with a first child only?), small gifts are made to other households in the settlement. Once, for instance, plantains and crystallized sugar were distributed by the women of the house, excluding the pregnant woman herself. Pregnant women perform their usual domestic and agricultural work virtually until the onset of labour.

9.2 Childbirth: An Example

Childbirth takes place in a suitable spot outside the actual dwelling, such as a private porch or veranda. A woman returns to her natal home for her first confinement, even if this is another household in her husband's village. She may return for later births too, but this becomes progressively less likely.

The midwife is usually an older relative. If complications arise the Barber's wife is summoned, but this is avoided if possible because she has to be paid. People said that in really serious cases they would go to a hospital, but I know of no occasion when this was done. No men can be present, or even close by, during the delivery. This applies above all to the father, who is kept well out of the way.

Example

Konar: Isakkiyammal's third child was born on the veranda of her marital house.[1] The midwife was Palammal (Isakki's *pāṭṭi*), helped

[1] These observations were made by Alison Good, as I was of course unable to be present.

by Cellammal (*madini*), Sanmukattay (*attai*), and Isakki's mother (*and* HZ)[2] Sanmukattammal. All are married women or widows. *Kuruvai* shouts marked her baby son's first cry (this is not done for a baby girl). Cellaiya Pillai the shopkeeper, who was waiting at the street corner with his watch, shouted the exact time of birth and departed.

The baby was washed. This should be done exactly 'one minute' after birth. The cord was then cut, and tied with thread as the women gave three *kuruvais*. Palammal spread sand over the verandah to soak up the blood, and swept this up into a basket, on top of which she laid the placenta. Meanwhile, the mother was taken inside to have her stomach rubbed with coconut oil. The baby was soon bathed again, in warm water mixed with holy ash. Palammal held him by his feet and shook him, tossed him in the air, blew in his ears, and sucked out the contents of his nose and mouth. Isakki lay down on a straw mattress on the veranda, while her mother dug a hole in the back yard and buried the contents of the basket.

Sanmukattammal woke Mekalinka Konar, our landlord, who bathed and went round to the birth house. My wife Alison was asked to take her ball-point pen as a dropper, and Mekalinka fed three drops of palm sugar solution (*karuppaṭṭi*) to the baby. Alison fed him three drops, and his father Murukandi was summoned from the back of the house to do likewise. *Kuruvai* shouts accompanied each act of feeding. A father first sees his child 'exactly one hour' after birth. The baby was given more *karuppaṭṭi* by Palammal, who washed his face, rubbed him with coconut oil, and powdered him. He was laid beside his mother, on a mat of plantain leaves.

Mekalinka Konar is a terminological grandfather (*tāttā*) of the child, but any respected man of the same caste can be asked to give this first feed. A new-born baby is fed only *karuppaṭṭi* for the first two days, and not until the colostrum has given way to milk does the mother begin breast-feeding.

Next day Virammal, the (Nayakkar) wife of Muttukrisna Konar, gave birth to twin girls. Twins are described simply as *irandu kuḻandai* ('two children'), and there are no distinctive views or practices regarding multiple births.

[2] Isakkiyammal had married her MyB. The birth took place in his house, though her natal home was immediately next door. The attendants were senior women of her own caste, as usual, but because of the particularities of her family tree their identities were perhaps not entirely typical (cf. 14.4, below).

The death of a woman during labour is commemorated by the raising of a *sumaitāṅki* ('burden-supporter') stone which is worshipped by relatives at festival times, often for several generations thereafter. There were no such deaths during my stay, but there was at least one stillbirth and two deaths in early infancy. There may have been more cases, for little notice is taken outside the family concerned.[3]

9.3 Prestations at Birth

The expenses involved in having a first child are met by the mother's parents. These may amount to Rs 150 when all the temple visits and prestations are included. Deliveries of first children are usually performed by women of the pregnant woman's natal family, normally her mother and various *periyammāḷs* and *sittis* (MeZ, MyZ, FeBW, FyBW, etc.). Subsequent confinements usually take place at her marital home, and the birth attendants then include her HM and various *attais* (FZ, MBW, etc.). If the Barber's wife has to be summoned, she gets either Rs 5 or a sari. The Munsip records the birth, for a fee, but whether this is a modern innovation I am not sure.

9.4 Early Infancy

Mother and child are not wholly excluded from the house, but spend most of the time out on the veranda, which is washed daily.[4] A small lamp is lit beside the child at night. On the '10th' day after the birth the mother leaves the house-site for the first time, to bathe.[5] On her return, she resumes her full working and social life.

Certain special foods are prescribed for a new mother. On the seventh day she should have chicken curry and liquor (*sārāyam*), mixed in 3:1 proportions. On the ninth and thirteenth days she eats chicken curry again, and on the 16th both curry and liquor, together with asafoetida mixture (*paḍikāyam*). This contains turmeric, mustard

[3] A stillborn child is buried without ceremony. Very young children have simple funerals (see 10.6, below).

[4] This is normally done only once a week, on Friday morning.

[5] Isakki gave birth on 20 June at 2 a.m., but according to local reckoning days do not begin until sunrise. Both first and last days are counted, so the '10th' day was 28 June.

seed, asafoetida, ginger, pepper, basil, jaggery, garlic, and *narukkumūlam*, a kind of root. On the thirtieth day she has curry, liquor, and asafoetida again.[6] This is the only situation in which women drink liquor, and one of the few occasions when meat is available except at temple festivals. Pillai women do not eat curried chicken after giving birth, but do take liquor. Isakkiyammal merely had chicken curry and *sārāyam* on the tenth day, after her bath. This is the most common procedure in practice.

Birth has a cooling effect on the mother (Beck 1969: 562), so the immediate emphasis in her diet is on heating foods to return the 'social temperature' of her body to normal. All foods are regarded as 'heating' or 'cooling' to a greater or lesser degree (Beck 1969: 566–70). Of those listed above, both chicken and liquor are heating, and asafoetida mixture is a blend of heating and cooling according to Beck's list,[7] with the former predominating. The new-born infant, on the other hand, is hot and has to be cooled by bathing.

All babies are breast-fed. Almost no one could afford powdered milk or baby food regularly, even if they wished to. From birth, though, a child is given both palm sugar and weak coffee. Children are not weaned systematically, but start taking solid food (usually boiled rice) before the age of one. They often continue taking mother's milk (*tāypāl*) until they are 2–3 years old; the limiting factor is usually the timing of the next pregnancy. Pregnant women often continue to breast-feed the previous child as long as possible.

9.5 Naming and other Ceremonies

According to the Sanskritic literature, a whole series of life-crisis ceremonies (*saṁskāras*) should be performed for a child between birth and puberty (cf. Kane 1941: ii. pt. 1, pp. 228–69). Some of these are done locally, although local ceremonies generally bear little resemblance to those described in the texts.

The first important event in a child's life is the giving of its name. This is usually chosen on astrological grounds, which is one reason why it is so important to know the exact time of birth. At some

[6] These timings are approximate, as meat is never eaten on Tuesdays, Fridays, or the last Saturday of a Tamil month.

[7] I could not collect such systematic data, but the ideas involved are perfectly familiar locally.

auspicious time when about one month old, the child is taken to a temple for worship. On returning home, the mother announces its name for the first time.

On 18 July 1977, Isakkiyammal took her son to the Terku Vandanam Amman temple, accompanied by her older children and their friends. The Priest performed worship using materials which she provided. No special attention was paid to the child himself, but when they returned to the house it was announced that his name was to be Sanmukaraj. Five days later, his father went to the Mariyamman Temple at Irukkankudi to have his head shaved, together with the beard he had grown during his wife's pregnancy.

Other significant events in the life of a small child include a visit to an important temple at the age of about 1, when its hair is shaved off and offered to the deity. The ear-piercing (see 4.3.4, above), accompanied by another head-shave, generally happens a few months or years later. The initial head-shaving, before which the child generally has deliberately unkempt hair, often takes place at a temple where the mother had made a vow, or about whose deity she had dreamed before the birth. A favourite local choice is the famous Murukan temple on the sea-shore at Tirucchendur. Another popular temple, involving less expense, is that at Irukkankudi. Coconuts and plantains are offered to the deity, and when the family return to the village they present small quantities of holy ash and parched grain to relatives and neighbours.

9.6 Discussion

Although menstruation, pregnancy, and parturition all represent temporary abnormalities in a woman's status, they are treated differently. Whereas first menstruation involves seclusion and elaborate ritual purification (see 7.2, above), the only disability which subsequent menstruation entails is exclusion from temples. A menstruating woman cannot prepare ceremonial rice offerings (*poṅkal*), but she can cook normal food in the home, from which she is not excluded. There are no restrictions of any kind for pregnant women, but there *is* impurity as a result of the birth itself. The new mother and her child are confined to the house-site, though partially excluded from the house itself.

It is not immediately apparent why birth should generate impurity, as it is such an auspicious event. It is, of course, similar to menstruation in that blood is discharged. In general, just as substances passing into the body (food, for instance) must be of carefully controlled purity and extremely restricted provenance, so substances passing out of it are almost invariably treated as impure, though not necessarily inauspicious or lacking in power (semen, for example).

It is not possible to speculate any further, in the absence of clear local views on such matters. However, the idea that giving birth involves impurity is of great antiquity in Tamil Nadu. Hart (1973: 234–6) notes that *anaṅku*, the sacred power women were believed to possess, was present especially in the breasts. He links the impurity of women after birth with the ban on sexual intercourse during the suckling period,[8] and sees both as designed to prevent the husband's masculinity being weakened by physical contact with the breasts, and especially the breast-milk, of his wife.

There is a strong case for seeing birth and its associated rituals as yet another stage in the ceremonial cycle which began with the mother's Sadanku and continued through her Kaliyanam. Like the Sadanku, but in contrast to the Kaliyanam, birth is polluting and is followed by seclusion. Moreover, a woman always has her first child at her natal home. In other words, the very same categories of women—often even the same individuals—who officiated at her Sadanku and Kaliyanam now help bring her first child into the world. The significance of this is discussed at greater length below (13.4, 14.4).

[8] This prohibition is supposed to apply locally.

10
Death Ritual

10.1 Introduction

For descriptive purposes it is convenient to divide death rituals into three stages: (1) the disposal of the corpse; (2) the rites in the cemetery one or three days later; and (3) the subsequent purificatory rites at which prestations are exchanged, and which typically happen sixteen days after the first stage. These must ultimately be analysed as a whole, however, and some elements appear at different stages in the funerary cycles of different caste-groups.

For most Hindus cremation is the preferred method of disposal, though Harijans always bury their dead. Each village has a cemetery (*suḍukāḍu*, 'burning wilderness', or *māyvuvāḍi*, 'death enclosure') to the north,[1] and each Harijan caste has a separate cemetery to the east. All these consist simply of untended plots of straggling thorn bushes and bare earth, with perhaps a few ashes or shards of pottery to indicate that a funeral has recently taken place. Kavundars set up inscribed stones near the Terku Vandanam Amman Temple. Women who die in childbirth may be commemorated by standing stones (see 9.2, above). Otherwise, the dead have no permanent monuments.

10.2 Cremation: An Asari Example

In this section one particular case is described in detail. The subsequent section will then give a generalized account of Hindu cremations and burials, mentioning systematic variations from caste to caste.

Example A

Aiyan Asari, a Blacksmith, died on 18 January 1977, aged 58. He had been ill for months and was very emaciated. A Cakkiliyar band from Sikampatti—three drummers, an oboe (*nākaṣvaram*) player,

[1] The Christian Nadars have a cemetery of their own.

and a cymbalist—played outside the house all next morning, with forays to meet relatives from elsewhere. A pavilion was built at the front door. Many villagers called to offer condolences and contribute to the expenses. Ponnuccami, the Village Blacksmith (eBS of the deceased), directed preparations.

The *nīrmālai* ('water garland') rite began at 13.30. A white vesti with a tuft of grass tied in each corner was held aloft by four bearers. Under this canopy stood the dead man's sons, Velccami (aged 19, the chief mourner) and Cellaperumal, holding small brass vessels. The dead man's three eBSs followed them, carrying large water pots. Led by the Musicians and the Barber blowing a conch shell, they left the village across its ritual boundary near the Pillaiyar temple. The mourners drew water from the Amman temple well and bathed. The Barber decorated the two small pots as *kumpams* (cf. 7.2, above). Coconuts were put on the large pots, too. The Oduvar Pusari laid flowers over the pots (the garland of the title?).

The Barber put ash on the mourners' foreheads. The two sons put on white threads as worn by Brahmans, but over their *right* shoulders rather than their left. The music restarted. All five mourners circled the pots thrice clockwise, led by the Barber blowing his conch, before picking them up and starting home. Two Pallar men, one leading the procession and the other blocking its path, fought each other with long staffs (*silampu viḷaiyāḍu*, 'stick sport') at the ritual boundary. The procession edged forward as its attacker slowly gave ground. With a final flourish on the drums, the house was reached. The pots were set down, and the music stopped abruptly.

The body was laid, head to the south, on a wooden board just east of the pavilion. The women inside began a keening cry which continued with increasing intensity until the cortège finally left. Screened by a red sari provided by the Washerman, the Barber shaved the dead man's beard. The widow, Laksmi, poured oil which the Barber rubbed into her husband's hair. Water from the big pots was used to wash the body, which was then sprinkled with water from the sons' smaller vessels.

The Barber tore strips off a new, white vesti to bind the limbs, and tied the remaining cloth tightly to hold the body upright in a cross-legged posture. He draped a sacred thread over the body and rubbed sandal-paste on the face and arms. He filled the eye-sockets with turmeric paste, fixed a coin to the forehead with oil, and rouged the lips with kumkum.

At 14.15 the music resumed. The Pallars swept the pavilion and brought a large grindstone to make a backrest for the body. They spread cow-dung thickly on the floor, and laid a mat on top of it. The coconut from the eldest son's pot was removed and kept by the Barber.

The widow bathed in front of the body, which was seated on a pannier of woven palmyrah leaves (*pāḍai*). The widow and other female relatives crouched at its feet, the wailing and drumming rose in intensity, and the elder son burst into tears. Sticks of incense were lit. The elder son and Ponnuccami went thrice clockwise around the body sprinkling water.

Led by the band, and with the white canopy held above them, both sons walked out to the ritual boundary, carrying a pot of rice wrapped in cloth. The Barber usually leads them round three clockwise circuits of a piece of knotted straw, after which they worship to the east. In this case they merely went to the boundary and came straight back. The episode is called 'bonds worshipping' (*kaṭṭu pārttal*)—presumably a reference to the earthly bonds of the deceased (cf. 10.3, Ex. C; 11.3, below).

The dead man's eBD placed the rice-pot on her head. With three others—two ZDs, including Ponnuccami's wife, and a ZSW—she circled the body three times clockwise. The elder son did likewise, led by the Barber. Each of the women offered the dead man yellow rice from the pot. The widow was given new clothes by the dead man's "brothers".[2]

The wooden bier.(*maritēr*, 'death car') resembled a sedan chair. Its red canopy was provided by the Washerman. The body was placed inside it in an upright position against a straw-filled palliasse. A live rooster, feet tied together, was laid beside it.[3] Eight men of various castes picked up the bier, led by the Musicians and followed by the Barber, male mourners, and other male villagers. The female relatives stayed at the house, and women near the route were ordered away. The pall-bearers ran to the ritual boundary, shouting 'Kovinda, Kovinda'.[4]

[2] This was how Ponnuccami put it: actually they were his BSs.

[3] This happens only on Wednesdays (and on Saturdays in some places). The dead man is said to want another body to accompany him to the cemetery. If this is not done, someone else will die almost immediately (Chettiar 1973: 87).

[4] This is a name of Visnu, even though most people are Saivites and Siva is the deity associated with the cemetery.

The bearers tried three times to surge up the slope out of the village, but seemed to be held back by some invisible force. They finally managed to run out of the village towards the cemetery, still shouting. The Musicians tried to keep pace, and the mourners followed more slowly. Any children present were forcibly sent back.

The band halted at the cemetery entrance. A pile of logs had been prepared by Pallar men, acting as Vettiyans (see 4.3.6, above). As soon as the bier was set down to the west of this, the band stopped playing and withdrew. The Barber and mourners placed the body on the pile, head to the south. The rooster was hung by its feet from a nearby bush. A Pallar man had brought two earthenware pots made by the Velar. One held water, the other embers from the household hearth, to ignite the pyre. Both Washermen were present; they dismantled the palanquin, and collected the cloths.

The Barber removed a strip of cloth from the dead man's vesti and handed it to Kalaiyan (F(2nd)WBS of the deceased). The Barber blew his conch and led Kalaiyan back to the house. Their arrival was the signal for the widow to don white clothing for the first time.

On his return, the Barber removed the coin and garlands from the body, on which the Pallars piled cakes of cow-dung. He untied the cloth over the mouth, and Ponnuccami fed *vāykkarisi* ('mouth rice') to the body, as did several affines (*sammandi*) of the dead man, and several from other castes. Each donor washed his hand, sprinkled some rice, and dropped a coin into the rice pot. Altogether, Rs 1.85 was collected. This *vāykkāsu* ('mouth money') is the perquisite of the Vettiyan. The Barber then covered the corpse's head with the vesti. While he shaved the faces (not the heads) of Ponnuccami and the dead man's sons, the Pallars covered the pyre with straw and mud. The Barber does this for most castes.

The *kalikuḍam uḍaittal* ('trickling-pot breaking', Chettiar 1973: 200) rite followed. The Barber punched a small hole in the water pot, and the elder son carried it clockwise round the pyre on his head, so that water dripped inwards towards the pyre. The Barber made a second hole, and the younger son joined in a second circumambulation. A third hole was made, and the sons were joined by Ponnuccami in a final circuit. The pot was thrown down and broken at the south end of the pyre. The three relatives wept together, and the sons removed their white threads. Dubois (1879: 212) says that this rite serves to mark the chief mourner as the deceased's heir.

The mourners withdrew to the cemetery entrance, leaving the

Pallar to light the pyre through a small hole in its mud coating. The Barber brought the chicken away, and it was later released unharmed. The functionaries were then rewarded (cf. 10.7.1, below). Before returning home, everyone who had been to the cemetery bathed at a tank or well. It was necessary at least to wash one's feet, hands, and face. Cooking was resumed in the bereaved household later in the day.

10.3 A General Description of Local Funerals

All funerals (except sometimes those of children) happen in early afternoon, and have the following general structure: (i) the mourners bathe and collect water; (ii) the body is prepared; (iii) the ritual boundary is visited; (iv) the cortège proceeds to the cemetery; (v) the pyre is prepared and ignited; and (vi) the functionaries are rewarded. As usual there are detailed differences from case to case. Systematic variations between castes are described below, as appropriate.

(i) *Mourners' Bath*: The chief mourner for a married adult, man or woman, is the closest possible *makaṉ* of the deceased, ideally the eldest son. The chief mourner of an infant is its father. After bathing at the well, chief mourners (including Harijans) wear white threads until the water-pot is broken in the cemetery. At Pallar funerals, a cow-dung Pillaiyar is made beside the well, after drawing water. The god is offered a coconut and the clothes to be worn by the deceased. The 'fight' is peculiar to Asari funerals.

At Reddiyar funerals, while the male mourners are collecting water, the women perform a 'bewailing' rite (*māraḍittal*).

Example B

At Sankaralinka Reddiyar's funeral in Kalinkapatti, there was a 'green pavilion' (*paccai pandal*), comprising a square of plaited palmyrah leaves 8 feet above the ground, under which hung the white vesti later used to dress the body. From its corners and sides hung strips of turmeric-stained cloth, and strings of chillies, turmeric roots, and *koḻukkaṭṭais*.[5] On the ground below were baskets of raw rice and Bengal gram, around which stood seven Reddiyar women.

[5] These are boiled rice-cakes, associated with offerings made by women at midnight ceremonies during certain months, from which men are excluded. Reports of naked dancing (Thurston and Rangachari 1909: vii. 387–8) seem fanciful.

Not all were close relatives of the deceased, and they included mature girls, married women, and widows. They moved slowly clockwise, singing. The song continued after the men had returned, while the body was shaved by Sanmukam, the Terku Vandanam Barber. Gram was distributed to the children, who were then chased out of the courtyard. The rest was eaten by the women, who also shared out the rice.

(ii) *Preparation of the Body*: This is similar for all castes. Harijans have their own Barbers to do it (see 4.3.1, above). A woman's body is prepared inside the house by the Barber's wife. The corpse is dressed in a new coloured sari (white for a widow), and garlands and cosmetics are applied as for men.

(iii) *Visit to the Ritual Boundary*: Harijans have separate ritual boundaries at the entrances to their own quarters, at which distinctive rites take place at this stage.

Example C

At the funeral of Kanniyammal, a Pallar woman, a 'bond breaking' ceremony (*pattam eḍuttal*) replaced the *kaṭṭu pārttal* of other castes. Three small grass baskets were filled with the 'nine grains'.[6] The widower carried two baskets, and his son, the chief mourner, took the other. Walking under a white canopy, they followed the Musicians to the bier, which had been built at the northern edge of their settlement.

The bier's canopy was spread on the ground, and a lock of the widower's hair was placed on it. The two men circled the bier clockwise, and set the baskets down on the cloth. They picked them up, circled the bier again, then tipped the baskets out on to the cloth. A lock of the son's hair was added. The grain was scooped back into the baskets, which they picked up, carried once more around the bier, and then carried back home.

The body was subsequently carried to this spot on a mat. The Paraiyars, too, avoid bringing the bier into the settlement. The Pallar Priest, Veyilmuttu, said the grain was scattered over the cemetery next day, but someone else said the seeds were allowed to germinate in the baskets.

[6] The nine grains from which cooked cereal (*sōṛu*) is made are (i) *arisi*, rice; (ii) *cōḷam*, Sorghum vulgare; (iii) *kampu* (Bajra), Pennisetum typhoideum; (iv) *keppai* (Ragi), Eleusine coracana; (v) *kuruḍavalli*, Panicum frumentaceum; (vi) *tiṉai*, Setaria Italica; (vii) *kadakkaṉi*, a millet; (viii) *varaku*, Panicum miliaceum; (ix) *sāmai*, a millet.

(iv) *The Cortège*: Castes differ in the extent of female participation. At the Pallar funeral (Ex. C), the eZ of the dead woman went all the way to the cemetery to remove jewellery from the body. A Tinda Vannar woman may go to the cemetery too, if needed to assist her husband or son.

Asari, Pillai, and Reddiyar widows, among others, perform the last obsequies at the house, whereas Maravar, Pallar, and Paraiyar women go as far as the ritual boundary and perform them there. If her rites take place at the house, the widow bathes in front of her husband's body. She and/or his BDs and ZDs then circle the body thrice, carrying a pot of yellow rice with which they 'feed' him. If the widow goes as far as the ritual boundary, she performs a 'trickling-pot' rite like that at the cemetery except that she circles the bier *anti*-clockwise. For a widower, his D may perform this duty. Afterwards the female relatives return to the house.

Some castes reverse the orientation of the bier, so that the body faces back to the house before crossing the ritual boundary, and faces forwards towards the cemetery afterwards (cf. Dumont 1957*b*: 247).

(v) *The Cremation or Burial*: All cremations follow the pattern described above (see 10.2, above). Even at a burial a fire pot is taken to the cemetery, as in the following case.

Example C

The Pallar woman's grave was dug by Cakkiliyars, in a north–south orientation. The body was laid at its western side. The deceased's eZ removed jewellery from the body, and its feet were untied. The Barber shaved the chief mourner's head, and the widower's right wrist. The corpse was fed yellow rice by the widower, his son, the dead woman's father, and others. Each sprinkled three handfuls of rice with his left hand, then washed his hand and threw coins on to the woman's chest. The money went to the Barber.

Cuts were made in the palms of the woman's hands. She was laid in the grave with her head to the south. A pot of embers was placed at the north-west corner. The widower and his son threw in handfuls of earth, and the rest was shovelled in, together with some branches. The garlands from the body were hung on posts, two at the south end and one at the north. The son did the trickling-pot ritual, joined by his father for the last two circuits. The palliasse from the bier was hacked with knives, and thrown backwards and forwards across the grave. Thorn branches were laid over the grave to protect it from animals.

(vi) *Prestations*: For most castes in Terku Vandanam and Kalinkapatti, the rewarding of specialists is presided over by the Karnam. At Harijan funerals, higher-caste village servants are not involved either as mourners or recipients, and a senior member of the caste takes charge (see 10.7.1, Ex. C, below).

10.4 The Second-Day Ceremony

Circumstances prevented me seeing this rite, but according to informants' statements it happens as follows. The Barber and Cakkiliyars (or the Pallars at Asari funerals) stay in the cemetery all night, tending the pyre so that it burns away completely. Next afternoon the Barber, blowing his conch, leads the male mourners there for the 'fire pouring' (*tī aṭṭutal*). They take nine kinds of cooked grain (n. 6, above), paddy, pulses and vegetables, a coconut, incense, cow's milk, and cow's urine. The grains are scattered by the mourners, and the liquids are poured. The nut goes ultimately to the Barber. No bodily remains are brought back or otherwise preserved.

The Paraiyar and Pallar ceremony, on the third day, is called 'grave-milk feeding' (*kuḻipāl ūṭṭal*). The Tinda Vannar leads male relatives to the grave. Food is offered to the birds, and milk is sprinkled on the ground. The cooked rice goes to the Vannar. The offering to the birds occurs during the sixteenth-day ceremonies of higher-caste groups.

10.5 Karumati: The Final Ceremony

Ideally, the final stage takes place thirteen or sixteen days after the funeral. It is called *karumāti* ('the source of *karumam*', from the Sanskrit *karma*, 'fate, actions in a previous birth'), or *karumāntam* ('end of *karma*'). It is by no means certain, though, that the word *karma* retains its literary significance locally (see 10.9, below). There are several local forms of Karumati. The most common of these takes the following form.

Example D

Kalyaniyammal, a childless Pillai widow, was cremated on 31 March 1977. The chief mourner was Vedam (BDH, *makaṉ*). The Karumati, delayed by Tamil New Year, was on the morning of 16 April. The Barber, blowing his conch, led the way to the Amman temple, followed by Vedam, Durairaj Tevar (a neighbour), the Oduvar, the Karnam, and a Brahman officiant.[7] Durairaj cooked rice and vegetables[8] while Vedam bathed, had his head shaved, and bathed again. A tumblerful of paddy was given to the Barber.

The Karnam built a 'pole-grave pavilion' (*kālkuḻi pandal*) about a foot high, out of sticks (Fig. 10.1). A Paraiyar man dug a shallow pit in front of it, using the earth to build up the pavilion floor. A cloth was draped over the frame, leaving only the eastern side open. This is called the 'Aiyar vesti', and goes to the Brahman afterwards.

Vedam donned a white thread and sat facing the pavilion, across the pit. He rubbed ash on his body, and washed his hands. Beside him, the Brahman anointed two mud bricks with milk, sandal-paste and water, wrapped them in turmeric-stained cloth with their tops protruding, decorated them with sandalwood and kumkum, and laid them on the raw rice inside the pavilion.

The Brahman placed sesame seeds in Vedam's right hand, then chanted a mantra containing Vedam's father's name. He washed off the seeds, then repeated the process for Vedam's mother (both parents are dead). He repeated the cycle, invoking the deceased. This is called *eḷḷuntaṇṇīr umiṛaikka* ('pouring sesame and water'; Winslow 1981: 183).

The Brahman laid a plantain leaf across the tray, and set three piles of cooked food on it. He added a peeled plantain, then broke a coconut and put the halves inside the pavilion. He burned camphor on the front leaf and offered worship, throwing petals into the pavilion.

Vedam rose and turned round on the spot three times clockwise, with his palms pressed together in worship. Two relatives who had arrived during the proceedings came forward and worshipped. The

[7] The Brahman bore Vaisnavite markings, indicating the lack of sectarian concern among even the most orthodox local caste. The Karnam was present as a relative, not ex officio.

[8] The fact that a man of lower caste-status was entrusted with preparing the food on this formal, intra-caste occasion, illustrates yet again the unimportance of hierarchy locally.

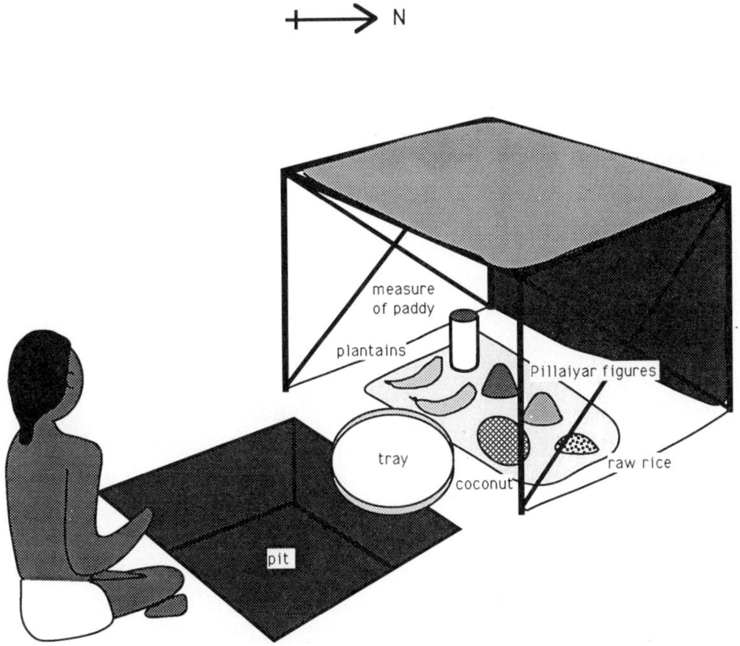

FIG. 10.1 The 'Grave Pandal' at a Pillai Karumati Ritual

Barber blew his conch as Vedam waded into the tank, carrying the two bricks. He turned to face west, and threw them back over his head into the water. Then he removed his white thread, and bathed again at the well.

Cooked gram and lentils were added to the food on the plantain leaf. The Barber dismantled the pavilion and threw the grass and sticks into the tank. Vedam carried the food tray northwards as the conch sounded, and laid it on the ground. He returned, and everyone watched until a crow flew down and began eating. The tidying-up then resumed. The Barber took the rest of the food and the coconut. Vedam bathed yet again at the well, into which the two Pillaiyars were thrown.

The bricks are shaped like the square-pyramidal *puḍams* which represent deities in village temples, and the way they were anointed suggested divine unction (*apisēkam*). The Oduvar said that they represented goddesses, but the Barber, who makes them, said they were Pillaiyar figures. He added, somewhat inconsistently, that one was like a man, the other like a woman. The worship and disposal of male and female bricks has been reported from elsewhere (Thurston 1906: 161, 170; Thurston and Rangachari 1909: ii. 7; vi. 112). Everyone disagreed with my suggestion that the bricks represented the mourners' ancestors.

According to the Barber, who is the expert on these matters, Konars, Asaris, and Cettiyars have Karumatis similar to this one. Velars and Maravars perform their rites at home, without the bricks. Kavundars erect stones at the Amman Temple on the sixteenth day. The Terku Vandanam Nayakkars have an idiosyncratic ceremony which merits a more detailed description.

Example E

The Karumati of Ponnaiya, the Terku Vandanam Munsip's father, was conducted near the Amman Temple by senior Nayakkar men on 12 September 1976, nine days after the cremation. A mud figure like a 'gingerbread man' was made on the ground, head to the south, with mud platforms at each end. Pebbles were placed on these, three at the head and one at the foot. Yellow rice was thrown over the figure, and it was sprinkled with water. Chains of flowers and turmeric-stained string were draped across it.

Five plantain leaves were set out, and piled with cooked millet, rice, sweets, and betel (Fig. 10.2).[9] Unlike other castes with public Karumati rites, Nayakkars prepare the food at home. The dead man's grandsons added more food to every leaf, and his three sons each threw water from west to east beside the well. Each took a plantain leaf from the head of the figure, and carried it northwards. No birds came, so the leaves were moved south. The ceremony did not resume until crows began eating the food.

The Washerman broke up the figures, threw the mud in the tank, and poured well-water on top of the fragments. He kept the contents of the other two leaves, and the rest of the food. Male guests of all castes were served food in the school, after bathing at the well. The Nayakkar women watched everything from under a distant tree, but took no part in the rite.

[9] The idea is to provide the deceased's favourite foods.

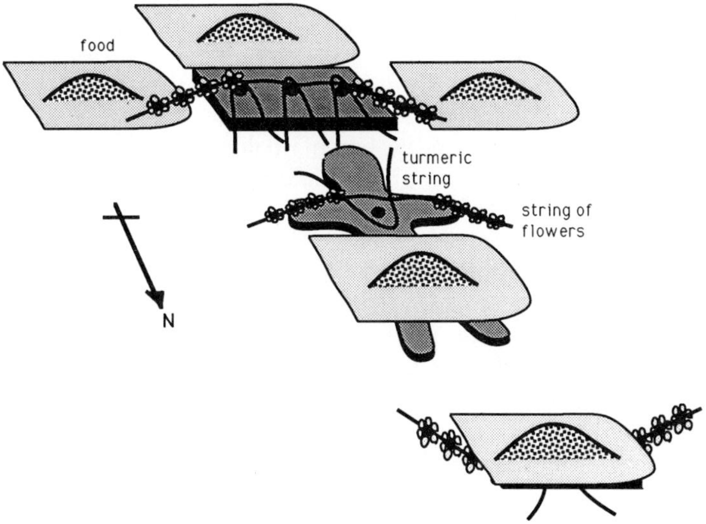

FIG. 10.2 The Mud Figure at a Nayakkar Karumati Ritual

The Barber shaved the beards and armpits of the dead man's sons.[10] They were presented with clothes by affines (*sammandi*), including their MBs, WBs, ZHs, and DHs. Such prestations are discussed below (10.8.1), for cases where I have more complete details.

Harijans do not perform a Karumati, though some elements of the rite (feeding the birds, for example) are incorporated into their second- or third-day ceremony. There is an attenuated rite on the sixteenth day, which the Pallar call *urimaikkaṭṭu*.[11] The Tinda Vannar attends but performs no duties. He is given cooked food, however, as are local relatives.

[10] I was told that Nayakkars also have their forearms shaved. This was not done here, but may have happened at the cremation.

[11] Literally 'claim binding', or 'duties and obligations of relatives'. The term *uṛumāl kaṭṭu*, 'tying the turban' (Dumont 1957*b*: 249), fits the Kallar ceremony but not this one.

10.6 The Funeral of an Infant

The rites described so far are for 'full members' of society, that is, married adults with children. If the deceased has no surviving children, burial is more likely than cremation and the rites may even be marked by levity. The chief mourner—a distant *makan̲* rather than an actual son—may be the butt of ribald joking. I even saw one such person pushed into the grave, while other mourners pretended to cover him with earth. When a child dies the situation is quite different, as there is real sadness. Yet children are not full members of the community, and the younger the child the more attenuated its funeral becomes. A stillborn or unnamed baby is buried with no ceremony whatever. There follows an account of the funeral of an older infant, which had undergone the naming ceremony.

Example F

The daughter of Cellaiya Pillai and Murukanantammal died on 16 December 1976, aged 3 months. Most of the mourners were neighbours, but Cellaiya is an important figure, so the Karnam, the President's brother, etc., also attended. The body was in the cowshed, held by a Konar widow, a neighbour. The mother sat with her hair loose, crying and beating herself with her fists. The body was smeared with turmeric paste and washed. The ear-lobes were pierced with thorns.[12] The mother held the child to her breast briefly, then it was enveloped in a white cloth.

Ponnaiya, the child's MF, picked it up. A few men followed him and the Barber down the street. The women went off to bathe, though Murukanantam herself did not seem to bathe that day. The procession crossed the ritual boundary without ceremony. The tank was full, so they had to wade through waist-deep water. The cemetery was under water too, so the funeral was held on common land north-west of the village.

A shallow grave was dug by friends, as no Vettiyan was present. Ponnaiya laid the body in it, head to the south, and Cellaiya threw in a handful of earth with his right hand. The remaining earth was replaced. Thorn bushes and stones were piled over it. Everyone bathed before returning home.

[12] The child was too young to have had an ear-piercing rite.

Cellaiya's shop reopened within a couple of hours. Neighbours took food in to the family for the rest of the day. Next morning they were selling home-cooked food as usual, but it was several days before Murukanantam reappeared in public. There were no subsequent rites of any kind.

Some ritual was necessary because the child had been named, yet she was too young to have had her ears pierced, so no specialists other than the Barber were involved. There were no subsequent prestations among relatives. These do occur for older children. A Pillai adult would of course be cremated.

Example G

Suppulaksmi, a 1-year-old Nayakkar girl, died on 26 January 1977. She was buried at once, and no cooking was done that day. At the 'seventh day feast' (*ēḻunāḷ āyviṭṭadu*) on 31 January, her parents, father's siblings, and father's siblings' spouses had oil-baths (*talaimulukku*). The Barber and Washerman were given cooked food. The parents received gifts from the child's affines (see 10.8.1, below), and feasted all their relatives.

10.7 Inter-Caste Prestations at Funerary Rites

10.7.1 At the Cremation

The central role in death ritual belongs to the Barber, Hocart's 'impure priest' (1968: 11). The Washerman, who provides the cloths for the bier and pavilion, assists him. For Harijans both duties are performed by the same specialist (see 4.3.2, above).

The grave-diggers (*veṭṭiyāṉ*) construct the funeral pyre, or dig the grave. Paraiyars do this for most castes in Terku Vandanam and Kalinkapatti, and also make and carry the bier at Vaniya Cettiyar funerals. Pallars do these tasks for the Terku Vandanam Asaris, as there is said to be a "father-son" link between them (Thurston and Rangachari 1909: v. 476). Cakkiliyars act as Vettiyans for the Pallars. They also stay with the Barber in the cemetery overnight, after high-caste funerals. A messenger (*tōṭṭi*) has the duty of informing the deceased's relatives in other villages. Terku Vandanam no longer has one, but the Pallars use Cakkiliyars as Tottis.

Funerals usually require Musicians. The local Pulavars are drummers but this particular task is too low-status for them, although they *do* drum in the cemetery itself at local Kavundar and Reddiyar funerals. Cakkiliyar Musicians cannot enter high-caste cemeteries. The local Cakkiliyars are not musicians, so Cakkiliyar bands are hired from Sikampatti[13] or Kuttal Urani.

All Terku Vandanam householders except Harijans and 'village sons' (see 4.3.1; 4.3.2, above) donate 50 paise to funeral expenses. Wealthy bereaved households may waive this, and the amount is reduced for simpler funerals. The donation is made at the bereaved house before the ceremony, and recorded on a list (*moy*) by the Karnam. As usual, delayed reciprocity is the norm. The communal provision of a share of the financial burden is, as we have seen, characteristic of life-crisis rites.

The specialists are recompensed at the edge of the cemetery. Every adult male in the village joins the funeral procession, and waits by the entrance during the cremation rituals. Afterwards the Karnam spreads a white cloth on which the money is placed, and all the men sit round to watch its distribution. These prestations are thus given publicly and witnessed by the whole community, from whom most of the money has usually come.

The Karnam draws up a list of recipients: it too is called a *moy* (see Dumont 1957*b*: 231–2). He is guided by elders of the bereaved caste as to customary practice. The specialists are called forward. The Karnam uses his left hand to throw money to the Barber, who takes it in his right hand and passes it on with his left. Use of the left hand marks the inauspiciousness of the event: it is normally grossly impolite to give in that way. The Barber, however, expresses his social inferiority to the Karnam by receiving the money in his right hand.

Example A

Asari: At Aiyan's funeral there was no *moy* collection. The payments came to Rs 52.50, as follows: Rs 0.50 each to the Velar and Oduvar Priests, Blacksmith, and Carpenter; Rs 4 each to the Barber (Sanmukam) and Washermen (shared); Rs 10 to the Pallar Vettiyan; Rs 32 to the Musicians; and another Rs 0.50 to the Oduvar (known as *tirumālai*, 'garland').

[13] Alias Ottarasupatti: neither name occurs in the 1971 Census (Government of India 1972*a*).

I (*left*) 'Bride' and 'groom' at a Velar Sadanku

II (*below*) The 'bridal' couple at a Maravar Sadanku

III Temple Kaliyanam: a Maravar couple with the wedding priest

IV House Kaliyanam: a Maravar couple on the marriage platform

V Asari mourners fetch water, led by the band and village Barber

VI An Asari man, decorated for the procession to the cemetery

VII (*above, left*) A Paraiyar woman, prepared for her funeral cortège

VIII (*above, right*) Divine Wedding: the divine couple

IX (*right*) Divine Wedding: the seven steps ritual

Example D
Pillai: At Kalyaniyammal's funeral the *moy* was Rs 58.50, i.e., all non-Harijan households had given. Payments totalled Rs 11.40, as follows: Rs 1.10 to the Velar Priest; Rs 2.50 to the Washerman (Raj); Rs 3 to the Barber (Sanmukam, helped by Ramasuppu); Rs 0.30 as *tirumālai*; and Rs 4.50 to the Paraiyar Vettiyans. There were no Musicians in this case. Each prestation was made in two instalments, and the second was given only when it had become clear that there was enough to go round. Both were classed as *sāṣtiram*, but giving in two stages made the achievement of *sandōsam* more likely (see 4.2, above).

Example C
Pallar: At Kanniyammal's burial the Pallar Priest wrote the *moy*. Altogether, Rs 46.50 was paid out: Rs 32 to the Musicians, Pallars of the same sub-caste; Rs 8 to the Tinda Vannar; Rs 6 to the Cakkiliyar Vettiyans; Rs 0.25 to another Cakkiliyar; and a few coins to a beggar.

The largest payment goes to the Musicians. It is given to them collectively, and is unaffected by the size of the band. There is some haggling. Their spokesman takes the money but remains standing; he mentions the cost of the midday meal, the expenses of the journey, and so on. Finally he is given a little more, and *sandōsam* is achieved.

There are usually several Vettiyans, but again the whole sum is handed to one representative. The Barber and Washerman then get approximately equal amounts. Artisans and Priests have no special roles at funerals, and their small prestations seem purely nominal. At Maravar funerals only, the recipients include the Terku Vandanam and Kalinkapatti Talaiyaris. Few of these people serve Harijans, so Example C is rather different.

The most general prestations of all, the attendance and financial contributions of the rest of the population,[14] are of course reciprocated when the occasion arises. Women villagers cannot go to the cemetery, but they visit the bereaved house (other castes even visit Paraiyar families in Terku Vandanam), and participate in the lamentations before the cortège leaves.

[14] There is no general household collection in Kalinkapatti.

10.7.2 *At the Karumati Rite*

The Barber directs the *karumāti* ritual if no Brahman officiant is present, otherwise he takes a supporting role.

Example D
At Kalyaniyammal's Karumati, the Brahman received Rs 5, a coconut, plantains, betel, 1 *paḍi* of rice, and the vesti used in the rite. The Barber received the left-over cooked food.

Example A
Aiyan Asari's Karumati was on 30 January 1977, at the Aiyanar well. It resembled Example D (10.5, above) but was conducted solely by the Barber. He got half the cooked food, equivalent to ¼ *pakkā* of rice, and the bereaved family later gave him raw vegetables and 1 *pakkā* of raw rice.

Sanmukam, the Barber in both cases, said that Vaniya Cettiyars pay Rs 12 for the entire funeral, whereas all other castes give him Rs 4 or 5. All give him cooked food too, except that Asaris and Cettiyars give 3 *pakkās* of raw rice, half at the funeral and half at the Karumati. A similar pattern exists in routine prestations to the Barber, where again Asaris do not give cooked food (see 4.3.1, above). Just as at Sadankus and Kaliyanams, then, village specialists perform tasks at funerals involving their client families. There is no special *sampaḷam*, but their contributions are recognized by *sāṣtiram* prestations.

Once again, non-local specialists receive both *sampaḷam* and *sāṣtiram* components in their rewards. That is why the Musicians are apparently so much better paid than the Barber, even though he supervises or performs almost every stage of the funeral. His meagre reward at the cemetery is merely a *sāṣtiram* gift: after all, people explained, he and the Washerman are 'village sons' precisely *because* they perform the mourning duties expected of a son whenever clients die.

10.8 Intra-Caste Prestations

10.8.1 Local Examples

The funeral is the scene for the main inter-caste prestations. By contrast, prestations at the Karumati are not public. The village does not help furnish them and they are witnessed only by relatives, whose own gifts are much more prominent. A feast is provided by the mourners, who are presented with vestis and towels or shirts (not the turbans reported by Dumont 1983; 94–102; 1957*b*: 251–6; cf. 10.8.2, below). The donors are close affines of the mourners, described as their *sammandis*. This term, roughly translatable as 'marriage partners', has several meanings which differ in genealogical precision (cf. term 21 in Tables 5.1 and 5.2). This is annoying for ethnographers, who do not know without detailed enquiry how to understand the term in each new context, but it is of course no more confusing for local listeners than, say, our own use of the word 'family'.

The exact identities of the *sammandi* donors depend upon the stage of life of the deceased and chief mourner. As affinity is perpetual (Dumont 1983: 14; 5.3, above)[15] the same people are affines of both, but the relationship is between contemporaries in one case, and seniors and juniors in the other. In identifying the affines making prestations at a Karumati, it is therefore necessary to specify their relationships to both the deceased and the mourner(s).

Example G

At the Nayakkar seventh-day ceremony, the dead baby's father (the chief mourner) and mother received a vesti, sari, and Rs 5 from each of the father's four ZHs. Other relatives gave small sums of money, as always when attending any life-crisis feast. The father said, however, that no gifts were prescribed from his own *sammandis*, meaning his WF, MB, and FZH. The actual donors were by that reckoning the *sammandis* of the dead girl. She had a MB too (WB to the chief mourner), but he gave only money.

[15] I argued against Dumont's use of the notion of 'affinity' in terminological analysis (see 5.4, above). The notion does, however, seem helpful when applied to jural rules, as here (cf. 14.3, below).

Example C

At the Pallar *urimaikkaṭṭu* for Kanniyammal only one vesti was given, by her brother to her young son Mariyappan (i.e., from MB to ZS).

This particular gift is the most vital because it comes from the chief mourner's main *sammandi*. When the recipient is young and unmarried, as here, his foremost *sammandi* (Dumont's 'principal affine') is his MB. As the Nayakkar and Asari cases show, a married man's main donor is his ZH rather than his WB, irrespective of whether the caste has a MBDy or an FZDy *urimai* preferences. The ZH and WB are of course terminologically distinct in the commonest local terminology (Table 5.2).

Example A

This last point is illustrated by the case of donor Arumukam at Aiyan Asari's Karumati. Altogether, four recipients and five donors were involved in exchanges of vestis and towels. Table 10.1 includes the terminological relationship in each case, as stated by the recipient. The genealogical positions of these persons are shown in Figure 10.3.

Neglecting one case where the obligation had been inherited (cf. Dumont 1983: 89; 1957*b*: 259), gifts to the unmarried sons of the

TABLE 10.1. Prestations at an Asari Karumati Rite

Recipient[a]	Relationship to deceased	Donor[a]	Relationship to recipient
Velccami (1) and	*makan̲* (S)	Solaiyappan (1)	*tāymāman̲* (MB)
Cellapperumal (2)	*makan̲* (S)	Ponnaiya (2)	*māman̲* (FZH)
		Arumukam (3)	*māman̲* (FBWB)[b]
		Muniyakutti (4)	*māman̲* (FZH)
		Puvalinkam (5)	*maccinan̲* (FZS)[c]
Ponnuccami (3)	*makan̲* (eBS)[d]	Arumukam (3)	*tāymāman̲* (MB)
Pon (4)	*makan̲* (eBS)[d]	Arumukam (3)	*tāymāman̲* (MB)
		Umaiya (6)	*maccinan̲* (ZH)[e]

[a] The numbers refer to Fig. 10.3.
[b] This donor is the WB of the father's *half*-brother.
[c] The donor's parents (FZ and FZH of the recipients) were dead.
[d] Their father was the dead man's elder *half*-brother.
[e] The case of this man, who did not give anything, is discussed in the text.

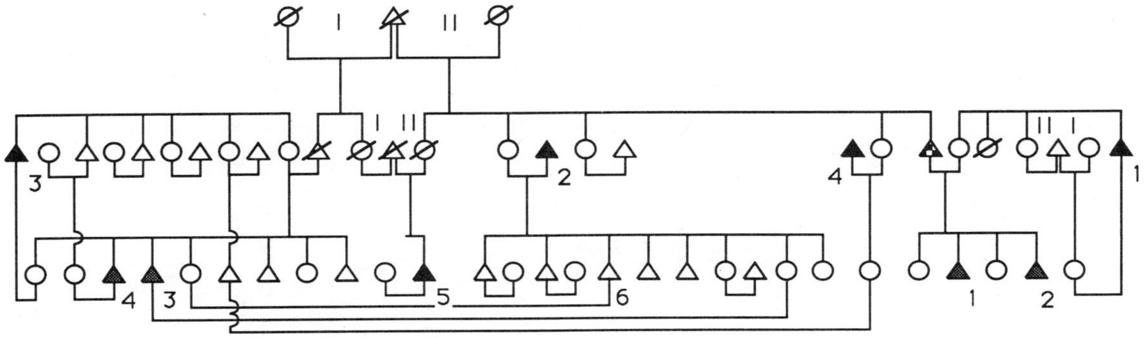

FIG. 10.3 Donors and Recipients in an Asari Karumati Ritual

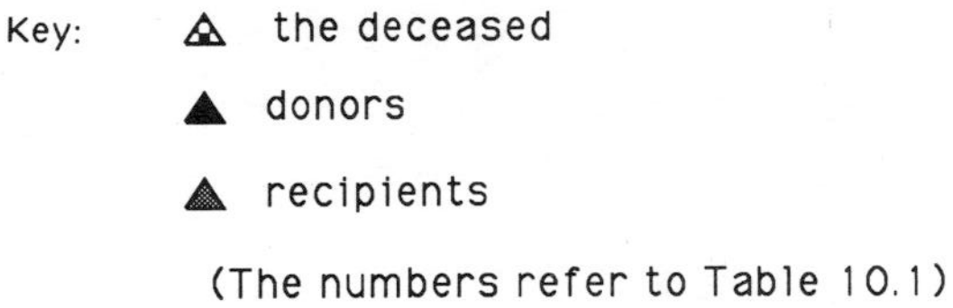

deceased all came from affines of the next senior genealogical level. For unmarried recipients, the senior MB made the most important prestation. Next in importance came the gifts of terminological *māmaṉs* or their 'heirs', and all the MBs and FZHs of the two boys made prestations.

The other two recipients were the married sons of the dead man's elder half-brother (same father, different mother). The general rule stated above would lead one to expect their main donor to be their ZH, and indeed Arumukam, having married his eZDy, is not only MB but also eZH to both men. Their other MBs, who were not also related in this other way, gave nothing. Arumukam's gifts to the dead man's sons seem secondary, and again were not duplicated by his brothers. It was as though, having given to the minor mourners—his WBs—he was obliged also to give to the chief mourners out of courtesy.

So far matters seem very clear. However, neither Ponnuccami nor Pon received anything from their other ZH, Umaiya (no. 6 in Figure 10.3), even though he was also Ponnuccami's WB as a result of sister-exchange. None of Ponnuccami's other WBs were involved either, but Umaiya's case raises questions which cannot be answered from the information available. For example, was Arumukam under greater obligation than Umaiya because he was also MB of the recipients? Would Umaiya have given had Ponnuccami and Pon been chief mourners? Was there any personal dispute between Umaiya and his affines?

The fact that the ZH rather than the WB is the main donor for a married mourner seems to reflect the importance of eZDy marriages. These create the genealogical identity MB = eZH, emphasizing that either relative may fulfil the role of 'principal affine'. The ZH is senior to the WB, given eZDy marriage: this is likely to be true terminologically whether genealogical eZDy marriage occurs or not, given the structure of the kinship terminology (see 5.6, above). Moreover, the ZH is of course the son-in-law of the deceased, and so much more closely related to him/her than is the WB.

A widow plays no active part in the Karumati and receives no gifts afterwards. However, she has already received gifts of clothing before the departure of the cortège, from her husband's "brothers" or their heirs (see 10.2, Ex. A, above). In other words, she receives gifts from her *sammandis* at the funeral, whereas male mourners do so at the Karumati.

10.8.2 Dumont on the Kallar and Maravar

Any account of Tamil funerary prestations is endebted to Dumont's pioneering analyses for Kondaiyankottai Maravars and Piramalai Kallars (1983: 93–102; 1957*b*: 251–64), but although the former sub-caste is found in Terku Vandanam, local practice differs markedly from that described by Dumont.

Terku Vandanam affines do not give turbans, but vestis and towels; there are no prescribed intra-caste gifts of food like those of Kallars (1983: 97); money is given by all villagers, not merely caste-fellows (cf. 1983: 97); lastly, neither of the groups studied by Dumont permits eZDy marriage. The question is whether, despite these substantive differences, the two cases have any structural features in common. I shall consider the chief mourner only.

One Kallar chief mourner—the son of the dead man—received turbans from four of his five ZHs; his WB and his WB's FFBSS; and his other wife's F. All these, plus the fifth ZH and some others, gave food too. The non-participation of the MB was a matter of pure chance (1983: 96). At a woman's funeral, the chief mourner was her eldest son: he received clothes from his ZH (who was also his MBS); his other MBS; his surviving MB; his MFBS; and his MFFB. The first two donors also gave clothes to his son, to whom they were FZH and FMBS (see the genealogy in 1957*b*: 254).

The obligation to give is more widely diffused among a chief mourner's genealogical affines' agnates than in Terku Vandanam. This may reflect the Kallars' greater patrilineality. For them the MB's gift takes pride of place, although the ZH gives an equal amount. This generationally asymmetric ideology seems at variance with the fact that such gifts are reciprocated if occasion arises, but as Dumont comments, the word *tāymāmaṉ* denotes 'more a role than a person' (1983: 96), and primacy may pass down to the MBS. The actual donor is preferably of the same generation as the chief mourner.

Dumont's only Maravar example is distorted by contingencies like emigration, and the fact that neither the deceased's F nor FF had any sisters (pp. 99–101), so rather than discuss it in detail, I shall merely refer to the quoted rule that a wife-taker's (ZH's) gift takes precedence over a wife-giver's (WB's) (pp. 101–2). I never heard this said locally, but local Maravars certainly shared the same patrilateral marriage preference, so their ZH is ideally also their MBS. The role of 'principal affine' then passes down from father to son.

In short, Dumont's findings do not conform exactly to mine but the resemblances are sufficient, bearing in mind the substantial differences in other respects, to indicate that similar structural principles are at work in both cases.

10.9 Local Views Concerning Death

Literary accounts of the Hindu view of death emphasize cycles of rebirth (*saṁsāra* in Sanskrit). One's *karma*, the accumulated balance of one's past good and bad deeds, determines the hierarchical position of each rebirth. The Tamil forms of both words are used locally, but with much more restricted meanings. As far as I know, *karumam* is used only in relation to the sixteenth-day death ceremony, and I only ever heard *samusāram* used as a respectful term for someone else's wife!

Charlene Allison (pers. com.) found that urban, orthodox Pillais in Tirunelveli Town knew of the rebirth doctrine but denied that they themselves subscribed to it. Many villagers to whom I spoke seemed unaware even of its existence. Queries about 'what happens when someone dies' were greeted with amused incredulity. The question seemed never to have occurred to them, at least in such general terms.

It was agreed that those who died violently became *pēys*, hideous demons which haunt particular trees and may be seen at night by the unwary. It was also agreed that the 'spirit' (*āvi*) left the body (*uṭampu*) at the moment of death. It did not accompany the cortège—'Only Siva is in the cemetery,' said Veyilmuttu, the Pallar Pusari—but remained in the bereaved household until the sixteenth day. The problem was, what happened to it subsequently? The few *ad hoc* suggestions offered (for example, that it 'went south') were clearly mere attempts to humour me. Not surprisingly then, local exegeses of funerals are fragmentary and inconclusive, and their analysis will depend largely on external, anthropological intuition (see 13.3, below).

11

Other Ethnographic Examples

11.1 Introduction

This chapter presents comparative material from other parts of southern India and Sri Lanka. It deals primarily with puberty rituals and weddings in the societies concerned, but birth ceremonies and funerals are discussed too, wherever possible. The aim is to set the practices reported in earlier chapters into their regional context.

Because I am interested in correlations between the socio-structural particularities of each group and the details of the rituals they perform, I shall naturally stress the differences between one group and another. By contrast, Kolenda (1984) emphasizes the similarities in wedding rites, not merely within the south but across India as a whole. To a great extent this contrast merely reflects our differing aims rather than any fundamental disagreement between us, yet it does seem to me that Kolenda goes too far. In the first place, her southern (Nadar) example (1984: 103–4) is unusual, and differs in several key respects from most ceremonies described here. More importantly, her comparison is premissed upon Lévi-Strauss's assertion that 'Generalized exchange extends over a vast area of Southern Asia' (Lévi-Strauss 1969: 269; Kolenda 1984: 98). As we saw (5.5; Good 1980: 489), this assertion is false.

My own comparison starts from the observation that female puberty rites are found almost everywhere in the region, and are often associated in various ways with 'mock' or 'real' marriages. In many places—but not Terku Vandanam—the time for which a girl is secluded is shorter for higher castes. The same applies to subsequent menstruations too (Ferro-Luzzi 1974: 122–9), though again not in Terku Vandanam. Seclusion times tend also to be longer in south than north Tamil Nadu.

Some rites coincide with the menarche and others precede it, but (*pace* van Gennep 1960: 65) this does not seem a fundamental distinction. The ceremony is at least partly aimed at assuring the girl her due place in adult life, safeguarding the status and purity of her relatives, and regulating access to her sexual and reproductive capacities. As long as she is not 'let out' into everyday, adult life before it has been performed, there is no logical reason why it should not occur at any time before, at, or even after puberty. Differences in timing are merely cultural variations.

The discussion deals only with Hindu and Buddhist groups. Muslim and Christian practices (Winslow 1980; McGilvray 1982*b*) raise other issues which there is no space to discuss here. Even so, by no means all the available accounts are considered. Thus, many cases are reported by Thurston (1906), Thurston and Rangachari (1909), Bhattacharyya (1968), and Puthenkalam (1977). These accounts suggest a high degree of uniformity, but their reliability is open to question, for even when discussing castes found in Terku Vandanam they make no mention of a 'bridegroom', or any other resemblance to marriage.[1] Nor is the sociological detail adequate: as we shall see (Chapter 14), the precise social identities of participants are crucial.

Furthermore, the literature is much less complete where birth and death rituals are concerned. Few of the writers on puberty rites and weddings have reported these other life-crisis rites in anything like so much detail. In some cases, therefore, I have had recourse to other sources dealing with the same regions but not precisely the same communities.

The ceremonies concerned are usually elaborate and complex, so my brief descriptions involve a lot of impoverishment and simplification, although I have done my best not to distort the significance of the material presented. In line with my comparative aims, I concentrate on sociological matters and pay less attention to the details of the rites themselves. In other words, I am concerned primarily with *who* does things, and *when* they do them, rather than with *what* they do.

Two further methodological issues must be addressed before proceeding. First, the 'ethnographic present' tense is used throughout this chapter, even for practices which are now defunct or modified. The aim is to develop a paradigm which reflects the *entire* range of possibilities in the region shown in Map 2, not merely those still found at present: this of course involves the working assumption

[1] Thurston and Rangachari discuss the Sadankus of the Maravar (1909: v. 40); Konar (ii. 358); Velar (vii. 343); Reddiyar (iii. 234); and Paraiyar (vi. 133), without mentioning any resemblance to a wedding.

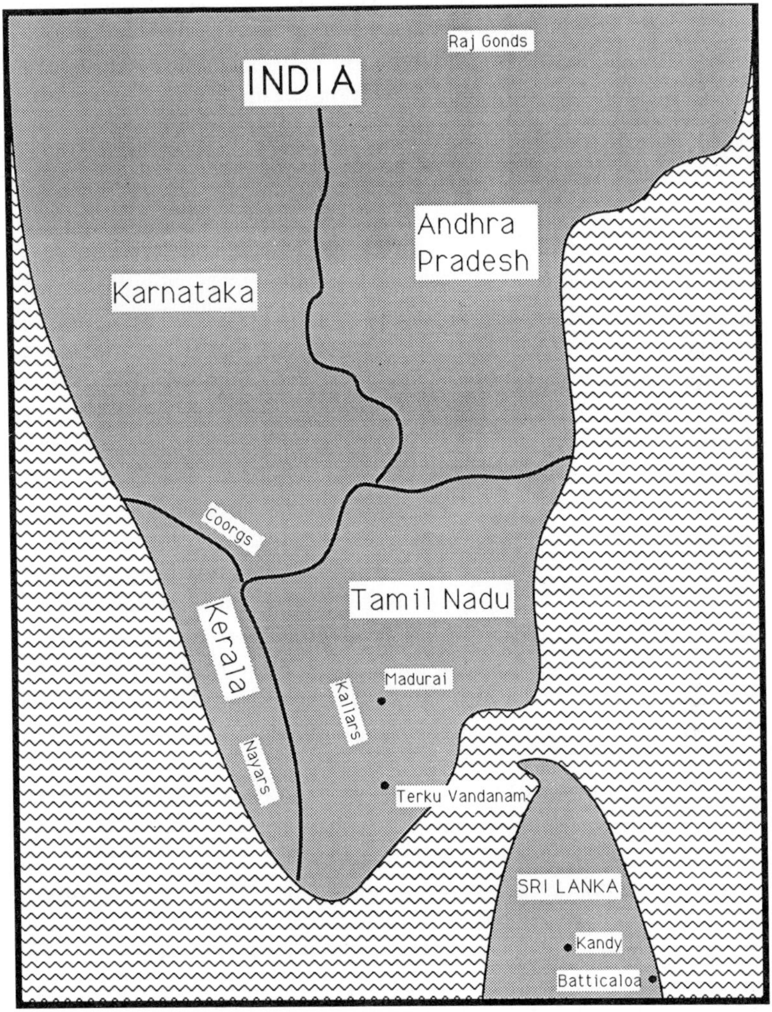

Map 2 Southern India and Sri Lanka

that these possibilities are the same now as they were in the past. Evidence for such continuity comes from the continued importance of the marriage practices analysed in Chapter 6, and from the enduring salience of the theological ideas discussed in Chapter 16.

Second, and to avoid misunderstanding, it is important to reiterate that when the terms "patrilineal" and matrilineal" are used below without further qualification, they should be understood as referring to the kinds of *de facto* unilineality discussed earlier (1.2).

11.2 Coorgs

The Coorg inhabitants of southern Karnataka have strongly defined units called *okkas*, which Srinivas (1952: 49, 51) describes as patrilocal joint families, each with its ancestral house and impartible landed estate managed by the eldest man of the senior branch. Later writers have argued that *okkas* are 'lineages' rather than 'joint families' (cf. Kalam 1987), but all agree that they are property-owning corporations. Ancestral landed property is not inherited by individuals, therefore, but a bride does get jewels and other gifts from her natal family which are returnable in case of divorce. Tambiah describes this as dowry of 'classical Indian form' (1973*b*: 102), but Srinivas himself notes differences from the 'similar, though not identical, Sanskritic custom' of *strīdhana* (1952: 154–5).

Coorgs have a standard South Indian symmetric prescriptive kin terminology, coupled with a rule of *okka* exogamy. There is a 'slight' preference for FZDy marriage or, more precisely, for a girl to marry into her mother's natal *okka* (Srinivas 1952: 146–7).

All auspicious life-crises involve *maṅkala* rites. They are done at girls' puberty ceremonies, at the ear-borings of boys,[2] and at weddings (pp. 70–1). If the principal subject is male, he is shaved, then bathed by three *sumaṅkalis* (married women with living husbands). He dons a special white gown. In the central hall of the house he thrice circles a three-legged stool, before sitting down. The *mūrta* rite is then performed: relatives present him with milk and money, and bless him; three *sumaṅkalis* do this first, led by his mother (pp. 72–4). At

[2] No details of the female puberty rite are given. Ear-boring is described as its male 'counterpart', which 'conferred social adulthood' on the boy. Men without ear-rings are barred from certain temples, and their ears must be pierced before their funerals (Srinivas 1952: 81).

weddings, two companions go through the shaving rite with the groom, and two other girls take part in the bride's bath (p. 80). The groom is assisted by his ZH, and the bride by her BW—a classificatory "sister" of the groom (p. 153).

On the first day of a wedding, separate *mūrtas* are performed at the natal homes of the couple, who are blessed by their own relatives and fellow-villagers. Next day, the groom's relatives accompany him to the bride's house to perform *mūrta* for her. Her relatives then do *mūrta* for the groom (p. 158).

The *sammanda* rite is then done by the 'family friends' of the couple. Every *okka* has enduring links of friendship with another *okka*—usually an affinal one—whose headman ideally plays this role (p. 56). The bride stands in the kitchen, with the groom outside. The bride's friend holds twelve 'pieces of gold' (actually pebbles), eleven of which are passed to the groom's friend to show that the bride is *almost* completely transferred to her conjugal *okka* but retains vestigial rights in her *okka* of birth (pp. 127–8).

The groom does *mūrta* for the bride, and leads her out of the kitchen. Her cross-cousin blocks the way and asserts his own rights over the girl. The groom gives him a gold coin, which he presents to the bride along with a coin of his own (p. 147). When she arrives at the groom's home, his relatives offer her *mūrta*. Extra-large sums of money are given to her by the groom and his mother (pp. 142–3). The groom receives large gifts from his MB, FZ and married Z: they make gifts at funerals, too (p. 150).

To demonstrate her membership of the groom's *okka* the bride gives coins to the children, fetches water from the well, and takes manure to the fields (pp. 92–5, 143). When she revisits her native *okka* after consummation of the marriage, she cannot be seen by fellow villagers until they have been feasted by her natal family, because she is now 'a new person' (p. 99). The two sets of relatives are kept largely separate during the wedding, and the couple's fathers do not meet again till months afterwards (p. 154).

A *maṅkala* is performed in the fifth or seventh month of a woman's first pregnancy (p. 100). Mothers are partially purified twelve days after giving birth, during the child's naming ritual performed by the Washerman (pp. 83–5), but they observe some restrictions until the sixtieth day, when they ceremonially restart fetching water from the well (p. 92).

Coorgs practise cremation for elders and burial for juniors. Each *okka* has a cemetery on its estate (p. 78). The corpse is dressed in a back-to-front *maṅkala* gown and lies on an upside-down mat (p. 118). Mourners also wear gowns, but do not put their right arms into the sleeves (p. 86). The chief mourner is the surviving spouse, and the eldest son's role is slightly less important (p. 112). Both of them, along with the deceased's opposite-sex sibling's son, do the pot-breaking rite, which severs links with surviving relatives (p. 151).

The chief mourner throws the first earth into the grave or lights the funeral pyre (p. 118). On the second day s/he pours water and milk in the cemetery (p. 94). Mourning usually lasts twelve to sixteen days. Daily food is offered to the spirit of the deceased (p. 84). The eldest son observes an ascetic regime for up to six months (p. 82). Junior *okka* members also mourn, but the restrictions are less onerous (p. 112). Special gifts are provided by affines, especially the native *okka* of a dead woman, or of a dead man's mother (p. 153).

11.3 Piramalai Kallar

Piramalai Kallar living in Madurai District, Tamil Nadu, also have strongly marked, exogamous patrilineages (*kūṭṭam*), although these are neither residential nor property-holding units. They act corporately mainly as followers of chiefs (*tēvar*), and as co-worshippers at lineage shrines. Property is owned by individual families, and inheritance is from father to son (Dumont 1957*b*: 168–74). Kallars have a MBDy *urimai* preference (Dumont 1983: 54).

Kallar puberty rites coincide with the menarche. A hut is built by a cross-relative, and the girl is led there at an auspicious time by a female cross-relative. She is armed with a sickle (cf. James 1974: 163). On the fourteenth day of seclusion, her MB arrives with elaborate gifts. The girl offers him an *ālatti*, and he garlands her. Everyone eats. Next day she tears down and burns her hut. She bathes at a well, and there is a communal meal in the house.

On later days neighbours take turns inviting her to eat. On the thirtieth day the household crockery is replaced and the house asperged (perhaps by a Brahman). The lineage priest and medium are invited to a meal. After another four or five days, the MB holds a banquet. He first gives Rs 1 to the girl, betel is distributed, and everyone bathes. Next day, other cross-relatives visit (Dumont 1957*b*: 243–4).

Kallar weddings (Dumont 1957*b*: 215–33) involve several movements to and fro between the natal households of bride and groom. At the bride's house, her MB leads her thrice round a platform inside a pavilion. The groom tours his own village and processes to the bride's house during the night, ideally on horseback. He sits in the pavilion while his yZ takes gifts in to the bride, and ties her marriage *tāli*. After a banquet the couple tour the village, the bride following her husband. After they leave for the groom's village, the bride's family have a *moy* collection.

At the groom's house the couple are welcomed by his MB. There is a banquet and another *moy*. The groom's yZ again ties the *tāli*, this time in the groom's presence. The couple return to the bride's village for a few days before taking up permanent viri-patrilocal residence. Apart from the groom's yZ, close relatives of the couple do not travel from one village to another, so the participants in the two places are almost completely different.

Tambiah claims to see a 'remarkable correspondence' between Kallar marriage prestations and classical dowry (1973*b*: 105), but in fact Kallar behaviour (Dumont 1957*b*: 228–33) resembles that in Terku Vandanam (see 8.5, above), and there is an overall balance in the prestations exchanged at marriage.

Looking at the cycle overall, we see that the Kallar puberty rites show no trace of the wedding episode which is so prominent in Terku Vandanam. Participation by cross-relatives is important, but the emphasis is almost entirely on the MB. The toing and froing during the wedding ensures, however, that Kallar girls *do* enjoy marital rites in their own homes, even though these occur at a later stage than in Terku Vandanam, and incorporate the real groom rather than a surrogate.

A woman returns to her natal home for the delivery of her first child. The Barber's wife officiates, and a man buries the afterbirth nearby. The Washerman informs the new father, who does not see the baby until next day. This messenger receives clothes and food. The mother is confined for seven days, and given heating foods (Dumont 1957*b*: 234–5).

Subsequent deliveries are at the marital home. The mother's parents and other relatives bring food on the seventh day to mark the ending of impurity (*tīṭṭu kaḷikkiṛadu*). The house is purified, the mother bathes, and a meal is cooked by her husband's FZ. Next day his MB's family bring food. There is another feast on the thirtieth day, when the child's ears should be pierced by the Goldsmith. Affines bring gifts. In particular, the child's MB provides gold earrings. The child is named when three months old, by the lineage priest (Dumont 1957*b*: 236–7).

Kallars bury their dead, but otherwise funerals closely resemble those in Terku Vandanam. The local Barber officiates. The band and other assistants are Cakkiliyars. Once the body is prepared the *pattam edukkiradu* (cf. 10.2, above) is performed. The mourners—garlanded, and carrying dishes of soaked rice—are led to the centre of the village by the Barber. They make one or three circles, then prostrate themselves thrice before their dish, facing north, while the Barber asperges them and chants 'attain heaven' (*suvarkkalōkam sēr*; Dumont 1957*b*: 247). The body is carried to the cemetery in a palanquin. At the centre of the village, the widow (or the daughter of a dead woman) performs the 'trickling-pot' rite (see 10.2, above). The chief mourner repeats this at the cemetery. The body is fed rice by mourners (cf. 10.2, above; Dumont 1957*b*: 247). Caste-fellows contribute towards the funeral expenses (Dumont 1957*b*: 248).

A second-day ceremony (*kādai ērrutal*; cf. 10.4, above) alleviates the impurity of the mourners. A 'turban tying' ceremony (*urumāl kattu*; cf. Ch. 10 n. 11) is held sometime between the fifth and eleventh days, after an oil bath. The identities of the donors and recipients were discussed above (10.8.2). A ceremony on the thirtieth day removes the remaining impurity (Dumont 1957*b*: 249).

Kallars practise one unusual and distinctive *male* rite, the circumcision of young boys. This ceremony (*sīppu kaliyāṇam*) is held every five years or so, for all boys of suitable age in the village. Each boy's affines are invited, and his MB arrives in procession with substantial gifts (p. 239). The boys wear mediums' hats, red vestis given by their fathers, and bridegrooms' garlands given by their MBs. They carry sticks to keep away demons attracted by the blood (p. 240). There is a feast for which the MB provides the rice. The main contributors to the *moy* collection are, in order, the MB, FZ, FFZC, MZH, and various agnates, starting with the FFBC. The gifts are large, and the hosts expect to make a profit overall (pp. 242–3).

The Barber performs the operation. Afterwards the boys are excluded from their homes for 30 days. They pass the time in a group, withdrawn from normal social life but able to collect tolls from market stalls and passing vehicles. These go towards the costs of the ceremony. From the tenth day onwards, they are fed by different households in turn. On the thirty-first day they give vestis to the Washerman, and bathe at a well. There is a meal at each boy's house, to which the Washerman and an elderly couple are invited (p. 240).

The boys are in an impure and vulnerable state during the thirty-day period (p. 241). It is interesting to note the clear parallels with female puberty (seclusion, impurity, etc.), and with weddings (the garland). The prestations at all Kallar rites seem larger and more elaborate than among many wealthier, higher-status groups. This may be partly attributable to the idealizations of Dumont's favourite informant, but the MB's responsibilities do seem more onerous than elsewhere.

11.4 Kandyan Sinhalese

Sinhalese are not Dravidian speakers, but they do have a South Indian-type symmetrical relationship terminology. Their kinship practices are hard to characterize because there are considerable variations both within and between localities. For most people kinship is bilateral. Kindreds (*pavula*) are important, and land is inherited equally by sons and daughters (Yalman 1962; Tambiah 1973*b*: 134). Marriages are unstable, and the husband's and wife's estates are kept separate for inheritance purposes. However, wealthier families stress patrilineal pedigrees (*vasagama*), and provide daughters with dowries in lieu of shares in the land (Yalman 1971: 136).

Although they are Buddhists, Sinhalese perform puberty rites quite like Kallar ones in structure, though different in cultural detail. In Yalman's account (1963) no locality is specified, but it presumably refers to Terutenne in the eastern highlands. In any case, very similar observations are reported from elsewhere (Winslow 1980: 607–8; Wirz 1954: 243).

The girl is secluded in a hut, alone or with a "grandmother". A rice-pounder is kept beside her. Her dirty clothes, eating leaves, and bodily excretions are put in a special cooking pot. An astrologer determines the length of her seclusion.[3] At the auspicious time the Washerwoman covers her head and leads her out to be bathed. The Washerman purifies the house with cow-dung and turmeric, and

[3] The girl gets a new horoscope at this time. That does not happen in Terku Vandanam.

places auspicious objects on to a pure cloth on the floor: raw rice; plantains; oil-cakes; a basin of water containing a coin; and an oil-lamp.

The girl is bathed thrice in water or milk. The Washerwoman breaks the polluted pot against a milk-exuding tree and dresses the girl in new clothes, keeping the old ones herself. The girl is covered again and led back into the house, where her MB breaks a coconut. Her head is uncovered, so the objects on the floor are the first things she sees. She looks into the water, puts out the oil-lamp, walks over the rice, and worships her relatives in order of seniority. The Washerman is given the items on the floor. There is a communal meal, at which her engagement is often announced (Yalman 1963: 29–32).

Gift-giving seems less pronounced than in previous cases, and the Washerman's role appears to be more important. Again there is no 'wedding' episode, but the girl's future marriage is directly referred to in the announcement of her engagement and the essential role of her MB. The absence of a mock wedding may not be too significant, as Sinhalese marriages often involve no ritual at all. If a woman begins cooking for a marriageable man, a perfectly respectable union is assumed to exist (Yalman 1971: 167–8). Even if there *is* a wedding, prestations are normally, by regional standards, limited in size and complexity (Tambiah 1973*b*: 133). On the other hand, we must again add the proviso that marriages between non-relatives or wealthy status-climbers may be extravagantly ceremonialized (Tambiah 1973*b*: 133; Leach 1982: 193–8).

The usual, and more highly valued, form of marriage (*dīga*) involves viri-patrilocal residence. Heiresses, or girls without brothers, may, however, marry uxorilocally (*binna*). The wedding—if there is one—is at the groom's house in the first case, and at the bride's in the second (D'Oyly 1975: 192).

At a *dīga* wedding the groom comes to collect his bride. His party includes a *nenda* (FZ, MBW, etc.) of the bride, who acts as the latter's mouthpiece and chaperone. The couple put on new clothes given by their MBs. The bride's MB breaks coconuts on the threshold, ties the couple's thumbs, and pours water over their bound hands. The large parts played by the MBs and *nenda* give 'the impression that the rites are in the charge of intermediaries' (Yalman 1971: 164–6). As the couple leave, the bride's cross-cousin shows his agreement to her marriage by accepting betel.

The published ethnography on birth and death practices makes no mention of any clearly defined affinal participation, although 'maternal kin . . . are given the most prominence' in Sinhalese rites of passage generally (Yalman 1971: 362). When a child is born, it is fed a little milk by a female relative or neighbour, then handed by the midwife to its father. The mother is secluded and subjected to dietary restrictions in the normal way. The duration of these is determined by the astrologer, who casts a horoscope for the child (Wirz 1954: 247–9).

Sinhalese practise both cremation and burial, depending on the wealth of the family. At the cemetery, Buddhist monks (*bhikkhus*) recite the Buddhist precepts before receiving the 'corpse's clothing' from the bereaved family—a white cloth which has been spread over the body. Water is poured to solemnize the gift. The monks then withdraw, and take no part in the actual funeral rites (Gombrich 1971: 241–2). The pyre, if there is one, is lit by 'nephews or sons-in-law of the deceased' (Ryan 1958: 104). After seven days the ashes are collected, and the relatives all provide a feast for the monks, who are invited to preach (Ryan 1958: 104; Wirz 1954: 192–3).

11.5 'Token Marriage' in Central India

Dube (1953) describes 'token pre-puberty marriages' which are performed in the Madhya Pradesh-Orissa border area, near the northern limit of the southern kinship system (Trautmann 1981: 111). These involve the 'marriage' of physically immature girls to objects such as arrows among tribal groups, branches among Raj Gonds (the 'aboriginal peasantry'), and wooden rice-pounders among Hindu castes.

This so-called 'first marriage' involves no marriage gifts, but during its two-day duration all the major wedding rites are performed: oil and turmeric are applied to the 'bride' and 'groom'; there is a procession; yellow rice is thrown; the couple go round the marriage post; there is a ceremonial bath.

A girl who does not undergo the ceremony before puberty is considered to be permanently polluted. The most intriguing feature, though, is that

> A real or classificatory brother-in-law (sister's husband) of the girl holds the token bridegroom in his hand and acts at the different stages of the ceremony

on its behalf. For this service he receives a special gift of money or cloth at the time of the girl's regular marriage. (Dube 1953: 19; original gloss)

It is not clear whether this 'brother-in-law' *has* to be already married; Dube may mean simply that any male cross-cousin can fulfil these duties. It is, however, significant that although the 'marriage' is ostensibly with the object, a 'potential spouse' acts for it and subsequently receives a prestation resembling that given to a man whose *urimaippeṇ* marries someone else (see 6.4, above).

In effect the 'marriage' of the human couple is nullified by the expedient of regarding the object rather than its bearer as the 'groom', an outcome achieved in Terku Vandanam by the choice of a female 'bridegroom' (see 14.1, below). The 'first' and 'second' marriages are said to be identical in structure, but no details of the latter are given.

11.6 Nayars of Kerala

The most famous 'pre-puberty marriages' are undoubtedly the tali-tying ceremonies (*tālikaṭṭukaliyāṉam*) practised by Nayars. The details vary greatly with sub-caste and region.

First, Sudra Nayars in Cochin (Gough 1955) live[4] in matrilineal, property-owning corporations (*taravāds*), headed by the senior male member (*kāranavan*). There is no co-resident conjugal unit. Men and women form sexual relationships (*sambandham*) with members of other *taravāds*, but sibling groups continue to live together along with the sisters' children. The relationship terminology is not of the standard symmetric prescriptive type (see 5.3, above; Gough 1952).

Several girls from a single *taravād* undergo the rite together. They may be secluded beforehand as if for a menstrual period, though the rite precedes physical puberty. A pavilion is built, a picture of goddess Bhagavati is drawn on its floor, and a milk-exuding branch is put in one corner to attract her. A bench is made of the same wood.

The ceremony is attended by allied lineages (*inaṅkar*), from among whom the 'grooms' are selected by astrologers. On the first morning the girls worship the lineage goddess. The 'grooms' are greeted at the

[4] Nayar society has undergone radical changes this century, but for comparative purposes (cf. 11.1, above) it is their earlier practices which are crucial. Their apparent exoticism serves in fact to highlight features widely present elsewhere too.

gate by the mature women of the lineage, and their feet are washed by its young men. At the auspicious moment, each girl is led to the bench by her brother. The Brahman officiant hands the *tāli* to her 'groom', who ties it round her neck. The couple are then secluded in the house for three days: there is disagreement in the literature about whether sexual intercourse might take place.

Next day the relatives sacrifice a cock to Bhagavati and there is feasting. On the fourth day every new couple takes a purificatory bath in the village pool before putting on their best clothes for a joint meal. The women eat first—a reversal of normal order. The 'groom' receives gifts from the head of the lineage, and then goes home. Sometimes a cloth is torn, with half going to the *tāli*-tier and half to the girl, as in divorce. The girl does not usually continue to wear the *tāli* after the ceremony (Fuller 1976: 103).

Nayar girls undergo rites (*tirandukaliyāṇam*) at their menarche too, but these seem mainly purificatory, with little sociological content (Fuller 1976: 101; Iyer 1909–12: ii. 29–30). The girl is secluded during her period, then bathed. The bath procession is joined by women from *inaṅkar* lineages. It may be led by her brother, who 'cuts' the water of the bathing tank with a knife to drive away evil spirits (Puthenkalam 1977: 60).

The *tāli*-tier can become a *sambandham* partner of the girl, though he is under no obligation to do so. For her part, she is now entitled to form several such relationships. Each of them has to be approved by both *taravād* heads and is then formally inaugurated. The man's party are fed at the girl's house. He is seated in the main room surrounded by lamps. Both partners pay respects to the elders and Brahmans, who bless them. The couple are then left alone: next morning, the man leaves money under her pillow (Iyer 1909–12: ii. 30–1; Fuller 1976: 107–8).

Whereas the *tāli* is tied by an affine in the Sudra case, Nayars of higher-ranking sub-castes have it done by a local Nayar chief, or a Nambudiri Brahman.[5] For some lower-caste groups, the *tāli*-tier is a woman: the girl's MBW or FZ, or even a Barber's wife (Gough 1955: 79).

One or other of a woman's *sambandham* partners meets the cost of her pregnancy (Fuller 1976: 108). This does not imply that he is

[5] Gough explains this in Freudian terms (see 12.1, below), but it seems likely that political considerations play a part in such choices and, even more, in the selection of *sambandham* partners (Mencher and Goldberg 1967: 89).

the child's genitor, or involve him in any subsequent paternal responsibilities. The Barber's wife acts as midwife and is paid with rice (Thurston and Rangachari 1909: v. 345). A mother is polluted for fifteen days after birth. She gets fresh clothes daily from the Washerwoman in exchange for rice (Thurston and Rangachari 1909: v. 346). She is excluded from temples for a further forty-one days, but none of her matrilineal relatives is affected in any way (Fuller 1976: 48). The child is named by the head of the *taravād* on the twenty-seventh day (Iyer 1909–12: ii. 44).

Gough says that Nayars have 'adopted many Brahmanical usages' (1959*b*: 254) in their funerary practices, but this seems merely an assumption stemming from the non-Sanskritic/Brahmanic dichotomy in terms of which her discussion is framed. The rites already had their current form by the sixteenth century (Gough 1959*b*: 255), which is more than can be said for certain about most others considered in this book. In other words, it seems perfectly valid to relate these practices to the particularities of Nayar kinship, just as in the other ethnographic examples cited here.

Nayars practise cremation, usually in the SW corner of the *taravād* garden (Gough 1959*b*: 272). A water-pot is broken, as in Terku Vandanam (see 10.2, above). During the sixteen-day pollution period, the chief mourner feeds rice balls to crows in the house courtyard (pp. 256–7). He follows an ascetic regime for up to a year, before disposing of the ashes in a sacred river (pp. 254–5). The chief mourner of a Nayar woman is her eldest son as normal, but for a man it is his immediate male junior in the *taravād*, i.e., his yB or ZS. The other *taravād* men are subsidiary mourners, and all *inaṅkar* lineages are represented (Gough 1961: 329). Spouses do not observe mourning or pollution for each other,[6] but in some cases a woman and her children *do* mourn when her *tāli*-tier dies (Gough 1955: 49–50).[7] The obligations of children on the death of their father vary from region to region. For example, in Cochin the chief mourner lights the pyre at the head end, and the deceased's son does so at the foot (Iyer 1909–12: ii. 92). Not surprisingly, the stronger the social link

[6] Gough is here discussing modern Kerala. Legislation in the 1930s gave Nayar wives and children the right to inherit a man's personal property, hastening decay of the classic systems described above (1959*b*: 241). Hence, in part, Gough's reference to 'spouses' rather than *sambandham* partners.

[7] This did not in fact happen in all cases (Fuller 1976: 111).

between them, the greater the involvement of sons when their father dies (Gough 1959*b*: 254–5).

Members of a low-ranking matrilineal caste, whose identity varies regionally, officiate at rites during the period of death pollution. A 'degraded sub-caste' of non-Nambudiri Brahmans officiates at subsequent rites, including the annual ceremonies required thereafter (Gough 1959*b*: 255). As is so often the case, the acceptance of food by affines (*inaṅkar*) marks the end of death pollution for the bereaved *taravād* (Gough 1961: 330).

The Tiyyar case is interesting in the present context. Tiyyars have localized *patrilineal* exogamous groups, though these may be cross-cut by dispersed, exogamous matrilineages (Gough 1955: 59–60); post-marital residence is virilocal; and inheritance is from father to son. At a girl's puberty ceremony, her *tāli* is tied by a boy from a lineage into which she may marry. The rite (Thurston and Rangachari 1909: vii. 80–1; Iyer 1909–12: i. 285–7; Aiyappan 1944: 159–60) resembles a wedding in many ways, and the *tāli*-tier may indeed marry the girl subsequently. All in all, this seems a kind of intermediate case between Nayar rituals and those in Terku Vandanam.

11.7 Matrilineal Tamils of Batticaloa

Tamils in Batticaloa, eastern Sri Lanka, also have exogamous, matrilineal clans (*kuḍi*), but these lack the corporate structure of Nayar *taravāds*. Married couples form separate, monogamous residential units, so their relationship is much closer to the South Asian norm. However, property passes through the female line and residence after marriage is uxorilocal (Yalman 1971; McGilvray 1982*a*; 1982*b*). Inheritance occurs by way of dowries which daughters receive on marriage. A man does not inherit from his own parents but his position differs from that of *binna*-married Sinhalese men (see 11.4, above), because after marriage his wife's parents move out, leaving her in sole ownership of her share of the estate, which he manages.

The onset of menstruation is strongly emphasized. Proverbs refer to it, its timing is astrologically significant, and the girl is bathed.[8] The thirty-one day seclusion ends with another bath in turmeric-water or sea-water, done by auspicious married women (*sumaṅkalis*).

[8] As far as I know, there is no such bath in Terku Vandanam.

These usually include the girl's MZ and MBW, but the only firm rule is that women of her own household, who share her pollution, do not participate. Some say that the bathers should be her cross-cousins (McGilvray 1982*b*: 36), but they are not generally drawn from any one generation, are not exclusively either members or wives of members of her matrilineage, and may not even be relatives.

The girl dresses in a sari and jewels for the first time. As in Terku Vandanam she is escorted by a junior female cross-cousin, described not as a 'bridegroom' but as a 'bride's companion' (*tōlipeṇ*). In other words, reference is again made to the girl's wedding, but the cousin is equated with the Male Officiant[9] or 'groom's companion' (*māppiḷḷai tōlaṉ*; McGilvray 1982*b*: 41), rather than with her future groom.[10]

There is an *ālatti* in which the girl's body is circled with lighted tapers. She re-enters the house and has a first, auspicious glimpse of various prescribed objects. She and her companion sit in a decorated seat to be congratulated by the guests, and receive gifts. A feast follows (pp. 40–1).

The parallels with local weddings are obvious and explicit (p. 41). The forms of decoration and dress are the same; the *ālatti* and ceremonial entrance into the house are similar, although of course the groom also takes part at a wedding; the decorated seat (*maṇavaṛai*) is the same; and both ceremonies are called *kaliyāṇams*. Not surprisingly, given the form of post-marital residence, both take place at the same house. The identities of wedding officiants are only vaguely specified, though the MBW/FZ may take a leading part (p. 47).

Batticaloa people say that the puberty rite removes the particularly severe pollution of first menstruation; protects the girl from malign spirits and evil eye; inaugurates her womanhood as auspiciously as possible; and publicizes her marriageability (pp. 34–5). A woman's periods are said to drain away the energy (*sakti*) which she would otherwise accumulate. Without this, men would be unable to retain control over their womenfolk (McGilvray 1982*a*: 52).

Batticaloa Hindus also used to perform a rite when a boy reached marriageable age, involving his first shave, the donning of adult ear-studs, and an *ālatti* (McGilvray 1982*b*: 50).

McGilvray's data suggest greater cultural and exegetic elaboration than in Terku Vandanam, though the rites themselves seem less

9 The significance of this will be discussed later (see 14.5).

10 In Vadakku Vandanam, the groom's companion is known as the *māppiḷḷai tōli* ('the litter in which the groom is carried'). The pun is characteristic of Tamil.

systematically integrated into the local kinship and caste systems. This may merely reflect our different methods of presentation, but I suspect the difference is a real one. It is certainly clear that the social identities of main participants are less rigidly circumscribed than in Terku Vandanam.

The local midwife is the Washerwoman or Barber's wife, but a woman's mother also plays a key role.[11] The new mother is secluded to protect her from malign influences. No one can be told the child's sex until the cord has been cut. Even then it is done through circumlocution so as not to attract demons. The new mother is fed heating foods and liquor (1982*b*: 58–9). Birth pollution lasts thirty-one days, but the most serious pollution and special diet last only until a special gift of 'twelfth[-day] rice' is made to the Washerman and the midwife. The Washerman and Barber receive food and clothing on the thirty-first day, too, when the mother takes a bath and the child is tonsured and has its ears pierced.

There is no published description of local death rituals, but thirty-one days of death pollution (*tuṭakku*) are observed by most castes (McGilvray 1982*a*: 56). This is generally said to affect matrilineal relatives most significantly, though views differ widely and there is some confusion. Thus, although the chief mourner is the eldest son, as elsewhere, most people say that only the *daughter's* children are polluted (McGilvray 1982*a*: 57).

11.8 Tamil and Nambudiri Brahmans

For reasons that will become clear later (15.1), it is necessary to include in this survey the life-crisis rituals of South Indian Brahmans, even though the published sources are less than satisfactory. Two groups will be considered: Tamil Saiva Brahmans, as representatives of South Indian Brahmanic orthodoxy; and Nambudiri Brahmans of Kerala, because of the unique features of their marriage practices, and because of their relationship with the matrilineal Nayar.

First of all, it is important to draw attention to certain unique features of Brahmans. They are strongly patrilineal—though purely in the Dumontian sense (see 6.2.1, above), for they lack the corporate,

[11] Post-marital residence is matri-uxorilocal (McGilvray 1982*b*: 27), so a woman naturally has *all* her children, not just the first, in her natal community. Her mother is therefore present on every occasion.

property-owning lineages of Coorgs (see 11.2, above). Thus, they have a strongly defined, global system of exogamous *gotras* (Tam. *kōttiram*, 'patriclan'). Moreover, women are so completely assimilated into their husband's lineage at marriage that they henceforth address all his relatives by the terms he himself uses (Gough 1956: 848; Mencher and Goldberg 1967: 87). None of the other groups considered here do this.

Brahman boys are 'twice-born' by virtue of the *upanayaṉam* ceremony, at which they are invested with the sacred thread. The heart of the ceremony is the transmission of sacred knowledge from father to son (Gough 1956: 836). Afterwards the boy would formerly have become a student (Sanskrit: *brahmacārin*) until he reached marriageable age. From a comparative perspective this looks like a male equivalent to the female puberty rite among other castes. Before the *upanayaṉam*, Brahman boys are not subject to family birth pollution, and receive only truncated death rites (P. Logan, pers. com.).[12]

The same is true of unmarried Brahman girls. An orthodox Brahman should marry off his daughter before puberty to avoid responsibility for the monthly destruction of an embryo (Iyer 1909–12: ii. 197). Because Tamil Brahmans formerly practised pre-puberty marriage, it followed that all unmarried girls—like pre-*upanayaṉam* boys—were physically immature. Such marriages are now illegal, but their influence on Brahmanic ritual practice is still clear. Thus, there is still no pre-marital rite for Brahman girls. A single wedding ceremony is all that is needed to inaugurate a permanent, monogamous union.

A Tamil Brahman girl is completely separated from her natal kin at marriage. Even before that she will not observe ritual pollution for natal family members, who in turn make no offerings if she dies. According to former custom, daughters could not under any circumstances return after marriage to live permanently in their father's house (Gough 1956: 841). Under such circumstances, affinal links are less important than for most Tamils. For instance, they are intransitive: even one's BW's family are not considered affines (p. 839). Moreover, marriages create status differences, although these too are intransitive, unlike in North India. Wife-takers regard

[12] There are no modern published accounts of Tamil Brahman life-crisis ceremonies. I am most grateful to Penny Logan for generously supplying unpublished material on contemporary marriages in Madurai.

themselves as superior to their wife-givers, and although these distinctions are not extended to wife-givers' wife-givers, so that a fully-fledged caste-wide system of hypergamy does not develop, they *are* transmitted down the generations. Thus a man respects not only his ZH but also his FZH, and 'patronizes' both his MB and his WB (p. 844).

Nowadays, Tamil Brahman weddings are largely completed in a single day. The ceremonies (Logan, pers. com.) begin with a procession. This formerly went from the groom's house to the bride's, where most ceremonial would have taken place, but nowadays goes usually from a temple to a wedding hall.[13] The groom is first given sandal-paste, red kumkum, a garland, and clothes by the bride's eldest brother. At the wedding hall he meets the bride, who is given a sari by his father and sandal-paste, flowers, betel, and a plantain by his eldest sister. The wedding ceremonies proper begin with the *viratam*, at which bride and groom have *kāppu* amulets tied to their wrists by their respective fathers. These tyings are done separately, sometimes before they set out for the hall.

The groom, dressed as a student, makes as if to embark on a pilgrimage, but is stopped by the bride's father. The bride arrives and they exchange garlands (given by their MBs) three times. In the past, when the couple were children, they were carried on their MBs' shoulders during these exchanges.

The bride's father then makes the 'gift of a virgin' which plays such a central role in Brahmanic marriage ideology, and leads also to the giving of large dowries. The rite is called *dārai vārttu* ('water pouring'). He holds his daughter's hands and chants a mantra stating his intention of giving her to the groom, then places her right hand on top of the groom's. His wife pours water over their linked hands (cf. Thurston and Rangachari 1909: i. 281–2; Iyer 1909–12: ii. 295–6). The groom's father supports his son's hands during this, but the groom's mother has no specific role.

The bride changes into the wedding sari provided by the groom's parents. She is accompanied throughout by the groom's eZ. At the *tāli*-tying, the groom may tie one knot and his eZ two, or vice versa. This rite is less important than among non-Brahmans, however, and the marriage is made binding only by the 'seven steps' which the couple take around a sacrificial fire. The bride's brother provides

[13] Many urban Tamils hold marriages in such halls nowadays, rather than in the home.

sweets and ghee, which she offers to the fire to ensure long life for her husband. The groom's sister(s) then put on the bride's toe-rings.

Thurston and Rangachari mention a procession 'on the fourth day', sponsored by the bride's MB. It does not occur in contemporary Madurai, but is particularly interesting because of the following episode:

> The bride is dressed up as a boy, and another girl is dressed up to represent the bride. They are taken in procession through the streets, and, on their return, the pseudo-bridegroom is made to speak to the real bridegroom in somewhat insolent tones, and some mock play is indulged in. (1909:i. 290–1)

A 'female bridegroom' appears in a quite different context here, for this episode comes after the wedding and it is the bride herself, not her female cousin, who takes the part. These differences are partly explicable when set into a comparative framework (cf. 14.5, below).

The afternoon used to be taken up with games-playing by the newly-weds, but this is rare nowadays. In the evening, the bride's brother presents betel, nuts, and lime to the groom, for himself and his bride; and to the groom's sister, for her own husband. He is supposed to roll up the marriage bed next day.

All this would formerly have happened before the girl reached physiological puberty, and this is no doubt one reason why Brahmans have no elaborate, public ceremony marking the menarche. There *is* a coming-of-age rite (cf. Iyer 1909–12: ii. 311–12) but it is a comparatively simple, unspectacular event. The girl is secluded in a separate room for four days. She has an oil-bath, then a *sumaṅkali* presents her with a new sari given by her MB or FZ. She is dressed elaborately, and sits on a ceremonial platform. An odd number of women, older than her and including at least five *sumaṅkalis*, sing songs about divine marriages. Her FZ and MBW are the ideal participants, but their presence is not—as on some occasions—obligatory. Men are not usually present, simply because there is nothing for them to do, but her father should come in to see her at some point.

First and, ideally, later births occur in the natal home, where the expectant mother goes after the *sīmantam* ('hair-parting') ceremony in the sixth or eighth month. Birth pollution lasts up to 40 days, but is strongest before the purification (*puṇyasāṉam*) on the eleventh day. The expenses of this are borne by the father or, for a first child, the paternal grandparents. The two grandmothers perform an *ālatti*. Gifts come from the child's MB and FZ: the latter gives silver anklets. In theory, and to some extent in practice, Brahmans perform more life-crisis rites (*saṁskāras*) for children than do other castes (Kaṇe 1941: 201–67; Thurston and Rangachari 1909: i. 270–3).

The eldest son is the chief mourner at Tamil Brahman funerals. The widow circles her husband's body three times before it is put in the funeral bier. The chief mourner lights the pyre and does the trickling-pot ritual (Thurston and Rangachari 1909: i. 300–1).

Turning now to Nambudiri Brahmans, they formerly emphasized primogeniture to such a degree that only the eldest son married a Nambudiri bride and produced heirs to the estate. Girls might marry before or after puberty, but although Iyer spends several pages discussing the whys and wherefores of post-puberty marriage, he nowhere mentions any puberty ceremony for a girl whose marriage was delayed (1909–12: ii. 183–4, 196–9).

Younger sons formed *sambandham* liaisons with Nayar girls, which from a Nambudiri viewpoint were not marriages at all, but akin to concubinage. If many Nambudiri men stayed unmarried, then clearly some Nambudiri women also had to remain single. Such women, according to some sources, were kept in life-long seclusion, and underwent a form of marriage at their funerals. Mencher and Goldberg say, however, that Nambudiris in South Malabar and Cochin allowed polygyny with up to three wives, so that most Nambudiri girls *did* eventually marry, if only to very elderly men (1967: 105).[14] Nambudiris explained their practices as a way of keeping intact the landed property of the patrilineal 'house' (*illam*; Mencher and Goldberg 1967: 89).

Nambudiris lack several key features of the 'Dravidian' kinship system delineated by Dumont (1983). Affinal links are even less important than among Tamil Brahmans. In particular, cross- and parallel cousins are not distinguished. Neither type of cousin is marriageable, and unlike Tamil Brahmans, Nambudiris do not permit marriages between close cross-relatives. A man can marry into his M's or FZH's lineages only if the girl herself is distantly

[14] Mencher and Goldberg's statement that *all* Nambudiri girls eventually marry contradicts Thurston and Rangachari (1909: v. 197) and Fuller (1976: 3). Iyer (1909–12: ii. 198) cites the *Malabar Marriage Commission* to the effect that some Nambudiri women 'die in a state of celibacy, but . . . the corpse undergoes all the ceremonies of a marriage', but adds that Nambudiri acquaintances denied this.

related (Mencher and Goldberg 1967: 97): that is, prior links of affinity can only be at group level, not between individuals.

The brother–sister bond is not close, and brothers-in-law have no mutual obligations. Consequently, the MB and MBW are of little importance in a child's life. Indeed, there are no relationship terms for affines. A man uses teknonymy, and a woman addresses her husband's relatives by the terms he himself uses. The separation of married women from their natal families is so complete that the son of one wife in a polygynous household is permitted to marry his father's other wife's sister. Not surprisingly, the terminology is not prescriptive, and there are no positive marriage rules. Marriages are arranged over great distances through mediators, and involve large dowries (Mencher and Goldberg 1967: 94–7).

The groom first processes to the bride's natal *illam*. He is welcomed by her father, who formally invites him to accept his daughter. The bride's father ties the *tāli*,[15] and her mother garlands her. She gives the garland to the groom. The priest pours water three times into the bride's father's hand, whence it falls on to the bride's hand and then the groom's. The bride hands the dowry to the groom. Her brother leads her thrice round a fire and water-pot, then the groom does likewise. The couple perform the 'seven steps', making the marriage binding. Some of the rites are repeated at the groom's *illam* (Iyer 1909–12: ii. 185–92; Thurston and Rangachari 1909: v. 204–10).

At births, the Barber's wife acts as midwife. The new mother gets heating foods. On the eleventh day she is partly purified, and on the fortieth she is freed from remaining restrictions. No formal gifts are associated with these events (Iyer 1912: ii. 201–2).

Nambudiri death rituals closely resemble those of Nayars. In fact, Gough assumes them to be the model upon which present-day Nayar practices are based (see 11.6, above). Not surprisingly, however, the mourners' identities differ at the funerals of men. Ideally the chief mourner is the eldest son, but if the deceased was a younger son with only Nayar offspring, his eBS officiated. His Nayar children were not involved in any way. Nambudiri spouses observe mourning for each other (Gough 1959*b*: 253, 255). During the cremation, the chief mourner does the trickling-pot ritual (Thurston and Rangachari

[15] Iyer (1909–12: ii. 191) says that Nambudiris are unique in having the bride's father tie the *tāli*, although 'nowhere among the Brahmans [is this] looked upon as a marriage rite'.

1909: v. 218; 10.2, above). On the fourth day, he pours milk and water in the cemetery. The period of intense mourning ends on the eleventh day, but the chief mourner and the deceased's spouse live an ascetic life-style for a full year (Iyer 1909–12: ii. 268–9).

12
Modes of Interpretation

The previous chapter described some of the diverse ritual practices associated with female sexuality in South India and Sri Lanka. Several different styles of analysis have been used in the past to interpret such rituals. The present chapter will evaluate these, and suggest yet another possible approach.

12.1 The Psychoanalytic Approach

In the Nayar case, Gough found it impossible to explain sociologically either the identities of participants in *tāli*-tying rites, or even the need to hold them in the first place. She concluded that such problems could be solved only with reference to 'unconscious motivations . . . in terms of a psycho-analytic hypothesis' (1955: 45–6).

Gough saw the rite as 'a symbolic defloration' (p. 62). A 'marked horror of incest' causes a girl's male relatives to 'renounce the rights in her mature sexuality before she is in fact mature' (p. 64). Even among matrilineal groups, 'a "normal" Oedipus complex must develop in early infancy' (p. 66), but the 'suppressed hostility of a boy towards his father [is] transferred to the mother's brother' (p. 67), as shown, apparently, by the fact that the boy observes ritual pollution on his MB's death. This curious use of sociological evidence to buttress a psychological argument is an attempt to reconcile the Oedipus complex with matriliny: unconsciously, the MB is regarded as the genitor as well as the pater.

High-status Nayars or Nambudiri Brahmans are called in to 'symbolically deflower' the women of certain Nayar sub-castes, because the taking of virginity is dangerous. The virgin's male relatives control her sexuality but cannot use it, so she is

> feared by men of her own age-group . . . A father-figure common to the whole society is therefore summoned, symbolically (and sometimes actually) to deflower the girl, release her, in respect of her sexuality, from the

ownership of her natal kinsmen, and leave her . . . a normal mature woman. (Gough 1955: 71)

I shall not follow the details of Gough's analysis here, for several reasons. First, there is no direct evidence for her interpretation. As she admits, psycho-analytic data on Nayars 'are not . . . at present forthcoming' (1955: 46). Second, the argument seems internally inconsistent. It is not clear why the high-caste 'deflowerer' is unafraid of the virgin, nor are his 'motivations' discussed (p. 72). Third, the posited transfer of Oedipal hostility is implausible. It is true that the MB is central to a Nayar child's life, whereas the putative genitor (he who paid the midwife) has little contact with it, but the relationship between its M and MB is quite different from that between the mother and father in more usual domestic units. It has, for instance, no sexual component. Finally, the alleged 'horror' of incest is at odds with the lack of words for it in Dravidian languages. There are only composite phrases which connote offences of various kinds, not all sexual in nature.[1]

Besides these internal difficulties, there are powerful general arguments against all attempts to explain rituals in psychological terms. A universal phenomenon, which the Oedipus complex is claimed to be, necessarily 'loses its force in the "explanation" of . . . particular ceremonies' (Yalman 1963: 38). Moreover, whatever 'unconscious motivations' govern *individual* responses to collective rituals, the fact remains that rituals are social events which cannot be completely accounted for in terms of the desires and motives of individual participants. Rites may of course satisfy psychic needs, but they necessarily do so in different ways for different participants, so one can hardly argue that they stem from or express particular needs. Nayar rituals form part of the very social order which brings about the participants' alleged motivations. But if the social order produces these motivations (Gough 1955: 66–7), it seems tautologous to use them to explain the social order.

12.2 The Ethnosociological Approach

In recent years South Asianist ethnographers have devoted increasing attention to indigenous accounts of the biological processes connected

[1] In Tamil, incest is *muṟaimasakku* ('order confusing').

with puberty, marriage, conception, and birth. Although few such studies deal directly with the actual rites of puberty and marriage, they are clearly relevant in so far as they concern the biological processes which these rites are said to control or even to bring about.

The Kondaikatti Velalars (KV) of Tamil Nadu say that they all share common blood (*irattam*) of characteristic purity. This purity undergoes limited fluctuation during normal bodily processes (eating, defecation, menstruation, etc.). There are also relatively minor, permanent variations in blood purity between different ranked, exogamous kindreds (*vakaiyāra*). A child gains blood from both parents. The father's blood produces its body (*uṭampu*), and the mother's its spirit (*uyir*). The KV also have unranked, exogamous patrilineal clans (*kōttiram*), so marriage partners come from the same kindred but different clans. At marriage a woman joins her husband's clan, and undergoes partial transubstantiation. Her *uṭampu* becomes identical to her H's, but her *uyir* remains the same (Barnett 1976: 143–9).

Among Jaffna Tamils, too, caste-fellows are said to share the same blood *vis-à-vis* outsiders, but to differ slightly in blood among themselves. Similar theories of conception and *uṭampu–uyir* are found, but the wife's transubstantiation is said to be complete, so that although the child's *uyir* derives from the blood she contributes to the foetus, this is identical to her husband's blood. Again the transubstantiation occurs during the wedding. The bride's mother pours water over the couple's hands, 'unbinding' the links of shared substance between the bride and her natal family. Then the groom binds the bride to him, and brings about her biological union with him, by tying the *tāli* (David 1973: 522–3, n. 7).[2]

McGilvray reports—with several caveats—a contrary view among Batticaloa Tamils, who say that blood does not differ according to family or caste. Moreover, 'spirit' is implanted at conception by an all-pervasive 'life-wind' (*pirāṇa vayvu*) coming from neither parent (1982*a*: 50).[3]

Such accounts are extremely interesting, but some authors unfortunately go beyond merely reporting local notions, to argue that these have methodological (David 1977*b*: 220) or even ontological

[2] None of this applies to Terku Vandanam, where the bride's mother is usually absent and the *tāli* is tied by the Female Officiant.

[3] This recalls the role of Vayu, the wind, in the birth of Murukan (O'Flaherty 1973: 290; see 16.3.1, below).

(Marriott 1976: 195) priority over other types of data and other styles of analysis. Thus, using Schneider's terminology (1968), Marriott and Inden assert that the 'cognitive nonduality of . . . code and substance' is a 'universal axiom' of Indian thought (1977: 229). The distinctive code for conduct of each caste (*jātidharma*) is present in some physical property—'bodily substance', 'blood', etc.—common to the entire *jāti*, which is reproduced by a combination of physical and moral acts, especially sexual intercourse and marriage. These acts must obey certain rules so that the correct, complementary bodily substances are mixed and passed on to the offspring. Castes are thus characterized by the internal transmission of 'hereditarily shared substances' (1974: 983–4; 1977: 231).

Such arguments raise a number of difficulties, however. For example, many South Asians prove to be ignorant of these ethnobiological theories, or hold views which contradict them. Notions of blood were never mentioned to me spontaneously, and although some people agreed with *my* suggestion (culled from David 1973) that a woman's blood changed at marriage, others seemed unfamiliar with the idea. Moreover, when one man did try to explain to me in terms of blood the alleged incompatibility of MBDy and eZDy marriage, his argument was internally contradictory (see 6.8.2, above; Good 1978*a*: 436). Similar contradictions are cited by Barnett (1976: 146 n.). Such findings support the view that local opinions usually constitute 'a more complex, more disjunct, more contextual, and more open-ended ethnosemantic field than the parsimonious theories of purity and natural substance would tend to imply' (McGilvray 1982*a*: 58).[4] This being so, there is nothing particularly sacrosanct about notions confined to 'older KVs, especially women' (Barnett 1976: 147), still less the opinions of '*an* informant whose systematic thinking was complemented by a very wry sense of humour' (David 1973: 521; emphasis added).

Even if indigenous theories are unanimously held, they are still of limited use for comparative purposes. They are merely localized cultural theories about widespread structural facts, such as the cross-parallel dichotomy in the terminology. One such theory cannot be compared with another except by way of a structural comparison, because if the kinship structures differ the theories are *ipso facto* non-comparable anyway. Different rules of descent necessitate

[4] McGilvray is taking Dumont's approach equally to task: there is no space here to pursue that aspect of his discussion.

different cultural theories, for instance: the ideas of the KV or Jaffna Tamils would lead to total contradiction for the matrilineal Tamils of Batticaloa.

Comparison must therefore begin at the level of structure, albeit with the provisos discussed at the start (see 1.2, above). Once the relevant degree of structural correspondence has been demonstrated between two localities, it becomes permissible to compare the cultural notions held in one place with those held in the other. Even more usefully, it becomes possible to see whether ideas expressed in one place throw any light on certain practices which have been observed in the other, but for which no local explanation is forthcoming. Even then, local theories are just as much rationalizations of practice as those produced by anthropologists (Bourdieu 1977). The latter, having set out to acquire information systematically, are not confined to the perspective of a single participant, and know—as informants may not—that similar practices elsewhere are explained differently. This allows, potentially at least, the production of a more general, and more widely applicable analysis.

12.3 The Socio-Structural Approach

Life-crisis rites bring about transformations in the social statuses of the central participants. Instead of positing matrilineal Oedipus complexes, or abdicating the analyst's role in favour of folk-biology, one can examine directly the social context in which a ritual takes place. Gough (12.1, above) gave up too soon, for subsequent writers have shown that it is perfectly possible to develop a sociological analysis, not only of Nayar ceremonies, but of South Asian 'puberty' and 'marriage' rites in general. To do this, one must first consider the social structure as depicted in and reconstituted by the ritual, emphasizing those features—primarily the caste system but also the rules governing the choice of marriage partner—which span the entire geographical region concerned (Yalman 1963: 25).

For example, Dumont sets the *tāli*-tying rites of aristocratic Nayar into this wider context (1964: 82; 1980: 114; 1983: 109–10),[5] by pointing out that in India sexual liaisons are first of all defined as either 'legitimate' or 'illegitimate', as in the distinction between

[5] Dumont's distinctions are based upon observations among the Piramalai Kallar (1957*b*), but are intended to apply to South Asia generally.

'wives' and 'concubines'. Legitimate unions are then further subdivided into those of 'high' and 'low' status.

From a male viewpoint, the key distinction here is that between 'principal' (senior or first) wives and 'subsidiary' (or subsequent) ones. But whereas men can undergo several marriages with full rites, women can usually only marry once 'in the strict sense and with the full ritual' (Dumont 1964: 82). Any subsequent unions, even if legitimate, involve truncated marriage rites and are in this sense 'secondary' or inferior. 'Full' marriages, which are both the 'principal' union of the man and the 'primary' union of the woman, are most strictly regulated with regard to the identities of both parties (Dumont 1964: 83), but unions which are 'subsidiary' for the man and/or 'secondary' for the woman are often less rigidly circumscribed. Concubinage is the least regulated of all.

In applying these insights to the Nayar, Dumont concentrates on the aristocratic sub-castes, whose practice of hypergamy means that their procedures are uncomplicated by considerations of affinity. He points out that caste boundaries are not absolute, but merely among the most important of a whole variety of social cleavages (1964: 83). Two further factors must be kept in mind. First, Nayars are matrilineal whereas most castes, even in Kerala, are patrilineal. Second, a given rite may inaugurate a subsidiary union for the male party, while simultaneously marking the primary marriage of the woman.

In such a context, the relationship between Nambudiris and Nayar aristocrats represents a kind of symbiosis, in which two contrasting systems of descent interlock. A Nayar girl's *tāli*-tying is the equivalent of her primary marriage. Nayar aristocrats seek to have it performed by a Nambudiri Brahman, because this enhances the status of their family. It is less important for them to control 'secondary' (*sambandham*) unions—within, of course, the limits imposed by the ban on hypogamy. As for Nambudiris, only eldest sons make 'principal' marriages with Nambudiri girls. Younger sons enter 'subsidiary' unions with lower status women such as Nayar aristocrats. For patrilineal, isogamous Nambudiris, only the offspring of their principal marriages can possibly have Nambudiri status. For matrilineal, hypergamous Nayars, on the other hand, the children of unions with Nambudiris are unequivocally Nayars. Their status is if anything enhanced by that of their genitor.

The argument can be extended to other Nayar groups too. The aristocrats constitute the upper limit of a structure which links a whole series of matrilineal, hypergamous Nayar sub-castes (Dumont 1983: 128). The relationship with the *tāli*-tier is more complex here, though, because the caste identity of the two parties imposes a degree of common kinship upon them. In short, then, the Nayar system is not a bizarre and unique phenomenon, but is consistent with pan-Indian practice, albeit in a rather idiosyncratic way (Dumont 1983: 133).

This approach brings out the structural logic of the system but is still (one might say) too wedded to substantive notions of 'marriage'. Fuller carries socio-structural analysis yet further, and his discussion is particularly relevant because it starts from the same premiss as my own, namely that:

> The problem . . . is not to decide whether the *tāli*-rite was a marriage; it is rather to determine what was 'stated' in the rite, and then to compare these 'statements' with similar or identical ones made in other communities. (1976: 105)

Fuller also devotes much more attention than earlier writers to the *sambandham* relationship, and treats puberty, purity, and marriage as a single cultural and structural complex. He first refines Iyer's suggestion (1909–12: ii. 27–8) that normal Hindu marriage comprises a 'betrothal' and a 'consummation', and that the Nayars' *tāli*-tying and *sambandham* inauguration correspond, respectively, to those two stages. Fuller points out that the 'betrothal-consummation' nomenclature does not really apply to the Nayars and suggests, purely for convenience, the labels 'first' and 'second' marriage (1976: 105).

This seems unnecessarily confusing in view of Dumont's terminology, to which, as Fuller notes, his own distinctions do not correspond. I agree completely, however, that the two rites should be considered as a whole, and that the *tāli*-tying is in part a subsidiary rite of passage within this whole. As Fuller points out, though, it is more than this, at least in cases where there is an enduring relationship of affinity between the families of the girl and her *tāli*-tier (Fuller 1976: 105–6).

Dumont (1983: 118) argues that for most Nayars (not those with Nambudiri partners) the relationship between *sambandham* partners, and between their respective lineages, is one of typical South Indian 'affinity'. He seems over-anxious to prove that 'affinity' is *identical* in all cases, but like Fuller (1976: 114) I feel that he is right to see a basic similarity. Relationships between affinal lineages (*inaṅkar*) resemble those found in Tamil Nadu, although the links between individual men and women are less important.[6] It seems to follow that one aspect of most *tāli*-rites is the concern to recognize (and continue?) these links of affinity.

Fuller concludes that a Nayar woman's 'second marriage' is 'principally concerned with the continuation of her or her husband's line through the birth of legitimate children' (1976: 105). In short, the *tālikaṭṭu* ensures the status and purity of the girl herself whereas the *sambandham* inauguration does so for her children. This valuable insight will be followed up below (15.2).

In Fuller's opinion, though, the 'first' and 'second' marriages are not separate for most South Indians: 'They are both included within one "ordinary" marriage, which is thus a rite of passage for the bride, as well as a ritual concerned with sexual relations and the progeniture of children' (1976: 105). This position seems to need revision in the light of female puberty rituals in Terku Vandanam and elsewhere. In short, the Nayar are less idiosyncratic than even Dumont and Fuller think.

12.4 The Symbolic Approach

Several writers have analysed the symbolism of the rituals themselves. One of these, Yalman, starts from the premiss that 'highly formalised collective rituals . . . reflect the structure of the collectivity' (1963: 54). Caste, as the 'general unifying structural framework' (p. 25), is therefore the prime factor to be taken into account, and indeed, that framework makes such rituals especially crucial. Given the importance of the caste system, it is obviously essential to be able to determine unequivocally the identities of all persons living under that system. It is particularly necessary to safeguard one's purity, and that of one's relatives, by restricting social contact with persons of doubtful or inferior purity. The regulation of marriage and sexual intercourse is an especially crucial way of avoiding status ambiguity.

This regulation may take various forms. Where endogamy is emphasized, as among the Sinhalese (Yalman 1960: 88, 91), status

[6] Most writers tend to elide the distinction between enduring bonds of 'affinity' linking entire *inaṅkar* groups, and the individual, temporary links set up by *sambandham* liaisons.

depends upon the 'caste blood' received from *both* parents.[7] As endogamy becomes less important, more emphasis is given to the status of one particular parent. In the limiting case of affiliation through only one of them, as among Nayar aristocrats, 'status differences can be kept up by unilineal pedigrees without recourse to endogamy rules' (Yalman 1963: 40).

In such limiting cases it is less important whom the status-bearing individual marries, with the important proviso that inter-caste marriages can only occur hypergamously. If caste affiliation is acquired solely through the mother, the fact that the father is of higher caste will not matter, and may even be a social asset. At the same time, provided that her offspring are barred from claiming his status, there is little to deter a man from a liaison with a lower-caste woman. There is thus a structural asymmetry. The father must always be at least equal in status to the mother, and to this extent group membership still depends on the statuses of both parents. It is through women that the purity of matrilineal groups is most directly vulnerable, however, and through women, therefore, that it must be most strongly protected (Yalman 1963: 42). Hence the unusually great emphasis on female purity among Nayars.

This socio-structural argument is the background to Yalman's analysis of the puberty rite itself, at the heart of which is a comparison between the Nayar *tāli*-rite and Sinhalese puberty ritual (see 11.4, above). Dumont argues (1983: 138) that such a comparison is inappropriate, since a rite like the Sinhalese one 'which is widely found in South India . . . has nothing to do with marriage except in sofar [*sic*] as it solemnizes, and almost advertises . . . the maturity of the girl to be subsequently married.' It would be more appropriate, in Dumont's view, to compare the Nayars with South Indian Brahmans, who until recently practised fully fledged pre-puberty *marriage* (see 11.8, above) for their daughters. This calls into question not only Yalman's analysis, and to a lesser degree that of Fuller (1976; 12.3, above), but also the position taken up in the present book. However, I shall argue that Yalman's procedure is more justifiable than Dumont is prepared to allow.

Dumont thinks that Sinhalese and South Indian puberty ceremonies 'cannot be considered as similar or homologous to a marriage as

[7] When phrased in terms of 'caste blood' this argument is not universally applicable. David (1973) and McGilvray (1982*a*), among others, report local views in which 'blood' is *not* seen as derived from both parents.

Yalman would have it' (1983: 138). Plainly, however, this is untrue of the ceremonies in Central India (11.5, above) and Batticaloa (11.7, above), to say nothing of Terku Vandanam (7.2, above). One problem seems to lie with Dumont's surprisingly rigid notion of "marriage". Rather unexpectedly, even when drawing up his typology of forms of Indian "marriage" (12.3, above), he seems by default to ally himself with the Gough rather than the Leach camp (cf. 1.3, above). Only from such a substantivist perspective, surely, could one be so dismissive of the resemblances between 'puberty rites' and 'marriages'?

The central assumption of the present book is that all South Indian and Sri Lankan ritual practices marking female puberty are, like those of the Nayars, 'Indian facts' (Dumont 1983: 105) which must be understood from a broad comparative perspective. Arguments over which puberty rites *can* be seen as resembling weddings, and which cannot, are therefore sterile. All such ceremonies have much in common, as regards both the structures of the rituals themselves, and their sociological concomitants (14.5, below), so although it is true that Sinhalese 'puberty rites' lack the direct and superficial resemblances to 'weddings' which are apparent elsewhere, Yalman seems entirely justified in comparing them with Nayar *tāli*-ceremonies.

Whether the results are completely satisfactory is of course a different matter, to which we shall now turn. Yalman analyses the Sinhalese ceremony (11.4, above) as follows:

> (a) The infertile child is polluted by menstrual blood. (b) She is segregated in a dark room where she becomes fertile but impure. (c) She is reborn out of the dark room with a new horoscope as a fertile but still impure woman. (d) She is cleaned but positively charged. (e) Her re-entry over the threshold into the 'community' as a fertile and pure woman is marked by the breaking of the coconut. (f) The positive charge goes into the water basin and other objects on the floor. (g) The washerwoman takes these away . . . The ceremony is a public statement that a girl has reached the marriage market. (1963: 32)

He also discusses the nature of menstrual pollution; the symbolic meanings of menstrual blood, semen, and milk; and the phallic symbols involved in the rite, such as the rice-pounder, plantains, and oil-cakes (1963: 29–31). He argues that the structure of the Hindu temple, with its central shrine which only the purest may enter, illustrates the importance of female purity, for this shrine is a symbolic womb which also contains the *liṅkam* or phallus of Siva. Inside the shrine, ' "purity" is created by the union of the gods' (p. 44).

Leach has accused both Gough *and* Yalman of presenting intuitive arguments which are 'incapable of validation' (1970: 821). Several of his specific criticisms of Yalman seem mistaken,[8] but his positive arguments take full account of the fact, noted but not followed up by Yalman, that the ceremony is a typical rite of passage culminating in the girl's aggregation into a new social status. The infant girl, he argues, is in a 'normal, neuter' state. On menstruating she becomes 'abnormal, impure, neuter', and so is isolated. After her seclusion she is bathed and becomes an 'abnormal, pure female'. When she returns to the house and walks over the rice to increase her fecundity, she becomes an 'abnormal, pure, fertile female'. Finally, her exceptional purity is transferred to the ritual objects, and she becomes a 'normal, adult female' (Leach 1970: 824–5).

Leach sees the rite as above all a transformational process. Its component acts and artefacts are dynamic agencies, bringing about social change rather than passively embodying 'meaning'. The rice-pounder, which Yalman saw as phallic, is interpreted by Leach as the instrument whereby a neuter infant (unhusked paddy) is transformed into a fertile woman (husked rice; 1970: 824–5). The argument is ingenious, and although it seems no less intuitive than Yalman's, it is certainly more structured and abstract. Rather than superseding Yalman's analysis, it throws a different, complementary light on the same event.

12.5 The Performative Approach

The rather static insights of earlier sections can be expanded upon in the light of Leach's realization that life-crisis rituals actually *bring about* socio-structural changes, rather than merely conveying rather banal 'symbolic messages' about them. This section makes some initial procedural suggestions in that regard, which I shall try to implement in Chapter 13. My starting-point is Leach's recognition that 'beyond a certain point, the gimcrack operations of Lévi-Strauss's cultural *bricoleur* require no "explanation" at all' (1970:

[8] For example, he accuses Yalman of ignoring the Sinhalese view that a coconut has male and female ends (Leach 1970: 824), yet Yalman discusses that very point (1963: 55).

828). In other words, one should not push too far in searching for 'symbolic' meanings in a South Asian rite of passage.

Firstly, some of the ritual acts and artefacts which make up such rites, though broadly consistent with what is taking place, may well not be specifically related to that particular context. A concern for status-advancement, for instance, may lead to the performance of acts, and the presence of objects, unconnected with the social transformations actually occurring.

Secondly, substantial differences are apparent even between different performances involving the same sub-caste. In fact, the problem of exactly how a rite is to be accomplished is generally solved in *ad hoc* fashion as it proceeds. There are frequent pauses for debate, during which knowledgeable or officious bystanders suggest alternative courses of action, often with considerable vehemence. Even the Brahman officiant requires prior guidance from family elders as to their particular, customary practice.

In view of this, how useful is it to think of rituals as vehicles for conveying hidden messages, contained in the substances and artefacts employed and the manipulations performed on them, and which can be revealed by 'cracking' the appropriate 'symbolic code'?

The definitive anthropological exploration of the meaning of ritual symbols[9] is probably that of Turner (1967), yet Sperber has queried the very basis of this enterprise, the notion of "meaning" itself. It is, he says, 'in [Turner's] eyes a descriptive category, in mine a misleading metaphor' (1975: 33). There is no analytical meta-level where absolute connections between symbols and meanings can be established, and symbolic 'analysis' is merely a process of re-symbolization in terms more accessible to a new audience. This is a crucial point, but unfortunately Sperber's own solution, which is to postulate a 'symbolic mechanism' feeding back from 'passive' into 'active' memory, is even less convincing (1975: 141).

It seems more fruitful to accept that rituals and symbols *do* convey meanings, explicitly and implicitly, but to recognize that this is not their only, or even their most important characteristic. Such is the message of the performative approach, which draws upon Austin's typology of speech acts. According to this, *locutionary* linguistic utterances are factual statements to which criteria of truth and falsity

[9] I use the word 'symbol' in a very general sense, to refer to objects or acts which 'represent something else' (*Chambers Twentieth Century Dictionary* 1973: 1367). This has the advantage of leaving open the question of 'meaning'.

can legitimately be applied; *illocutionary* utterances, such as 'I apologize' or 'Bless you', bring about the state of affairs to which they refer by the mere fact of being said; and *perlocutionary* utterances, such as political speeches, are attempts to persuade listeners of their validity (Austin 1976).

The performative approach is based on the premiss that, just as not all speech acts are purely, or even partly, locutionary, so rituals do not always merely 'symbolize' social transitions but may also sometimes 'effect' them. Rituals need not only be locutionary, but may also be illocutionary (Tambiah 1973*a*; 1979) or perlocutionary (Kapferer 1977; 1979*b*). That is, they not only 'state' things, but may simultaneously 'accomplish' things, and 'validate' things. In particular, the enactment of a life-crisis ritual not only makes 'statements' about the rights and responsibilities of adulthood, matrimony, and so on, but also brings about the social transformation concerned. To do so successfully it must convince the participants and onlookers of its efficacy (Tambiah 1973*a*: 220–2). In order to be effective, therefore, such rites must be seen to be adequately performed, or felicitous (pp. 223–4).

One can analyse rituals as performances while still recognizing that the expression of 'meaning' is part, though sometimes only a minor part, of what is going on. Thus, there is clear continuity between Turner's 'dominant symbols', which 'refer to values that are regarded as ends in themselves, that is, to axiomatic values' (1967: 20), and Kapferer's 'symbolic types', which 'unify context and transform it in terms of their own consistency' (1979*a*: 11). The second are largely a dynamic reformulation of the first, but with some important differences which make them more appropriate to the Indian context.

If dominant symbols express axiomatic values, that implies a degree of consensus among ritual participants as to what these values are. Yet even in the famous case of Ndembu milk-exuding trees, men and women seem to have different perspectives on the place of matriliny in their society (Turner 1967: 25). If such differences exist among even the comparatively homogeneous Ndembu, how likely is ideological consensus in a society as culturally diverse as India? In my view, one cannot expect to find dominant symbols in the Indian context, because the necessary cultural and exegetic uniformity is lacking in such a heterogeneous environment. Universals in Indian rituals have a rather different character.

First, there is a set of symbolic materials which have pan-Indian general significance, whatever the contexts in which they are put to use. These artefacts and substances resemble Turner's 'instrumental' symbols, which are the 'means of attaining . . . explicitly expressed goals' (1967: 32). I shall call them *reagents*, since their significance lies mainly in their capacity to effect particular kinds of transformation. Whereas chemical reagents are used to acidify, to buffer, etc., those in Indian ritual serve to cool, to purify, and so on.

Ritual reagents like betel leaves, sandal-paste, turmeric, and camphor seem to have comparable uses almost everywhere. These partly reflect their physical properties of edibility, shape, colour, and inflammability. In use, such reagents have both *import* and *purport*, that is, both intrinsic and extrinsic significance. The import of a reagent is the transformative effect it is conventionally said to produce. This remains more or less constant: curled-up betel leaves represent reciprocity (Dumont 1957*b*: 231), sandal-paste represents coolness, and so on. The purport of this depends upon the context in which the reagent is brought to bear, however. Cooling with sandal-paste may be necessitated by abnormal impurity, as when it is applied to a menarchal girl, or by close contact with divinity, as when temple worshippers smear themselves after a *pūja*.

Second, there is a shared repertoire of basic ritual procedures, which may be ordered sequentially, combined, superimposed, or otherwise transformed so as to construct rituals which 'state', 'accomplish', and 'validate' in a contextually appropriate manner.

Some of these manipulative procedures can themselves be classed as reagents. Others, of particular importance or unusually wide-spread occurrence, recall Kapferer's 'symbolic types'. His formulation has the advantage, for the South Asian context, of emphasizing constancy of form as much as consistency of meaning. Moreover, he sees symbolic types as only semi-autonomous in both these respects: though capable of transcending particular contexts they are none the less partly shaped by them (1979*a*: 11). Blood sacrifice, for instance, takes on or emphasizes particular significances according to the context in which it occurs (temple worship, house building, exorcism, etc.), but is none the less virtually universal geographically, remarkably constant in structure, and justified on the basis of the same mythical corpus.

Not all symbolic types are pan-Indian in their incidence, though. Elsewhere I have discussed the important *poṅkal*-cooking ritual of

Tamil-speaking South India (1983). The most striking finding was an association between *poṅkal* and transition. *Poṅkal* is a complex manipulative process rather than a material substance or artefact, but it none the less has a constant import in all contexts where it appears. However, what distinguishes *poṅkal* from, say, sandal-paste or betel leaves, and makes it a symbolic type capable of transforming context rather than merely being shaped by it, is the fact that *poṅkal* also possesses immanent properties which mere reagents do not.

Structured configurations of reagents, whether substances, artefacts, or acts, display properties absent from reagents alone. For example, sandal-paste in isolation, like the word 'cooling' taken out of verbal or non-verbal context, has import but no purport.[10] But when applied to a puberal girl's skin during a purification ceremony, sandal-paste has both import and purport, like a phrase such as 'cooling helps remove impurity'. *Poṅkal*, too, consists of a configured set of symbolic reagents, though of greater complexity.

The distinction between 'reagents' and 'symbolic types' is that the latter have purport as well as import, locutionary and illocutionary as well as perlocutionary force. It is because blood sacrifice and *poṅkal* state and accomplish something *in themselves* that these statements and accomplishments carry over into every context in which these symbolic types occur.

Though heuristically useful, the distinction between 'types' and 'reagents' is of course not absolute, particularly when several such types occur in conjunction.[11] For example, the purports of the *poṅkal*s at Tai Ponkal (the winter solstice festival) and at the annual goddess festival have opposed, as well as common features. Although both are concerned with barriers between humanity and nature, the aim is in one case domination of, in the other surrender to, natural processes (Good 1983: 242).

The implication of all this is that the analysis of life-crisis rituals should focus not so much upon the 'meanings' of the artefacts employed, as upon the uses made of them, and upon the social identities of the users. A chemist employs acids or bases not for their

[10] In my view (*pace* Sperber), ritual performances *can* usefully be compared to communicative utterances.

[11] Similarly, the significances of many 'reagents' are less one-dimensional than this might imply. Reiniche (1979: 178) notes that although both lemons and turmeric are 'cooling', the two are not fully interchangeable because each has subsidiary connotations peculiar to itself.

specific, individual properties but merely for their common ability to change the pH of any solution. Likewise, the ritual officiant uses water to purify, or turmeric to cool, the person on whom the rite centres, irrespective of the nature of the rite itself.

Consider the *ālatti* ritual at a Sadanku (see 7.2, above). The wholly-interchangeable auspicious items used by the Female Officiant to encircle the girls, are reagents. The meaning of the act derives from its social and spatial context—the significance of the platform as a temporary temple, the social identities of ritual participants in light of the local kinship system, etc.—rather than from any *specific* symbolic properties inherent in the items themselves. Moreover, performing the act actually achieves something. It marks out the sacred space occupied by the couple, and creates a barrier to protect them from evil eye or other malign influences which might subvert the ritual,[12] but it will not achieve these aims unless properly performed by an appropriate person using appropriate material reagents. It is the fact that these reagents are used by a *sitti* to encircle a puberal girl, that makes the action efficacious.

The reagents employed, and the actions of participants, must therefore be appropriate to their context, although other reagents and actions could often have perfectly well been substituted for them. To that extent such details are sociologically irrelevant. Only when the rite is adequately performed by the correct personage does it bring about the desired social transformation, and the achieving of that transformation is the 'highest common factor' present in all the various ritual forms. One almost gets the impression that Ndembu rites are constructed around their central, immutable symbols.[13] The emphasis in Indian ritual seems the other way round: material reagents are introduced where appropriate into a primarily social, transformative performance.

[12] We might be tempted to view the sacredness of the platform, and the existence of evil eye, as themselves metaphorical or symbolic notions. This would, I think, be an error. Evil eye is as real to local people as, say, malaria. They protect their children against it with a special ritual every Friday, just as we gave our daughter her weekly dose of Daraprim.

[13] For example, Turner says that dominant symbols have 'considerable autonomy with regard to the aims of the rituals in which they appear' (1967: 31).

13
An Analysis of the Ritual Cycle in Terku Vandanam

13.1 The Sadanku

The insights gained in Chapter 12 can now be applied to the ritual cycle described in Chapters 7–10. Every stage in that cycle refers both backwards and forwards in time, reasserting kinship links set up in earlier stages or preceding generations, and setting the scene for the renewal of these links in future stages or succeeding generations. Moreover, any given ritual marks different points in the personal ritual histories of each of its various participants, so the cycle has no clear beginning or end. The main concern here is with the female upon whom most of these rituals are focused, however, and for convenience of presentation we begin with her Sadanku.

At the most superficial level, a Sadanku ritual consists of a sequence of events in time. The most important are the onset of menstruation, the seclusion, the bath, and the 'wedding' with the female 'groom'. The underlying socio-temporal sequence is, however, not linear and continuous but quantized and sporadic. First, rites of passage involve liminal periods of 'social timelessness': second, ritual performances occupy finite time-spans but, often, 'the message is transmitted as if everything happened simultaneously' (Leach 1976: 44).

Life-crisis rituals do not merely symbolize or send messages about the changes taking place, however; they actually *bring them about* (see 12.5, above). These changes will be considered one by one, and the conclusions are summarized in Figure 13.1.

First, there is the transition *immature* → *mature*. Biological and social maturity are notionally simultaneous in Terku Vandanam, although comparative evidence shows that this is not true everywhere. Before menarche a girl is immature, but by the end of the Sadanku she has become mature. This maturity is the result of the actual onset of menstruation, and is at once made manifest in her clothing. Prior

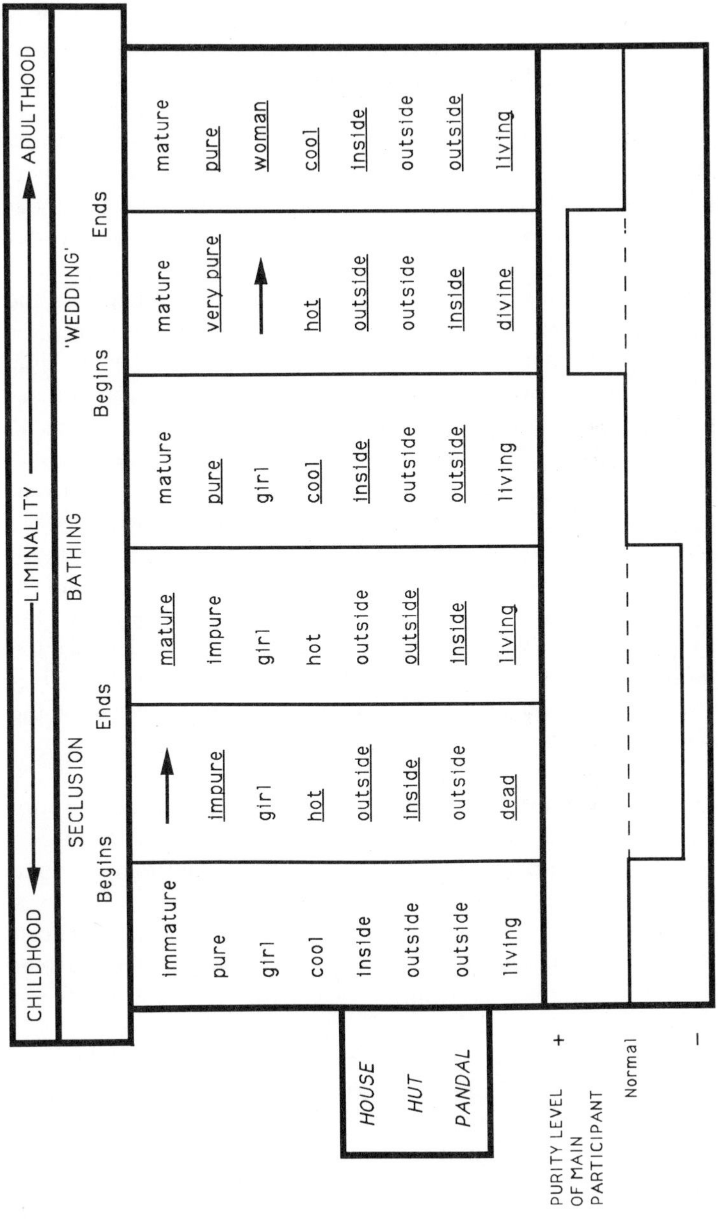
CHILDHOOD
LIMINALITY
ADULTHOOD
SECLUSION
Begins
Ends
BATHING
'WEDDING'
Begins
Ends
HOUSE
HUT
PANDAL
immature
pure
girl
cool
inside
outside
outside
living
impure
girl
hot
outside
inside
outside
dead
mature
impure
girl
hot
outside
outside
inside
living
mature
pure
girl
cool
inside
outside
outside
living
mature
very pure
hot
outside
outside
inside
divine
mature
pure
woman
cool
inside
outside
outside
living
PURITY LEVEL OF MAIN PARTICIPANT
+
Normal
−

FIG. 13.1 Structure of the Sadanku Ritual in Terku Vandanam

to her seclusion she wears a blouse and long skirt; subsequently, she always wears a sari. While secluded she just wears an old, dirty garment, but after her bath she dons a new sari given by her MB.

With regard to the *pure/impure* opposition things are more complex, because there is not just one, irreversible change in orientation. The mature woman is in a state of normal purity after the Sadanku, like the immature girl before menstruation began, but the intermediate phase is divided up as follows. Menstruation generates impurity, which causes the girl to be placed in seclusion, and is later removed by the bath and its associated ritual. However, everyday purity is itself impure relative to the 'sacred' purity attained in the 'wedding' episode, which has to be dissipated at the very end.

There has been a tendency in South Asian anthropology to elide the distinction between purity and auspiciousness (cf. Dumont and Pocock 1959: 33). The case of the Sadanku adds to the increasing body of evidence (Marglin 1985*a*) that such a view is too crude. Although impurity (*tīṭṭu*) is explicitly associated with the menarche, it is equally clear that the event is auspicious. This is evident in the occurrence, at *all* stages of the ritual, of the *kuruvai* cries which mark auspicious transitions and defend participants against spiritual attack (Tapper 1979: 13). The more formal titles (see 7.1, above) for the Sadanku specifically describe the occasion as auspicious. Given the value placed on female fertility it could hardly be otherwise, although as we shall see this fertility is viewed with some ambivalence by the girl's natal family.

The *girl* → *woman* transition also involves a single, irreversible change, but cannot be equated with the acquisition of maturity discussed above. If that were so the bathing alone would suffice to complete the transformation, yet in practice the climax of the ceremony is still to come. It is the 'wedding' episode which brings about the onset of womanhood, thereby forming a subsidiary rite of passage within the total Sadanku. It also anticipates to some extent the state of affairs later realized by the Kaliyanam, namely, the assumption of responsibility by the girl's marital relatives.

This *girl* → *woman* transition is the social counterpart of the folk-biological change implicit in the *immature* → *mature* transition. Pre-puberty marriage is a high-status, Brahmanic custom, so the performance of a form of 'marriage' at or before a girl's puberty may represent a claim to high caste status by the group concerned, although no one ever suggested this to me. More certainly, a sexually mature but unmarried female is an anomalous creature. The ritual relieves her natal family of some of the burden imposed by this anomaly, and recognizes that their affines will eventually resolve it by accepting her in marriage. Thus, the 'female bridegroom' is wherever possible the Z of the girl's *urimai* partner (Table 14.1).

Liminal states are 'hot' (Beck 1969: 564). Cooling elements are required to prevent the heat of the main participants from spreading, so the rite ends with the cooling of participants and spectators. This *hot/cool* opposition is clearly manifest in the Sadanku. Although my informants were less explicit than Beck's, they consistently used 'cooling' substances like water, cow's milk and urine, turmeric, sandal-paste, and margosa, to control and ultimately remove the girl's excess heat. Such heat arises in conjunction with both abnormal impurity (the seclusion) and abnormal purity (the 'wedding'), hence the application of sandal-paste, ash, etc., after both events.

Three spatial oppositions are directly observable, the first being *inside the house/outside the house*. The pure girl (inside) is excluded (outside) when she first menstruates. After the bath she regains normal, everyday purity and goes back inside. A 'mature girl' is still socially anomalous though, and has to go outside for the 'wedding' episode. At the end she reverts to normal purity and goes inside again.

The opposition *inside the hut/outside the hut* is more straightforward, for she enters the hut at the onset of menstruation and leaves it forever at the end of her seclusion. Clearly, the house is associated with everyday, normal purity and the possession of definite social status, whereas the hut represents liminality in a negative, impure context.

The marriage pavilion (*pandal*) on the other hand, represents positive, pure liminality. Weddings temporarily exalt the status of the bridal pair (Dumont 1980: 53). Likewise, the girl begins the Sadanku 'wedding' as a normally pure individual, who is then installed in the pavilion and further purified by the Brahman. The significance of this is discussed more fully in the next section. She is then 'hot', and so has to be cooled before she leaves the pavilion again. Hence the third spatial opposition is *inside the pavilion/outside the pavilion*.

Leach argues that liminality may be regarded as a state of social death, whereby a liminal individual is temporarily or permanently removed from normal society (1976: 79). The seclusion can indeed be seen in this way, and the eventual re-emergence then represents a rebirth. It seems inappropriate, though, to interpret the Sadanku 'wedding' or the Kaliyanam in this fashion. Rather, they are periods of temporary divinization, and the pavilion is a kind of temple—literally so in the case of a Kovil Kaliyanam (see 8.3.2, above).

13.2 The Kaliyanam

Fuller stresses the need to view Nayar rites of puberty and marriage as a single entity (1976: 107). Similarly, Leach argues that such rites can usefully be looked at synchronically rather than diachronically (1976: 44). Here, too, one should not be misled by the considerable time gap between the Sadanku and Kaliyanam, which are in fact two stages of the same process. From this wider perspective, a female is in a liminal, transitional state from the onset of the menarche until the completion of her Kaliyanam. This view is supported by the fact that a few wealthy families in Terku Vandanam seclude mature, unmarried daughters, although this seclusion is not always total, and is justified by a desire to keep girls out of the sun, making them fairer of skin and more desirable brides.

Because of the very obvious similarities between the two ceremonies, many points made in the previous section can be applied directly to the Kaliyanam, although in the absence of impurity things are actually rather more straightforward. Once again the female is in a state of normal *purity* both before and after the Kaliyanam. In between, however, she again experiences a temporarily exalted purity and auspiciousness, achieved thanks to the initial purifications carried out by (ideally) a Brahman. He subsequently performs acts of worship resembling the services (*upacāram*) offered to temple deities.

The *hot/cool* opposition appears in the same way as in the Sadanku 'wedding'. Again the bride's exalted state makes her ritually hot, and this heat is first controlled, then dissipated, by the Main Officiant. In this case, though, there is much more emphasis on the groom. Whereas the girl was earlier the centre of attention, he is now the focal point of all ritual operations, and takes precedence over his bride.

The close resemblance between the Sadanku 'wedding' and the Kaliyanam extends to the 'reagents' employed (see 12.5, above). Sometimes, indeed, these seem specifically intended to refer forward or back to the other ceremony. What else are we to make of the presence of water-pots on the Kaliyanam platform (Fig. 8.2), or indeed of the entire 'wedding' episode at the Sadanku?

The use of the rice-pounder in the *mukūrttakkal* rite (see 8.2, above); the layers of rice and paddy between the plantain leaves which cover the platform at Sadankus (Fig. 7.1) and Kaliyanams (Fig. 8.1); and the burning of paddy husks in the fire, all recall Leach's dynamic analysis of the Sinhalese puberty rite (see 12.4, above). The rice-pounder dehusks paddy and converts it into rice. Paddy and rice thus represent, respectively, the 'before' and 'after' states of the entire rite of passage from immature girl to mature wife.

Only two of the spatial oppositions identified in the Sadanku are relevant here. In the absence of impure liminality there is no impure threshold equivalent to the hut, but the house and pavilion have the same significances as before. The house is associated with normal purity and possession of a definite social status, whereas the marriage pavilion represents pure, sacred liminality. The central participants' movements to and fro between these value-laden social spaces require the assistance of the Main Officiants. They occur in similar ways at the Sadanku 'wedding' and Kaliyanam, though only in the latter is there a *triple* circuit of the platform.

Hindu temples stand upon the cosmic axis (Eliade 1955: 12 ff.; 1964: 259 ff.; Shulman 1980: 40). In performing a *piradakṣiṇam*—a clockwise[1] circuit of a temple's main image—one is therefore circling the entire universe. Nor are temples the only possible sites for circumambulation. The gods themselves reverse the procedure and circle the village at festival time (Good 1985*a*: 131). Appropriately then, bridal couples circle their marriage platforms, the sacred spaces within the confines of which they become temporarily god-like.

Whereas a Sadanku involves a transformation in status from girl to woman, the transformation at a Kaliyanam is from *woman* to *wife*. This completes the process begun by the Sadanku, namely the social transfer of the female from her natal to her marital family. Moreover, although local biological theories vary considerably (see 12.2, above), there is a widespread feeling that a bride acquires

[1] Das (1982: 91) takes Srinivas (1952: 118) to task for using the 'non-native' term "clockwise" to describe circumambulation. For her the key point is that the shrine, etc., is kept on one's right-hand side throughout. It is true (Das 1977: 26 n.) that there are parallels between linear and circular ritual movements which Srinivas's classification tends to obscure, but the *raison d'être* of the *piradakṣiṇam* seems to require that it be directed successively towards all the cardinal points.

certain biological characteristics in common with her husband's family, while simultaneously losing this link with her natal relatives.

This suggests another possibility which was unfortunately not raised with informants at the time. Jaffna Tamil wives are of the same 'substance' as their husbands, and one purpose of a wedding is the effecting of this transubstantiation (David 1973: 521). Such ideas have only restricted currency in Terku Vandanam, but if transformation *does* occur it must clearly be accomplished at some point during this ritual cycle. Moreover, Yalman and Fuller argue that the puberty rite safeguards the purity of the girl's natal kin, personified by her father (see 12.3, above).

It seems, then, that the Sadanku 'wedding' is a first step towards combating the threat which a mature but unaffiliated daughter poses for her natal household's purity. It initiates both the social process of removing her from her father's jurisdiction, and the physiological process of transforming her blood or body. It achieves both these aims by linking her with the family of her ideal future husband, the *urimai* man, so that she ends the Sadanku identified more with her cross-relatives and less with her father. This accords with the presence of the female 'groom', the choice of Main Officiant, and the gifts from the MB (see 14.4, below). All these anticipate the permanent transfer of the woman at her Kaliyanam. The final opposition, then, may be that between *father's blood* and *husband's blood*. It would be interesting to know the views of various South Asian groups on this matter, and how these correlate with the extent to which 'puberty' is stressed relative to 'marriage'.

13.3 Death Rituals

Whereas the analyses of Sadankus and Kaliyanams overlap to a great extent, funerals require a different, though by no means wholly unconnected approach. The manifestations of the *purity/impurity* and *hot/cold* oppositions in death ritual need particularly detailed discussion (see 13.3.1, below), but it is first necessary to look briefly at the spatial values involved.

As previously, *inside the house* is clearly associated with normal social status. The body is taken outside to be bathed and dressed, as the first step in separating it from the social identity of the deceased. Similarly, the actions of the living within the house are temporarily circumscribed. They cannot cook—the prime domestic activity—for example, because their own new social identities are not yet fully resolved.

Once again a pavilion serves as a threshold on which the deceased is made ready for his journey to the *cemetery*. Just as the house is associated with normal secular status, the Sadanku hut with impure, auspicious liminality, and the wedding platform with pure, auspicious liminality, so the cemetery is associated with impure, inauspicious liminality. Indeed, it seems to have just the characteristics expected of a 'double negative'. At the annual festival of Karaiyadi Madan, a form of Siva, the medium of the eponymous deity dances out alone to the Terku Vandanam cemetery and, I was told in awed tones, 'eats bones'. The cemetery, it seems, displays the same powerful ambiguities as Siva, its resident. Finally, yet another pavilion-threshold is constructed during the most common local form of the Karumati rite (see 10.5, Ex. D, above); here the liminality is pure but inauspicious.

13.3.1 Death and Impurity

Death is strongly associated with impurity (Hocart 1968: 12; Dumont 1957*b*: 250). It is commonly reported from many parts of South Asia, for example, that no cooking is done in the bereaved household before the final feast. Locally, however, the behavioural consequences of all forms of impurity are in general slight (see 2.2, above), and this applies also to taboos at funerals. At most no cooking is done on the actual day of the funeral, but the evening meal is sometimes prepared even then. Funerals are impure events none the less, and a subsequent bath is seen as essential for all who attend the cemetery.

Many features of death ritual reflect its impurity, such as the central roles of the Barber and Washerman, whose daily function is to remove organic impurity from their clients. Impurity is also recognized by various reversals: the use of the *left* hand, counter-clockwise circumambulation, the thread worn over the right shoulder rather than the left, etc.

By no means all such orientational behaviour conforms to the textual norms analysed by Das (1977), however. In particular, counter-clockwise circumambulation is less universal than might be expected. Dumont sees the Kallar's clockwise circuit of the grave as mistaken, since at impure events the circuit should be anti-clockwise

(1957*b*: 248). Here, only Harijans circle counter-clockwise in the cemetery; other groups vehemently denied my suggestion that clockwise movements were inappropriate. It therefore seems closer to the spirit of events in Terku Vandanam to emphasize the sacredness of the body rather than its undoubted impurity, a point developed below (13.3.2).

As usual, departures from everyday purity generate 'heat' (see 13.1, above). This of course implies a spiritually and socially excited state rather than raised physical temperature, but high temperatures may serve to express the presence of this ritual heat, as with cremation itself. Moreover, cremation takes place in the hottest part of the day, and the temperature begins to fall about the time the mourners return home. Items like fire, Bengal gram, rice, and the colour red are all associated with ritual heat and liminality (Beck 1969: 566–70). Conversely, water, oil, the milk, urine and dung of cows, coconuts, sandalwood, turmeric, margosa, betel, and the colour white are all associated with ritual coolness and/or social normality (Beck 1969: 566–70). Bathing with water and oil; pouring of milk, water, or other liquids; removal of bodily hair; immersion of ritual artefacts in a well or tank; all these have the effect of cooling and purifying the deceased and/or the mourners.

The preparation of the corpse removes the impurity of physical death and prepares for the separation of the deceased from the community. This separation begins with the procession and is not achieved without difficulty, for the pallbearers have to struggle across the settlement boundary. The separation of the dead from the living is complete once the pyre has been lit or the grave filled in. The heat thus generated is dissipated next day by pouring liquids on the ashes or grave.

The spirit (*āvi*) of the deceased remains behind until the sixteenth day, when its separation from the human world becomes complete (see 10.9, above). By then emphasis has shifted to the mourners, whose prior social status was undermined by the death of their relative, and who themselves thereby entered a liminal state. Their impurity and heat are removed in stages by head-shavings[2] and baths during the sixteen-day period. The process is completed by the Karumati, when the prestations exchanged reconstitute their social ties. Previous links are renewed, and new statuses recognized. As

[2] Widows, too, have their heads shaved after their husband's funeral.

usual, the re-entry of an individual into everyday social life is accomplished by a gift from the prime representative of the social order, the 'principal affine'.

The deceased is also directly involved in the Karumati. In the Nayakkar case (10.5, Ex. E), the offering explicitly consists of his favourite foods. The use of a mud figure strongly suggests that the ritual is modelled on more orthodox rites designed to 'reconstruct a body for this ethereal spirit' (Parry 1980: 91), and thereby allow it to become an ancestor (Bhattacharya 1893: 656–7). Finally, Dubois says that the small stones on the rectangular mud platform represent Yama, Rudra, and the deceased himself (1879: 215).

The feeding of crows is reported from many parts of India, though explanations of it are vague (cf. Pocock 1973: 37; Babb 1975: 95). Srinivas (1952: 106) identifies the crows with the spirit of the deceased: if satisfied, it finally leaves the village. The fact that the *āvi* is said locally to leave the bereaved house on this day is consistent with such a view, but it was never explicitly stated to me.

Overall, 'end of mourning' rituals in South India present a complex and confusing picture. In the absence of authoritative local exegesis, it seems fruitless to attempt further analysis of the Karumati itself. A thorough comparative study is needed, of a kind for which data are presently lacking. I shall therefore leave matters at this inconclusive stage, and return to the funeral proper from a somewhat different perspective.

13.3.2 The Ritual Journey

Funerals contain obvious and important processional elements. The mourners go to a well to bathe and collect water. Their return trip is sometimes only completed with difficulty, after a fight. Next the mourners visit the village boundary, to break the earthly bonds binding the deceased. The cortège which conveys the corpse to the cemetery also has difficulty crossing the boundary. Next day, mourners revisit the cemetery to cool it. Finally, they proceed outside the village for the Karumati.

During local temple festivals, similar movements take place. The temple deities possess human mediums and process clockwise round the settlement: conversely, the villagers process to the temple and circumambulate it (Good 1985*a*). In this context the inhabited settlement within the ritual boundary represents ordered, secular human society, while the land outside is the home of the powerful but disorderly gods (Reiniche 1975: 199).

No deities are permanently present inside the settlement: the shrines of partly 'domesticated' family gods (*kuladeyvam*) are set amid agricultural land, while more powerful deities like the village goddess have their temples in the wilderness. Finally, 'only Siva is in the cemetery': it is an especially divine but dangerous place, visited by the incarnated deity Karaiyadi Madan (a form of Siva) during his annual festival.

Temple festivals involve fusion of these different spheres, marked by movements of deities into the settlement, and of villagers out to the temple. Both types of movement terminate in circumambulation, the focus of which is a sacred spot associated with transition from one world to the next. It seems reasonable to conclude that the body of the deceased, circled by women in the settlement and by men in the cemetery, likewise occupies a sacred axis linking this life with the hereafter. The bier in which it is transported from the settlement to the wilderness has the same name (*tēr*) as the 'cars' in which, during major South Indian temple festivals, effigies of the gods are borne clockwise round the surrounding town (see 16.3, below).[3] The movement in both cases is between the human and divine worlds, but whereas at a temple festival these two worlds temporarily coalesce, at a funeral they remain separate and the deceased has to be transported from one to the other.

As this implies, the route is the same both for gods descending and the dead ascending. In Puri, a major Hindu pilgrimage centre, the cremation ground is the *swargadvāra* ('gateway to heaven'), the very spot where Brahma descended to consecrate the image of Jagannath (Macdonald 1953: 517–18). Such places are vertices at which heaven and earth intersect, and time and space may be transcended. At Terku Vandanam funerals the body is transported northwards to the cemetery which is also the abode of Siva, and from which the village goddess 'descends' at the start of her annual festival (Good 1985*a*).

In Nepal, ritual journeys often occur in the vertical plane (Allen 1974: 10–11). The poles and ladders observed there are not in

[3] In village festivals, a human medium replaces the 'car' as the vehicle for the deity's circuit of the settlement.

evidence in Terku Vandanam, but the notion of vertical transition is by no means absent. In brief, circular movements mark the poles of the cosmic axis, whereas intervening linear movements take place *along* it. The entire cortège can thus be seen as a vertical journey along the *axis mundi*, projected onto the horizontal plane.

The mourners' preliminary visit to the ritual boundary, to break the earthly bonds of the deceased (see 10.2, above), takes place at the *ellaikkal*, the 'boundary stone' marking the ritual boundary of the village. *Ellai* also means 'death', and in this context the stone marks the boundary between this world and the next. Beside it, as at the gate of a Siva temple, is a Pillaiyar shrine which marks the entrance to Siva's other abode, the cemetery. The Kallar have a similar rite (see 11.3, above), which the Barber ends by saying '*suvarkkalōkam sēr*' ('conduct to heaven'). Finally, the mourners circumambulate straw during this rite. The Tamil word for straw, *settai*, also means 'putrefied flesh'. The straw may therefore be identified with the body of the deceased, on the boundary between one world and the next. The whole episode is a kind of rehearsal for 'conducting the body to heaven'.

All these journeys are led by drummers. There is a very widespread association between drumming and ascent of the cosmic axis (Eliade 1964). In South India, particular styles of drumming are always associated with transitions between this world and the next. Moreover, drummers themselves frequently display signs of possession, suggesting that they are balanced precariously on the borderline between the worlds.

Much of this evidence is highly circumstantial, and few of these points would stand up to scrutiny on their own. Taken together, however, they suggest a series of journeys to and fro along a notionally vertical cosmic axis. Moreover, these journeys conform to a much more general pattern.

The word *kāḍu* ('cemetery') also means 'forest grove', so the funeral cortège is a journey from a 'pavilion' (the *pandal* outside the house), northwards to a 'forest grove' (the cemetery). This recalls the canonical account of the Buddha's birth. He was born in a pleasure-grove, his mother's womb being depicted as a jewelled pavilion. After facing east and being worshipped by the gods, he 'examined the four quarters' (circumambulated) and took seven steps northwards under a white parasol (Thomas 1949: 33). After the seventh step he again inspected the four quarters and announced:

'This is my last birth. There is now no existence again' (Thomas 1949: 31).

Similar journeys took place subsequently in the Buddha's career, and the recurrent theme of 'pavilion', 'grove' and 'promenade' has been examined by Mus (1935: i. 476 ff.). He argues that circumambulation serves to encompass cosmic space, while the northward promenade represents vertical passage through the gateway to heaven. The Buddha's ascent is sometimes re-enacted during Buddhist festivals (Scott 1927: 328–33), and Macdonald (1953: 37–8) identifies this same structure in the contemporary car festival at Puri.

Terku Vandanam funerals conform to this structure, too, and also share the same general concerns. Moreover, their parallels with local temple festivals have already been mentioned. The mourners process under a white cloth (parasol) to the village boundary, where they circumambulate as well as facing east. Subsequently the cortège leaves the *pandal* (pavilion) and proceeds northwards (promenade) to the cemetery (grove), where circumambulation and cremation (ascension) take place. Of course these elements have other significances too, but taken together the parallels are quite striking.[4]

This is not meant to imply that local funerals are survivals of ancient Buddhism, merely that the Buddha's promenade and the Terku Vandanam cortège have the same aim, namely, ascension along the cosmic axis. Given a common repertoire of symbolic 'reagents' (see 12.5, above) with which to accomplish this aim, it is not surprising that such similarities exist. All over India, the dead or dying are transported to the village cemetery, the Ganges, or other holy places. For example, Babb describes a funeral whose resemblances to that in Terku Vandanam are very obvious (1975: 92). It seems natural that death should often be visualized in terms of movement from one world to another.

13.4 The Cycle as a Whole

The Sadanku safeguards the status of the girl's natal family and her affines in general, while the Kaliyanam links her to her husband's

[4] The correspondence is of course not perfect. For example, the number seven has no significance in local funerals.

family, thereby legitimating her future children.[5] Appropriately, then, the Sadanku takes place entirely at the girl's house, and the Kaliyanam at the groom's. By contrast, the matrilineal Tamils of Batticaloa hold both their 'puberty' and 'marriage' rites at the girl's natal home, where the couple subsequently reside (McGilvray 1982*b*: 43).

The Terku Vandanam Sadanku has two distinct phases. The impure liminality of the seclusion gives way to the pure liminality of the 'wedding'. The Kaliyanam contains no such duality and is unambiguously pure and auspicious. From the perspective of the cycle as a whole, the dual aspect of the Sadanku—whereby impurity is followed by abnormal purity—seems to be merely a secondary, encompassed reflection of the broader Sadanku-Kaliyanam structure.

Mothers-to-be are not impure, and pregnancy does not lead to exclusion from house or temple. Birth *does* generate impurity, however, and new mothers are secluded for ten days before returning to normal life (see 9.6, above). Parturition does of course involve 'the irruption of the biological into social life' (Dumont 1980: 61), and pollution may arise for that reason. Unlike death pollution, though, it does not normally spread to her relatives except, in minor respects, to her husband. Like a Sadanku, birth is at once impure yet auspicious. The delivery of a male child, in particular, is greeted with the *kuruvai* cries used only to mark auspicious transitions. A girl's birth is not so greeted, but is certainly not *in*auspicious.

It is interesting to note, given that 'heat' is generated by most states of abnormal impurity or purity, that birth brings about abnormal 'cooling' in a woman (Beck 1969: 562–3). She is fed with special 'hot' foods and liquor, to restore her bodily equilibrium (see 9.4, above). The baby, on the other hand, is born 'hot' and is at once cooled with water and coconut oil.

So the transition into motherhood is polluting, just like the earlier transition into womanhood. Moreover, a woman always has her first child at her parents' house, and they meet the costs just as they did at her Sadanku. A wife's status is ritually clarified by the end of her Kaliyanam, but in practice her new position in her nuptial household is not fully secure until she has borne a child, ideally a son.

[5] The distribution of functions between these stages is not quite the same as proposed by Fuller (1976: 105) for the Nayars. This is not surprising, given the other differences between the two cases (cf. 15.2).

It is by no means uncommon for a husband to use his wife's infertility as a reason for divorce or polygyny.

There is thus a strong case for seeing the rituals accompanying the birth of a first child as yet another step in the cycle begun by its mother's Sadanku. Subsequent children are increasingly likely to be born at her husband's house rather than her father's, but clearly a wife's incorporation into her husband's family occurs only slowly and gradually.

Finally, what of a female's role in funeral rituals, especially that of her husband? Ideally this should precede her own,[6] and given the required age disparity between them this happens more often than not. Several local households contain *two* generations of widows. Furthermore, widowers are permitted to remarry, and often do so, whereas widows almost invariably cannot (see 6.6, above). Overall, they outnumber widowers by 35 to 11.

A widow plays a largely passive role at her husband's funeral, and emerges from their marital home only to bid farewell. She circles his bier thrice anticlockwise, pouring water from a pot. These acts are clearly inversions and transformations of the water-pourings and circumambulations at her Sadanku and Kaliyanam. They are also repeated by the (invariably male) chief mourner, once the cortège reaches the cemetery. He goes around in the opposite direction, however, and local people insisted that this was not a mistake (cf. 13.3.1, above). In light of the foregoing discussion it is possible to offer a tentative explanation for the fact that the widow's circumambulation none the less *does* occur counter-clockwise.

The disabilities of widowhood in Indian society are too well known to need much comment here. A married woman with a living husband is a *sumaṅkali* ('auspicious woman'), and only she can, for example, cook *poṅkal* at village temple festivals (Good 1983: 227; 1985*a*: 137). A widow, by contrast, is an *amaṅkali* ('inauspicious woman'). She cannot even be present at *poṅkal*-cooking, and does not attend Sadankus and Kaliyanams, at least not in a major role (Reynolds 1980; 16.7). Her husband's death therefore brings about a drastic deterioration in a woman's lot. She experiences the effects of death pollution more strongly and permanently than anyone else. Her counter-clockwise circumambulation at the beginning of the funeral procession reflects its unmitigatedly negative implications

[6] A widower is left socially and ritually incomplete (Marglin 1985*b*: 53).

for her. Although birth and puberty, too, are polluting events for a female, her husband's death is both impure *and* inauspicious.

Once the cortège reaches the cemetery, the Barber and a mourner return to the house with cloth from the dead man's vesti. The widow's head is then shaved, she removes her jewels, and dons white clothing for the first time. Henceforth she never again wears a *tāli*, jewels, or coloured clothing (see 16.7, below).

	AUSPICIOUS	INAUSPICIOUS
PURE	Kaliyanam	Karumati
IMPURE	Sadanku Birth	Funeral

FIG. 13.2 Purity and Auspiciousness in Life-Crisis Rituals

One general point which has emerged repeatedly during this chapter concerns the need to treat purity and auspiciousness as independent variables. As Figure 13.2 shows, the rituals discussed illustrate all four possible permutations. Whereas Sadankus and childbirth involve auspicious impurity and Kaliyanams epitomize auspicious purity, funerals are both inauspicious and impure (cf. 13.3.1, above), especially for the female most centrally involved, the widow.[7] Like other rites directed at ancestors, Karumatis exemplify the fourth logical possibility, being pure but inauspicious (cf. Das 1982: 143). Overall, the *pure/impure* sequence found both in the

[7] Deaths which conform to the normal expectations of the life cycle—for example, a widower whose children are all married, or a *sumaṅkali* with grown children—may sometimes be seen as auspicious (Narayanan 1985: 58). This clearly does not apply when death brings about widowhood.

Sadanku and, on a larger scale, in the Sadanku-Kaliyanam sequence as a whole, finds an echo in death ritual, where the impure funeral is followed by the pure Karumati. Yet at the same time the two sequences are diametrically opposed with respect to the *auspicious/inauspicious* opposition.

14
The Social Identities of Ritual Participants

This chapter examines the genealogical and terminological relationships of the main participants and officiants in rites of passage. We shall see that the same social roles, the same personages, and even the same persons, appear over and over again in the life-crisis rites of a given individual, and of that individual's siblings, spouse and offspring.

The analysis will first deal with Terku Vandanam and its environs, and will then be broadened in order to seek conclusions applicable to the entire region. The emphasis will be on puberty rites and weddings, the events for which most information is available, but whenever possible birth, death, and other relevant occasions will also be taken into account.

14.1 Ritual Officiants in Terku Vandanam

First of all, Tables 14.1 and 14.2 give the genealogical and terminological identities of key participants in every Sadanku and Kaliyanam during my stay. Unless otherwise stated, Ego is the maturing girl in Table 14.1, and the groom in Table 14.2.

(i) *The Bridegroom.* The most immediately striking feature of a Sadanku is the role of the 'female bridegroom', or *māppiḷḷai.* In everyday speech *māppiḷḷai* is a relationship term used by male Egos for junior male cross-relatives (Table 5.1), but in the context of weddings it has the particular connotation of 'bridegroom', just as *peṇ* ('girl') means 'bride' in the context of marriage. The uses of *peṇ* and *māppiḷḷai* for the central figures in a Sadanku are just two of many explicit local acknowledgments of its resemblance to a Kaliyanam. When asked why a girl acts as 'groom', people reply that if a boy did so it would become a real wedding. This evades the basic issue of why the rite is necessary in the first place, and is not even superficially convincing in view of the fact that one local group—the

TABLE 14.1. Relationships of Main Participants in Sadankus

Caste[a]	Genealogical relationship to 'bride' of			
	Urimai partner	'Groom'	Female officiant	Sari donor
Maravar (Ex. A)	MBSe	FFBDD[b]	MBW (*attai*)[c]	MB
Maravar (Ex. B)	MBSe	MBD	FeBW (*periyammāḷ*)	MB
Maravar (Ex. D)	MBSe	FZD[d]	FZD and FBSW (*madiṉi*)	MB
Paraiyar (TV)	MBSe/FZSe	FMBD[e]	MyZ (*sitti*)	MB
Konar (Kovilpatti)	FZSe	MBS[f]	MyZ (*sitti*)[c]	MB
Velar (Ex. C)	MBSe[g]	MBD	FyBW (*sitti*)[c]	MB
Ayotti Reddiyar (KP)	MyBe	MBD	?[c]	MB

[a] The Examples are discussed in detail in Ch. 7.
[b] The 'bride' had no female first cross-cousins.
[c] A Brahman Priest was present on these occasions.
[d] The 'bride' had no MBD.
[e] The 'bride' had no unmarried first cross-cousins. Though genealogically senior, the 'groom' was 5–6 years younger.
[f] The 'groom' was a baby boy. The 'bride' had no FZS or FZD.
[g] Another Velar named the FZSe as *urimai* partner, but both emphasized that 'bride' and 'groom' should stand in the *urimai* relationship.

TABLE 14.2 Relationships of Main Participants in Kaliyanams

Caste[a]	Genealogical relationship to groom of			
	Bride[b]	Female officiant(s)	Leader[c]	Follower[c]
Konar (Ex. D)	MFBSD (*marumakaḷ*)	FFFZHBDSW[d] (*sitti*)	WyB[e] (*maccin̲an̲*)	yZ (*taṅkai*)
Konar (Ex. D)	FFFZHBDDHBD (*marumakaḷ*)	FFFZHBDSW[f] + WeZ[g] (*sitti*)	WFBSy (*marumakan̲*)	yZ (*taṅkai*)
Pillai (Ex. A)	FZSD (*marumakaḷ*)	eZ (*akkāḷ*)	WyB (*maccin̲an̲*)	eZ (*akkāḷ*)
Maravar (Ex. B)	MBD (*kol̲undiyāḷ*)	Two yZs (*taṅkai*)	yZH[h] (*maittun̲ār*)	yZ (*taṅkai*)
Maravar (Ex. C)	MFBSD (*kol̲undiyāḷ*)	eZ, yZ (*akkāḷ, taṅkai*)	yZH (*maccin̲an̲*)	eZ (*akkāḷ*)
Nayakkar (Ex. F)	FMZHZSD (*marumakaḷ*)	eZ (*akkāḷ*)	WFBSy[i] (*maccin̲an̲*)	eZ (*akkāḷ*)

[a] The Examples are discussed in Ch. 8: D was a double wedding.
[b] In all but the Maravar examples, the bride had referred to her groom as *māman̲* prior to the wedding.
[c] These columns refer to the triple circumambulation of the platform.
[d] The groom had no married Z in the Konar examples. Coincidentally, these were the only weddings not to involve a Brahman officiant.
[e] The groom sometimes calls this person *marumakan̲*. The terms in this column are virtually interchangeable, except for Maravar.
[f] The Main Officiant was also the bride's FBWBW (*attai*).
[g] The minor officiant was the groom's WeZ and WMBW, as the result of a previous eZDy marriage.
[h] The groom was earlier led out by his MB (*tāymāman̲*) for the distribution of new clothes.
[i] The bride had no B. The groom was led out by a different *maccin̲an̲*.

Konars—have a baby boy as 'groom' (Table 14.1).[1] In any case, some key stages of Kaliyanams are omitted from Sadankus, such as the *tāli*-tying, the binding of hands, and the final *triple* circumambulation.

The Konar 'groom' has to be very young, whereas girls are typically 16 or more at puberty.[2] Given the prescriptive requirement that a groom be senior to his bride, such a couple are not 'potential spouses' terminologically (Table 5.2). The large age discrepancy in the opposite direction might in itself be enough to invalidate the wedding, although no one explicitly said this. In short, the 'groom' is always a cross-relative of the puberal girl, but one who is unmarriageable for reasons of gender and/or relative age.

Table 14.1 shows that where possible the Sadanku 'groom' is the younger sister (in the Konar case, younger brother) of the puberal girl's *urimai* partner (cf. 6.4, above). In apparent contrast, none of the Kaliyanams in Table 14.2 followed the *urimai* rule. As it happened, however, no *urimai* partner was available for any of these particular brides and grooms. In all, about 10–15 per cent of local marriages do conform to *urimai* rules (Table 6.1). In many cases conformity is impossible, either because no partners exist or because they have already married someone else, but even if an *urimai* partner is available s/he is not always married. Potential spouses must satisfy not only categorical and genealogical requirements, but economic, political, and temperamental ones too, and even if not forced by demographic contingency, parents are likely to look further afield for sons- and daughters-in-law than when they are merely selecting a Sadanku partner for their daughter.

(ii) *The Sari Donor.* In every case, the Sadanku sari was given by the girl's senior MB (*tāymāmaṉ*), and the Kaliyanam sari by her groom. For most local castes the groom may of course be the bride's MyB or his terminological equivalent, so there are obvious parallels between the two prestations. Several factors urge caution here, however. First, Maravar MBs donate Sadanku saris too, even though eZDy marriage is forbidden. Second, the donor is ideally married. Finally, the ideal donor is the MeB, for whom the girl, as yZD, is not marriageable anyway.

[1] My assistant thought that in his Vaniya Cettiyar sub-caste the *tāymāmaṉ* (MB) acted as 'groom', though he had not actually seen this for himself. Similar practices are reported for some Vellalar (Thurston and Rangachari 1909: vii. 385; cf. 14.2).

[2] The very late onset of puberty probably reflects poor health and nutrition.

(iii) *The Main Female Officiant*. Even if Brahmans are present, Sadankus and Kaliyanams are largely conducted by female relatives of the main participants. The ideal Sadanku officiant is a genealogically close *periyammāḷ* or *sitti* of the girl, that is, a senior or junior FBW or MZ. Her assistants stand in the same terminological category. At a Kaliyanam the groom's married Z officiates. If he has none, a more distant "sister" takes charge. Unmarried "sisters" never do so, and are limited to bringing up the rear in the final triple circumambulation.

As a woman's husband is usually her *māmaṉ*, the officiant at her Sadanku, too, is a "sister" to her potential spouses. In other words, the Main Officiants at a given female's Sadanku and Kaliyanam should always be the same *personage*, and may perhaps even be the same *person*. Maravars forbid eZDy unions of course, so this argument does not apply to them as it stands. It is none the less noteworthy that in one case the Main Officiant, as *madiṉi* of the menarchal girl, was again a "sister" of her potential husbands. In another case, the puberal girl had no female cross-cousins: her 'groom' was a more distant cousin and the Main Officiant—most unusually—was the wife of the *tāymāmaṉ* who donated the sari.

(iv) *The Male Officiant*. At a Kaliyanam a man leads the groom out and heads the final triple circuit around the platform. He is called the groom's companion (*māppiḷḷai tōḷi*) or *macciṉaṉ*. *Macciṉaṉ* normally means 'junior cross-cousin, male speaking' (Tables 5.1 and 5.2), but in this context it refers to whoever takes the officiant's role in the Kaliyanam.

In every case, the Male Officiant was referred to as the *macciṉaṉ* when his role in the Kaliyanam was under discussion. However, Table 14.2 displays Ego's answer—often given months before or after the wedding—to the question, 'What is X's relationship to you?' These answers therefore refer to kinship relations in the abstract, not to roles in particular rites of passage. This explains why no fewer than three different terms appear in the appropriate column. Even so, the variation is less than first appears, because *macciṉaṉ* and *maittuṉār* (and *marumakaṉ*, for castes allowing eZDy marriage) are more or less equivalent terms of reference and address (Table 5.2).

Whatever the terminological situation, the genealogical position is clear enough. The ideal *macciṉaṉ* is either the groom's WyB, and so, obviously, the yB (*tampi*) of the bride, or his yZH, another "brother" (preferably a *tampi*) of the bride. In the absence of both these relatives, more distant terminological equivalents are called upon.

14.2 Previous Ethnographic Accounts

There are some puzzling references in the older literature to the custom of a mature woman marrying a young boy, her junior cross-cousin. The boy's father, her MB, then allegedly cohabits with her and sires her children. I know of no similar reports from modern fieldworkers, and such a practice would flout the age requirements of South Indian marriages. Two of these reports concern groups found locally, namely the Konars ('Idaiyar', Thurston and Rangachari 1909: ii. 360) and Reddiyars ('Kapu', Thurston and Rangachari 1909: iii. 240),[3] but I found no evidence whatever for such a custom among either. Thurston relates the practice to the absolute necessity of marrying the first cousin, but this merely indicates that he has misunderstood the classificatory nature of the prescription. I do not claim that such marriages never took place, especially in areas remote from my fieldwork location, but it is easy to see how second-hand accounts of Sadankus and eZDy marriages might mislead.

The Sadanku is spoken of as a 'wedding' and involves a child referred to as a 'bridegroom'. It might not be apparent if one had never actually seen such a ceremony that the 'groom' was often a girl, and the 'wedding' something less than fully fledged marriage. If the fact that women marry their "uncles" (who according to western commonsense are the fathers of their cross-cousins) was also known, it would be easy to jump to a wrong conclusion like that outlined above. On the other hand, several accounts say explicitly that the young 'groom' is the *pater* of the woman's children, and the "uncle" merely their genitor. I can only comment that the scope for misunderstanding Tamil statements about kinship is immense, particularly if one's knowledge of the idiom is slight. In any case, even if one *were* to see the Sadanku as the 'survival' of a custom of marrying a mature woman to a boy, which seems to me highly unlikely, that would explain nothing about the present status of the ceremony.

[3] See also the Kunnuvan (Thurston and Rangachari 1909: iv. 120); Malayali (iv. 423); Nattukottai Chetti (v. 265); Okkiliyan (v. 441); Tottiyan (vii. 184); and Konga Vellala (vii. 193).

14.3 Alliance and the Ritual Officiants

As we saw (5.3), a distinctive feature of local relationship terminologies is the categorization of relatives into two broad classes, which Dumont (1961*b*: 81) labelled 'consanguines' and 'affines' respectively, hence his formula, *kinship equals consanguinity plus affinity*. I tried earlier (5.4) to modify this view in the light of theoretical advances by Needham (1967; 1973), which are seemingly approved of by Dumont himself (1975: 145 n). That earlier critique dealt only with the relationship terminology, however, and must be extended to the jural level before we can fully understand the roles of the key participants in rituals.

For Dumont, the structural principle which relates the two terminological classes is 'alliance'. This connects groups rather than individuals, and hence has a diachronic as well as a synchronic dimension (1983: 14). Cross-cousin marriage is 'the perfect formula for perpetuating the alliance relationship' (1983: 14). One such marriage in every generation suffices to maintain the alliance link between Ego's consanguines as a group, and the whole group of his WB's consanguines (see 5.3, above).

Dumont himself speaks of 'consanguines' and 'affines' rather than 'parallel' and 'cross-' relatives, because the latter are not indigenous categories. But his chosen terms carry meanings too narrow for the contexts in which he uses them. There are parallel relatives—like Ego's cross-relatives' cross-relatives—who are in no sense 'consanguines' of Ego. Similarly, there are also cross-relatives who have no direct links of alliance with Ego's group (David 1973; 5.4, above).

The dualistic view which Dumont then held envisaged only two types of data, 'ideological' and 'behavioural' (1980: 343–4). Like Lévi-Strauss, he therefore saw the 'rule of alliance' as enshrined in the relationship terminology, and regarded both as aspects of ideology. Instead, it seems more fruitful to treat them as belonging to two different levels, the 'jural' and 'categorical' respectively (Needham 1973: 171; 5.1, above).

Despite his historically important realization that 'kinship terminologies have not as their function to register groups' (1964: 78; 1983: 12), Dumont's analysis in terms of 'consanguinity' and 'affinity' *does* necessarily refer to the identifying characteristics of groups. These very concepts accord primacy to genealogically close relatives, despite his avowed intention of doing precisely the opposite. For example, because of the way 'affinity' is defined, the term *māmaṉ* seems to apply only to members of the same agnatic group as Ego's MB and/or WB: otherwise, how could it meaningfully be said that 'one and the same' alliance relationship is transmitted down the generations (1983: 14)? In fact, though, "*māmaṉ*" is merely a terminological category: all usages of the term are equivalent, because the relationship it expresses is purely formal. I therefore argued that, when one was discussing the terminology, the alternative terms 'parallel' and 'cross-' were more helpful precisely because they were analytic abstractions, carrying no prior semantic burden for indigene or ethnographer (see 5.4, above).

However, the consanguine/affine distinction *does* seem valid when 'jural' phenomena like descent groups or local marriage rules are considered, with two reservations. First, these terms do not encompass Ego's entire kinship universe, but apply only to genealogically defined relatives of particular, close types. Second, they refer to the presence or absence of common 'blood' or 'substance', matters on which South Asians themselves often hold definite, though varied, opinions (see 12.2, above). The terms "consanguine" and "affine" should therefore only be used in ways consistent with the views of the group concerned, and are subject to the inherent limitations of all 'cultural' data. That is, they express ideas which are non-generalizable, and unevenly disseminated through the group. Dumont himself recognized the cultural variability of these concepts when, in debate with Radcliffe-Brown (1953), he argued that for the Nayar the father (M's *sambandham* partner) was an affine, and the MB (head of the *taravād*) a consanguine (1983 [1953*b*]: 20).[4]

My argument, then, is that diachronic, corporate 'alliance' is indeed present in many South Asian societies, but only at the 'jural' level. Links of 'alliance' or 'affinity' connect particular groups between which marriages have taken place in the present generation or remembered past. In short, 'alliance' is best seen as a jurally and genealogically based phenomenon, not as a feature of the terminology.

[4] *Both* protagonists were beside the point in this particular case, as the Nayars do not have a 'Dravidian' terminological structure (Gough 1952).

14.4 Diachronic Alliance and Ritual in Terku Vandanam

The ideal participants in local rites of passage do not merely fall into particular terminological categories *vis-à-vis* the principals, but are the genealogically closest members of those categories. This fact does not support Scheffler's contention (1977; 5.4, above) that 'Dravidian' terminologies display 'polysemy by extension'. Instead, it reflects jural considerations quite independent of the terminology. The *tāymāmaṉ* (senior MB), for instance, is so important because he, and in the next generation his S (*maccinaṉ* or *māppiḷḷai*), is Ego's closest male affine. Ego, together with his F, MB, and MBS, form a close-knit group who, if *urimai* rules are obeyed, actually exchange women in each generation and so become each other's brothers-in-law.

This example only mentions men—deliberately so, for women do not fit so neatly into the consanguine/affine dichotomy. In most cases they move from one domestic group to another, and the effecting of this transfer, often conceptualized in biological terms, is a prime purpose of the rites under investigation. Some people say that a girl starts life with one set of consanguines and is transferred to another when her blood changes at marriage, so to avoid ambiguity I shall refer to 'natal' and 'marital' relatives, rather than 'consanguines' and 'affines', when considering the female point of view.

It is with these structural and cultural points in mind that we should reconsider the role of the Main Female Officiant. Why is this personage so uniquely fitted to effect the status transformation of the puberal girl or bride? The ideal Sadanku Officiant is the girl's *periyammāḷ* or *sitti* (MZ, FBW). She leads out the girl, often bathes her, dresses her, leads her out again, officiates at the 'wedding', and leads the single circuit of the marriage platform. A similar personage (or even the same person) leads out the bride at a Kaliyanam, ties the *tāli*, and brings up the rear in the final triple circumambulation. On both occasions, she performs an *ālatti* rite to protect the girl from malign influences.

At both events, then, she literally and metaphorically leads the girl through the transitional phase between one social status and another. The overall transition has not been completed by the end of the Sadanku, of course, so it is fitting that the girl is led both into and out of the *pandal* (the sacred threshold) by the Main Officiant. The transition *is* complete, though not yet permanent, by the end of the Kaliyanam. The Main Officiant's task is then over, and appropriately she brings up the rear in the final procession.

If possible, the groom's eZ is preferred to his yZ, but in any case the Main Officiant is his consanguine by birth and affine by marriage. Being anomalous in this way with respect to the groom, she is the ideal person to effect the transformation which tying the *tāli* represents, for it is at this point that the change in the bride's ethno-physiological identity occurs (David 1973: 523). The groom has previously 'lost' his Z in a wedding at which he himself, as the bride's yB, may well have been Male Officiant. In return, as it were, his Z now provides him with a wife, who may even be her own D.[5] In any event, whether by donating her own D or transferring her "sister's daughter", it is the groom's eZ who ensures that he acquires a wife.[6]

She brings the bride to her brother, stands between them while they are seated on the platform, but is separated from her brother by the bride during the final procession. Having discharged her obligation to her brother, she ends the ceremony finally and definitively parted from him. The Main Officiant thus acts as a ritual broker between her brother and his new affines, in a way which reflects her own structurally intermediate position between two similar groups. This is so whatever the particular *urimai* rule of the group in question, though the precise details vary from case to case, as shown in Figure 14.1. An unmarried Z does not yet occupy such an intermediate position of course, and so would not be a satisfactory officiant from this point of view.

This analysis may be extended to cover the birth of the first child, for which a wife returns to her natal home. During her confinement she is assisted by the married women of that household—her M, and various *periyammāḷs* and *sittis* (see 9.6, above). The very women who play such crucial parts in effecting her transformation and transfer during her Sadanku and Kaliyanam officiate yet again at the completion of the process.

The role of the Male Officiant follows from this, whether he happens to be the groom's WyB or his yZH (these two are in any case

[5] Unfortunately I did not attend any eZDy marriages. It is possible that the eZ herself could not officiate in such cases, because of the bride's M's customary 'shyness' towards her son-in-law. On the other hand, the latter *is* her yB.

[6] From this point of view, eZDy marriage can plausibly be seen as the logical culmination of the role of an elder sister at her brother's wedding.

equivalent terminologically). His role is subordinate to that of the Female Officiant, and he can perhaps be seen as the opposite pole of the continuum along which the two women move at marriage. He shares the affinal characteristics which the groom's Z acquired at her own wedding, and which the bride is in process of losing. He thus represents a 'permanent affine', just as the groom himself is a 'permanent consanguine'. Moreover, his presence completes the symmetry of the dramatis personae. Not only the groom's Z but also the bride's B is involved, but whereas the Main Female Officiant is ideally the groom's eZ, the Male Officiant is the groom's—often even the bride's—junior. This seniority of the groom's side accords with the age requirements for spouses themselves.

This does not exhaust the implications of the parts played by these two officiants. One of them is likely to become parent-in-law of any child born to the marriage at which they officiate, given the *urimai* rules and the high incidence of first cross-cousin marriage (Beck 1972: 240–3). There is indeed, though too much should not be made of this given the smallness of the sample, a strong correlation evident in Table 14.2 between the genealogical identity of the Male Officiant and the direction of the *urimai* preference. For castes with a MBDy preference (Konar, Vellalar, Nayakkar), the WyB or nearest available alternative officiates. Conversely, for those with a FZDy preference (Maravar), the yZH is involved. In every case therefore, the Male Officiant's D will be the *urimai* girl of any son born to the marrying couple.[7]

Among Coimbatore castes with MBDy *urimai* preferences, claims over the future offspring of a new union are staked quite explicitly by the groom's Z (Beck 1972: 239–43). In Terku Vandanam, such claims are merely implicit in the fact that a "sister" of the groom delivers the first-born child; in the idea of the *urimai* link; and in the very existence of diachronic alliance.

Given repeated 'cross-cousin' or eZDy marriage, the same few individuals have *urimai* claims over one another, officiate at each other's Sadankus and Kaliyanams, deliver each other's babies, marry their children to each other's offspring, and exchange gifts of clothing when members of each other's families die. Figure 14.1 shows how any given marriage connects with and evokes the past, present, and future marriages of three generations of affines, whichever consistent

[7] It may also be relevant that the Maravar are the only caste in Tables 14.1 and 14.2 to prohibit eZDy marriage.

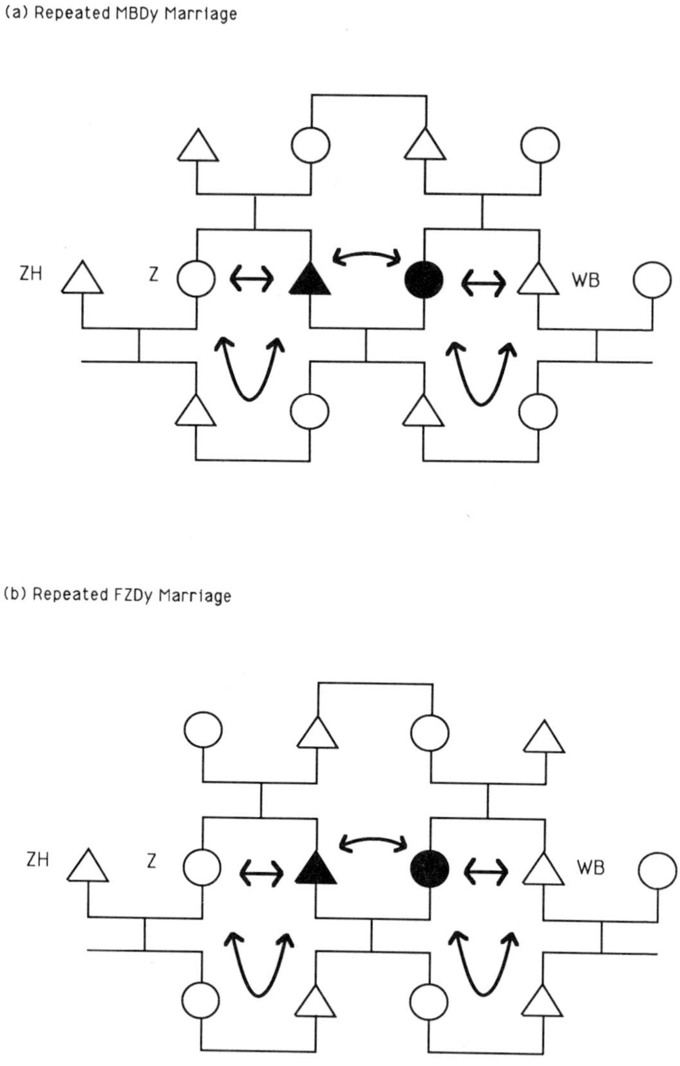

FIG. 14.1 Diachronic Aspects of the Alliance Relationship

(c) Repeated eZDy Marriage

Key:

Groom (Ego)	▲
Bride	●
urimai link	↔
Future in-laws	↶↗
Officiants	↔
(not known for (c))	

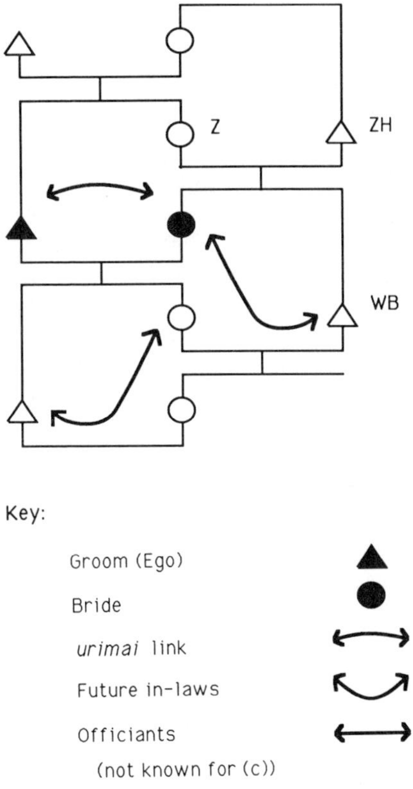

form of close genealogical marriage is practised. Given the degree of close intermarriage in Terku Vandanam, the empirical situation is not very different from this ideal picture even when *urimai* rules are not fully adhered to and when, as a result, the participants are slightly more distant genealogically.

As for the 'female bridegroom', she is the "sister" of a potential spouse and also, given eZDy marriage, the "daughter" of one (a *māmaṉ*). Without local exegesis, it is not clear what specific conclusions should be drawn from the latter point, but together they provide another acknowledgment of the *urimai* preference, and a reminder that the alliance relationship is not confined to a single generation. The 'bridegroom' stands in for her eB, the true *urimai* partner. The puberal girl's affines thereby provide an asexual 'mock-husband' for her 'mock marriage', who may be either an immature girl or an infant boy.

This role is not essential to effecting the desired transition, however, because it adds nothing not already implied by the social identities of other key participants. This must be so, for many groups in the region do without a 'groom' altogether. But a Sadanku is essentially a cultural performance, and due allowance must be made for the fact that a transition may need to be enacted over and over again if it is actually to be effected. As Barth remarks, the first blow of an axe communicates one's intention of felling a tree, but the tree is not thereby felled (1975: 209–10). Redundancy may exist in the message conveyed by a rite, but not in its performance.

Rituals of puberty, marriage, and birth are auspicious, whereas death and its ancillary ceremonies are inauspicious (see 13.4, above). There are corresponding sociological differences too. The first three events take place in the domestic arena. They are dominated by actors and officiants from the principals' own caste—by auspicious women (*sumaṅkalis*) and affines. Funerals happen in the wilderness, and are performed exclusively by men. Specialists from other castes predominate, and the key participating relatives are agnates of the deceased.

The chief mourner is always a parallel relative, and even this role is largely passive. Funerals are supervised by the Barber or, later, a Brahman. At no stage do relatives have the degree of executive responsibility so noticeable at other rituals. At births a midwife is not essential, and at Sadankus and Kaliyanams the Brahman is largely a technician hired to create an appropriately pure environment, who may in the last analysis be dispensed with altogether. This is not possible at a funeral: even at a child's burial (see 10.6, Ex. F, above) a Barber is actively present.

Not merely birth, but also the major public ceremonies of puberty and marriage are performed and supervised by women. This seems surprising at first, given their normal retiring domestic role, but it is actually perfectly intelligible in light of the anomalous status of women *vis-à-vis* the parallel/cross dichotomy. Yet women, even the closest relatives of the deceased, are totally excluded from the cemetery and even from the Karumati by nearly all castes, and play virtually no part in the process of disposing of the dead.

Affinal relationships epitomize the everyday South Indian social order in many ritual contexts (cf. Good 1985*a*: 155). This order is temporarily disrupted at life crises, so affines are at first little in evidence. When it comes to admitting the main participants to their new social statuses, however, they play the key roles. At a Sadanku where a Brahman is present, he supervises the ceremony up to and including the bath, but then leaves the Female Officiant to take over. The fact is clearest of all at death, where affines have no role at the funeral or Karumati. Only when the mourners come to be readmitted to normal domestic life do their affines play a significant part.

The affine mainly involved (*sammandi*; see 10.8.1, above) is the MB for a bachelor, and the ZH for a married man. For castes with FZD *urimai* preferences, the ZH is of course ideally the MBS, while in cases of eZDy marriage the same person could remain one's 'principal affine' throughout, because of the identity between MB and eZH. Even castes with an MBDy preference, for whom MBS = WB ideally, seem to regard the ZH as principal *sammandi*, possibly because he, unlike the WB, is also a close affine (son-in-law) of the deceased. Overall then, despite their differences from all other rites of passage, funerary rituals too ultimately recognize the importance of diachronic affinity.

14.5 Officiants Elsewhere

It remains to be seen how widely applicable this explanation of the roles of the key participants may be. Can the comparative material presented in Chapter 11 be interpreted in a similar way? Unfortunately the available information is by no means always complete: for instance, Dube (1953; 11.5, above) says nothing about officiants at local weddings. None the less it is possible to detect some broad trends, at least in outline.

In the *Coorg* case patriliny is so strongly marked, given the importance of the *okka*, that close affines are not an undifferentiated group, but—as the institution of the 'family friend' shows—are subdivided according to *okka* membership. Moreover, the groom's sister is more clearly separated from him at her marriage than in most non-Brahman cases (Srinivas 1952: 148), and is statistically unlikely to be linked with the particular *okka* from which his own bride comes, though she is still of course a potential mother-in-law to his future child. It seems consistent with all this that instead of the groom's Z acting as Main Officiant in a Coorg marriage, the transfer of the bride is managed by two *male* affines, the 'family friends'. The groom's ZH and the bride's BW also take part, however, and since the latter is of course equated terminologically with the groom's sister, things are not as different as might at first appear. The particularities of Coorg social structure lead to roles being allotted differently, but their underlying structural significance seems much the same as in Vandanam.

Piramalai Kallars, whose patrilineages are less corporate in character, also maintain clear separation between events at the bride's and groom's houses, and minimize contact between the two families during the ceremony, features which seem to be characteristic of strongly unilineal groups. The groom's sister ties the *tāli* round the bride's neck, however, so unlike his other relations she has to go with him to the bride's village. She also leads the bride into the marital home. It is usually the yZ who is involved (Dumont 1957*b*: 219), but otherwise the position of the Main Officiant is similar to that in Terku Vandanam. The ideal Male Officiant is the groom's MB. The bride's MB is involved too, in the rites at her natal home. Here, as in Terku Vandanam, there is therefore clear continuity between the officiants at puberty rites and weddings: at the bride's first menstruation, and the groom's circumcision, their respective MBs will have played key roles (see 11.3, above).

The fact that many *Sinhalese* girls go through no further ritual after their puberty ceremony correlates with the general unimportance of lineal pedigrees in that society. When there *is* an actual wedding, it is conducted by the two MBs, especially the bride's MB—a classificatory "father" of the groom—assisted by the bride's *nenda* (FZ, MBW). These are precisely the cases where the patrilineal South Indian pattern is most likely to be found, with landed property being inherited only by sons, and daughters receiving dowries at marriage (Yalman 1960; 1971).

The rites of *Batticaloa Tamils* put much more stress on the role of women. The ideal Female Officiant, in so far as she is specified, is the girl's *māmī* (FZ, MBW). Not only is she senior in generation to both bride *and* groom, she is also of the opposite terminological category to her counterparts in the Terku Vandanam and Kallar cases, being what would in Vandanam be called an *attai*, rather than a *periyammāḷ* or *sitti*. The difference is presumably related to the matriliny of this group (McGilvray 1982*b*: 47).

On the other hand, there are differences between the Batticaloa case and that of the *Nayar*. Although the 'married' women of the Nayar *taravād*—the girl's M, MZ, MZDe, etc.—are involved in both the *tāli*-rite and *sambandham* inauguration (Gough 1955: 49), they seem less important participants than the young men of the lineage—her B, MZS, etc.—and its head, the Karanavan. The *tāli*-tier himself is of course an affine (*inaṅkar*) in the most common, Sudra Nayar, case.

Among *Tamil Brahmans* the bride's father plays a key role, particularly in connection with his 'gift of a virgin' to the groom. The groom's eldest sister is also involved, but her role lacks the pre-eminence evident in Terku Vandanam: for example, although she assists at the *tāli*-tying, the importance of this is less than among non-Brahmans. This is consistent with the fact that she and her brother have a comparatively distant relationship.[8] She is completely transferred to her husband's lineage, and adopts his kinship usages. Consequently, she and her brother 'do not apply the same terms to each other's spouse's kin as they do to their own spouse's kin' (Gough 1956: 848). Moreover, marriage creates status differences whereby her marital relatives see themselves as superior to her brother. Under these circumstances, the logic of my earlier argument regarding the sister's role as Female Officiant (14.4) clearly does not apply to the same degree. Another notable feature is that the bride's brother, who plays a passive, secondary role in Terku Vandanam, is much more to the fore among Brahmans. Moreover, it is ideally her *eldest* brother who acts,[9] not the yB as in Terku Vandanam.

[8] This statement needs qualifying (Penny Logan, pers. com.). The B–Z link among Brahmans is formally more distant than for other Tamils, but is not unimportant. The situation resembles that in North India, where brothers and sisters are spatially and socially separated—often with more pronounced hypergamous connotations—but retain important ritual links. Thus, a North Indian sister gives her brother an amulet for good luck (cf. Mandelbaum 1970: 68), and at the annual *Raksha Bandhan* festival he makes a return gift. The nearest Tamil Brahman equivalent is the *Kanu* New Year festival, when women make offerings for the welfare of their brothers. Non-Brahmans have no equivalent ceremony (Logan 1980: 358). The role of the MB in Brahman weddings—though attenuated compared to, say, the Kallar case—shows that diachronic affinity does exist and that differences between Brahmans and other Tamils are only matters of degree.

[9] The eldest brother is particularly important as he inherits his father's obligations

In Terku Vandanam the 'female bridegroom' figures in the puberty ritual, and is played by the sister of the 'bride's' *urimai* partner, whereas among Tamil Brahmans this role used to appear in the wedding, and was played by the bride herself (Thurston and Rangachari 1909: i. 290; 11.8, above). Why this contrast? First, there are two separate rituals for girls in Terku Vandanam, whereas a Brahman girl, because pre-puberty marriage was normal until recently, only passes through one. Her wedding therefore condenses within it elements which in Terku Vandanam are spread between the two stages. Second, the Terku Vandanam 'groom' represents her own brother, with whom her connection remains quite close, with whom she is on a relationship of status equality, and whose kinship usages she shares throughout life. Among Brahmans, on the other hand, the brother–sister bond is more distant. It is the wife, not the sister, who shares a man's kinship usages and with whom, following her complete transfer at marriage, he is on equal status terms.

This does not of course explain why there should be a 'female bridegroom' role in these ceremonies in the first place. Given that the role exists, however, it does seem to make sense that it should be played by a man's sister in Terku Vandanam, and by his wife among Tamil Brahmans.

Nambudiri practices are markedly different from the standard South Indian pattern. Close cross-relatives are not permitted to marry, so links of diachronic affinity are almost wholly absent. Affines have little social contact, are scarcely recognized terminologically, and cannot perpetuate their alliance by arranging unions between their respective children (Mencher and Goldberg 1967: 97). The B–Z, WB–ZH, and MB–ZC bonds are distant and unimportant. Again, the bride's father takes the leading role in a girl's wedding. In this case, he not only makes the 'gift of a virgin', but even ties the *tāli* himself.

14.6 Overall Conclusions

The following picture emerges from all this. Where there is strong patrilineal descent and viri-patrilocal residence, a bride is completely

to make regular *cīr* prestations (cf. Dumont 1957*b*: 228) to his married sisters and their children (Penny Logan, pers. com.).

transferred—socially and possibly ethno-physiologically too—to her husband's lineage. There are then three possibilities.

In the Brahman case, first of all, she becomes merely an adjunct to her husband's social persona, to such an extent that she even changes her terminological usages and adopts his. Her father literally presents her to her husband, and takes the major officiating role in the wedding.

Among patrilineal non-Brahmans the transfer is less radical. A woman continues to be identified with her natal relatives and shares their terminological usages. She continues to call her father-in-law *māmaṉ*, for example. Thereafter there are two possibilities, depending on the extent to which patriliny takes corporate form (sense 2; cf. 1.2, above). Non-Brahmans with strongly defined, corporate patrilineages (such as Coorgs) emphasize the bride's transfer into her husband's group, but do not identify her completely with it. *Male* affines therefore conduct the ceremony. For people like Kallars and the castes of Terku Vandanam, on the other hand, who are patrilineal to varying degrees but lack corporate lineages, the ideal Main Officiant at marriage is a woman who has made (or will make) the same transition between patrilines as the bride undergoes during the wedding, but in the opposite direction—in other words, the groom's sister. Her exact terminological relationship to the bride depends upon whether eZDy marriage is allowed, and the precise genealogical link between the two women depends in part upon whether such a marriage has in fact occurred among their close relatives. This dynamic ambiguity in the position of the sister—who is her brother's consanguine by birth and affine by marriage—is resolved in the Brahman and Coorg cases, making her a less appropriate wedding officiant.

Where there is no stressed line of descent—the typical Sinhalese case—then again no transfer takes place, and there need be no wedding ritual and no officiant. There has, of course, already been a puberty rite in such cases, to resolve the girl's status *vis-à-vis* both her natal and (potential) marital relatives. Those Sinhalese who *do* aspire to unilineal pedigrees hold weddings in which the main officiant appears to be the bride's MB: as in the Coorg case, strong patriliny goes with a major role for male affines.

Where there is matrilineal descent and uxorilocal residence, as in Batticaloa, it is in a sense the women who remain structurally stationary and the men who are transferred, though it is perhaps not surprising to find no corresponding notion of male transubstantiation. In any event, the Main Officiant here is a member of another matrilineage *vis-à-vis* the bride, a 'permanent affine' who, as MBW, received a man from the bride's matrilineage in the previous generation. Having received a "husband", as it were, she now gives back a "son".

In the Nayar situation of matrilineal descent and no joint residence, on the other hand, neither men nor women 'move' between lineages. The rituals resolve the girl's status with respect to her own natal lineage only, and the exact identity of her 'groom' is unimportant provided it conforms to general, non-hypogamous status requirements. Members of the girl's own matrilineage, especially the men on whom responsibility for her rests, therefore effect the transformation.

These correlations between the identities of officiants at life-crisis rituals, and the socio-structural characteristics of the societies concerned, are not precise. They depend, for example, upon some rather subjective judgements about the 'strength' of unilineality in each case. But one hardly expects any societies, still less such complex and heterogeneous ones as these, to be reducible to mechanistic laws and principles of co-variance. It does at least seem clear that meaningful generalizations can be made as a result of such controlled regional comparisons. It now remains to be seen whether the same can be said regarding the forms, emphases and degrees of elaboration of the rituals themselves.

15
The Overall Pattern

15.1 Exo-Solutions and Endo-Solutions

In Terku Vandanam, the *saḍaṅku*, the *kaliyāṇam*, and the birth of the first child are stages in a single process, which both marks and brings about the passage of a female from infancy to motherhood. At every stage, the enduring chain of alliance is manifest in the choice of functionaries and the system of prestations. Every stage refers back to similar transitions in previous generations, and holds out the promise of others in generations to come. Analysis in these terms has proved applicable to other localities too, as far as the identities of ritual officiants are concerned. The problem now is how to set the particular ritual solution found in Tirunelveli into the context of the very varied Indian and Sri Lankan practices reported in Chapter 11, in order to bring out the essential unity of purpose which, it is argued, underlies them all.

This requires a form of structural analysis which avoids the substantive categories—such as "marriage"—conventionally employed in cross-cultural comparison. That latter approach is less staunchly empirical than it appears, for by labelling each ceremony a "puberty rite" or "wedding", it ends up emphasizing such categorical aspects rather than the particularities of the institution under investigation. Ultimately, such an analysis is founded not on empirical observation but on a typology. Let me reiterate that I use terms such as "wedding" merely as convenient labels, lacking this kind of analytic significance. Moreover, terms such as "patrilineal" and "matrilineal" are used in a polythetic way: the overlap in significant features may often be quite considerable, given the degree of underlying cultural unity across the region, but this is not, and need not be, assumed (cf. also 1.2, above).

Across this region, the various "puberty rites", "*tāli*-tyings", "prepuberty marriages", seclusions, and "weddings" which have been examined are related in an even more profound sense than Yalman

(1963) suggests. They represent different solutions to the same problems, solutions whose differing emphases should correlate with differences in other aspects of social structure. The basic issue, as Yalman says, is the regulation and control of sexuality, purity and reproductive capacity, which is crucial to the maintenance of caste identity but attainable in a variety of ways.

The examples described in Chapter 11 are not isolated ideal-types, however. Different practices shade into one another, and these individual cases are best seen as lying along a continuum of ritual practices and socio-structural forms. As usual when dealing with a continuum, the greatest degree of understanding is achieved by focusing initial attention upon its extremes.

At one of these extremes is the former practice of Tamil Brahmans (see 11.8, above), and many North Indians of whatever caste (Freed and Freed 1980: 404–8), namely pre-puberty marriage for females. There is then no need for a sociologically significant ceremony to mark first menstruation, and a single rite brings about the permanent, monogamous union of the couple concerned. This may be termed the *exo-solution* to the problem, because girls are thereby completely separated from their natal kin, 'physiologically' and/or structurally, long before they reach puberty. Indeed, there is a sense in which Tamil Brahman girls are never fully associated with their natal relatives, given, for example, the mutual non-observance of ritual pollution.

The situation is much the same for married Nambudiri Brahman women, although unlike Tamil Brahmans, Nambudiris do not permit marriages between close cross-relatives. However, only the eldest son of a Nambudiri marries a Nambudiri woman. Many Nambudiri women therefore remain single, at least temporarily, yet Nambudiris have no public puberty rite. Despite the wide discrepancies among the various accounts of Nambudiri practice (11.8, above), there is agreement that, although Nambudiri women may remain unmarried for long periods after biological puberty, no puberty rite is performed for them and they are instead secluded within the household. The purity and probity of unmarried women is safeguarded not by ritual, but by rigid, potentially life-long, seclusion. Some accounts say that such women undergo a form of marriage at their funerals, before their relatives finally lose control over them.

This may be called the *endo-solution*, in the sense that responsibility over the female is not relinquished even in the ritual sense by her natal kin, who instead protect themselves by keeping her a virtual prisoner. It is hardly surprising, incidentally, to find that Brahmans, whose womenfolk are the purest of all, display the two most extreme solutions to the problems of female sexuality.

15.2 The Model

Clearly, female sexual activity may pose a greater potential threat to one set of relatives than to the other. Accordingly, responsibility for directing and supervising that activity is ritually redistributed among her natal and marital relatives, so as to become largely the prerogative of the more threatened group. The labels 'exo-' and 'endo-' thus indicate that responsibility is assigned by the ritual to the girl's marital or natal relatives, respectively.

Empirically, responsibility is most easily observable in the degree of control exerted by these relatives over her conduct. Thus, a Nambudiri spinster is under the exclusive control of her father, and a Tamil Brahman wife is controlled by her husband and father-in-law. This is not a very sensitive criterion, however. It is hard to specify precisely what kind of evidence would enable us to say that one group 'controls' women more than another. Moreover, women necessarily live in one place or the other, and so are for all practical purposes the responsibility of one set of relatives exclusively. There are in effect two mutually exclusive possibilities rather than a continuously variable index.

A further problem is that the ritual which ostensibly marks this transfer of responsibility may take place long before the woman actually moves out of her natal household. This is true to some extent in Terku Vandanam, and is even clearer in cases of pre-puberty marriage, where the child bride generally continues to live with her parents after the ceremony, at least until the onset of puberty. Usually then, the reallocation of jural control over and practical responsibility for the female does not occur gradually during the ritual cycle, but takes place once and for all upon its completion.

The rites themselves accomplish something rather different, namely, the transformation and resolution of her *ethno-physiological status* with respect to her natal and marital relatives, and her future descendants. This process is completed over the puberty-marriage-birth cycle as a whole, except for certain loose ends which arise because affinity persists over time, and which are ultimately resolved, for one generation, by the marriages of the next. In the two polar examples, transformation occurs either all at once (exo-solution) or not at all (endo-solution). In all other cases the process takes several stages, which often emphasize to differing degrees the resolution of her status *vis-à-vis* natal, marital, and descendant relatives.

According to Fuller's formulation (1976: 105; 12.3, above), for example, the first ritual stage is mainly concerned with the status of the girl herself and her natal relatives, the second with the statuses of her spouse and future offspring—the latter being fully secured, in each individual case, by the birth rituals. A strong exo-orientation ought therefore to be associated with an emphasis on the second ritual stage. In such a case, by definition, the female's links with her natal family are clarified (or even severed) at once, so she never poses any threat to them. The danger threatens her marital relatives instead, and it is her wedding, Fuller's 'second marriage', which assuages it. Conversely, a pronounced endo-orientation, whereby a girl remains in her natal home permanently, or for a long time after puberty, places the burden of danger and responsibility upon her natal relatives. It ought therefore to be associated with an emphasis on the puberty rite, Fuller's 'first marriage'.

Fuller's model therefore points to the following conclusion: the greater the exo-orientation, the greater the relative importance and elaboration of the wedding; and the greater the endo-orientation, the more the puberty rite will be emphasized.

However, although my debt to Fuller's analysis is clear, and although it certainly makes sense of the Nayar data for which it was devised, its specific conclusions need not be directly applicable to all other contexts. It emphasizes one particular substantive difference in function, and one particular temporal separation—that between puberty rite and wedding, or, in his terms, between 'first' and 'second' marriages—but the very obvious gap between these stages generally found in 'secular time', may assume less significance, or disappear altogether, in 'ritual time'. Two diachronically separate ritual events may often be better analysed synchronically, as if they were simultaneous (cf. 13.1, above). Furthermore, if the intervals between the two stages are indeed unimportant in the context of the cycle as a whole, they might equally well occur at *any* point in the transformational process. There need not be the neat—though even there, not total—functional separation between first and second stages which Fuller demonstrates for the Nayar case. In short, one cannot simply view the cycle as a rite of passage in which the puberty rite represents 'separation' and the wedding 'aggregation'.

If so, why then is the cycle so frequently divided up into two stages, despite the wide differences in the distribution of constituent elements between them? This seems unanswerable on purely ritual grounds, and the solution may lie elsewhere.

Pre-puberty marriage has never been current among most non-Brahman Tamils. In Terku Vandanam, marriage under the age of 18 is disapproved of even for mature girls. Arranging a marriage is, moreover, a lengthy and fraught business, especially when the two families are not closely related. The actual wedding is costly, too. Most Sadanku expenses are recouped through the *moy* collection, but at a Kaliyanam the bride's father must provide a substantial *sīdaṉam*, without any *moy* receipts to offset this expenditure. It should be handed over at the Kaliyanam itself, and although in practice there may be some delay, most of the cash involved has to be saved, earned, realized, or borrowed before a girl's father can embark upon her marriage.

Marriage, then, is not something to be rushed through in a few days, after one's daughter begins to menstruate. And yet *something* has to be done: a sexually mature female cannot just go on living in her father's house as if nothing had happened.[1] The fact that the ritual has two stages appears, from this perspective, to be a kind of compromise between the exigencies of purity and status requirements, and more practical considerations. One does just enough to provide temporary prophylaxis against the contagious pollution and accumulating sin[2] which the girl's menarche would otherwise release into the midst of her family. One is then free to seek a permanent solution, at a leisurely, dignified, and careful pace more in keeping with the importance of the decisions involved.

Whether this particular rationalization seems plausible or not, it is reasonable to assume that the types of relationship given most emphasis at the very start of the ritual cycle will be those which are most crucial from the viewpoint of the relatives as a whole. A study

[1] A Nambudiri-type total seclusion is of course impractical for less wealthy people, who need their daughters to work in the fields or the home. Even for Nambudiris it is only a last resort if the girl has not married.

[2] The sin arises from the monthly death of the menstruating girl's ovum, which has been denied the chance of life by her non-involvement in legitimate sexual intercourse (see 11.8, above).

of the initial stages of the ritual cycles should therefore provide a flexible index of comparison, closely related to the notions of control and responsibility discussed above, but more easily evaluated.

Of any two societies, that in which the "wife" and/or "mother" is more directly crucial to the status or purity of her marital relatives and their descendants, should place more initial emphasis upon resolving her status *vis-à-vis* those marital relatives. It is therefore to be expected that patrilineal groups will stress the ritual resolution of status *vis-à-vis* affines, while matrilineal groups stress control by, and resolution of status with respect to, natal relatives. Bilineal or non-lineal groups should come somewhere in between. These stresses should be evident even in association with *de facto* (sense 3) unilineality, but should become even more pronounced in connection with categorical (sense 1) or *de jure* (sense 2) descent (cf. 1.2, above).

Lineality is not the only relevant factor. For example, hypergamy places yet greater stress upon the status of the status-bearing spouse. Moreover, all things being equal, the dangers and responsibilities facing natal relatives ought to be greater, and ritual resolution of their status more important, in societies with uxorilocal rather than virilocal residence. Finally, inheritance patterns, too, are likely to be relevant.

Exactly what *kind* of evidence is relevant here? I argued that a pronounced emphasis upon the puberty rite at the expense of the wedding, is not *in itself* evidence that the cycle is oriented towards natal relatives, although it may be suggestive in this regard. Nor is a strong cultural resemblance between puberty rite and wedding the only possible indication of an exo-bias. What is important is the extent to which the initial rite emphasizes affinal relationships, especially of those genealogical types associated, for the group concerned, with legitimate or ideal sexual unions. The greater this emphasis, the greater the exo-orientation. With this in mind, we can turn to a re-examination of the empirical data.

15.3 Application of the Model

The *tāli* rite of Nayar aristocrats (11.6, above) has obvious similarities to Brahmanic pre-puberty marriage, but this resemblance is superficial. The girl is merely united in a fictive sense to an individual with whom no prior relationship of affinity exists, and with whom her connection remains tenuous in comparison with the endo-link to her natal *taravād*, even if, as is by no means always the case, she subsequently forms a *sambandham* relationship with her erstwhile *tāli*-tier.

As Fuller says, the *tāli*-rite is really far more concerned with regularizing her position with respect to her natal kin, than with doing likewise for their affines. Nayar aristocrats therefore lie very close to the endo-pole of the continuum. There are, however, *two* ritual stages to be considered. Although the emphasis lies heavily upon the *tāli*-rite, the subsequent ritual inauguration of the *sambandham* relationship strikes some balance between natal and marital relatives, showing that these Nayars do lie some small distance along the continuum, away from the endo-pole itself.

Sudra Nayars give greater emphasis to diachronic affinity than their aristocratic caste-fellows. The *tāli*-tier is much more likely to be an affine (*inaṅkar*), and to become a *sambandham* partner of the woman concerned. Hypergamous *sambandham* is comparatively rare, because Sudras are far more numerous than aristocrats and other higher-ranked groups, but it remains a theoretical possibility. Several simultaneous *sambandham* liaisons are possible, but each must be with a member of a different exogamous group. This is because the affinal links between the lineages of the *sambandham* partners are usually reciprocal and lack the relativistic marriage-concubinage character of the corresponding Nambudiri-Nayar relationship.[3] All in all, the endo-orientation of Sudra Nayars, though strong, is less extreme than that of the aristocrats. Given that both Nayar groups are matrilineal, and that residence is natolocal for the *sambandham* partners and matri-avunculocal for their off-spring, the strong endo-emphasis is hardly surprising.

The 'token marriage' of the Central Indian groups assigns the crucial role of bearer of the inanimate 'bridegroom' to a man who is a potential spouse of the puberal girl, in the classificatory sense at least. Moreover, this 'token marriage' almost exactly mimics the wedding. These points suggest a relatively weak, but distinct, exo-orientation. The field of possible husbands is specified with some precision.

Affinity plays a more direct part in the Terku Vandanam Sadanku, where a living affine participates as 'bridegroom'. Moreover, by

[3] To be precise, the *tālikaṭṭu* ceremony involves the permanent affines of the girl's *taravād* as a whole (i.e. their *inaṅkars*), whereas *sambandham* inaugurations involve individually focused, temporary 'affinal' links.

emphasizing the *urimai* relationship, the Sadanku narrows down the affinal focus and makes it more genealogically specific. This activation of the *urimai* link increases, at least in the ritual context, the involvement of close affines in a girl's marital arrangements, even if the *urimai* preference itself is not ultimately adhered to. This also points to a greater exo-orientation.

The examples dealt with so far pose few problems. We turn now to two less clear-cut cases, those of Kandyan Sinhalese and Piramalai Kallars. As a group in which females are subject to relatively weak control in sexual matters, a state of affairs doubtless connected with the degree of economic independence which the bilateral inheritance of land often affords them, Sinhalese might be expected to lie midway between the endo- and exo-extremes. The emphasis upon affinal links in the puberty rite, and the degree of elaboration of the wedding, ought therefore to be greater than in either Nayar case, but less than for Terku Vandanam or the Central Indian groups.

Kandyan puberty rites confirm the first prediction quite well. There is a distinct and fairly specific affinal content. Whereas only diffuse relationships of inter-group affinity come into play during Sudra Nayar *tāli*-rites, the affines involved or invoked here have specific genealogical links with the girl herself. In particular, her MB participates, and the identity of her future husband is often revealed.

Generalization about weddings is more difficult, not only because of the wide variations from area to area, but also because—even within each area—weddings range from the highly ostentatious to the non-existent. There is also the complication that residence may be viri- or uxorilocal, in itself indicative of a central position on the continuum. It seems reasonable to assume that *binna* (uxorilocal) weddings will generally be less elaborate, because the wife continues to live in her natal home and is neither the responsibility of, nor even in regular contact with, her marital relations. All being equal, *dīga* (virilocal) marriage seems likely to require a more elaborate ceremony in view of the closer relationship between the wife and her marital relatives thereafter. Neither Yalman (1971) nor Leach (1961*b*; 1982) say specifically that this is so, although it seems implicit in many of their comments. It might also be expected on purely pragmatic grounds, too. After all, *binna* marriages involve grooms from poor families, who could not afford elaborate weddings anyway, whereas *dīga* unions include cases where the groom's family are engaging in status-climbing.

The richer the family, the more likely it is to have an elaborate wedding, and to follow the South Indian pattern whereby land is inherited exclusively by sons, and daughters merely receive movable property as dowries (Yalman 1971: 132). It is also more likely to have, or have adopted, patrilineal *vasagama* pedigrees (Yalman 1960: 88, 107). *Within* the Kandyan context, then, a greater emphasis on patrilineality goes hand in hand with greater elaboration of the second stage of the ritual cycle. Both tendencies are consistent with increasing exo-orientation. This case therefore fits the overall paradigm internally, as well as externally.

Given the pronounced patrilineality of Piramalai Kallars, one would expect either a strong, genealogically specific affinal component in the puberty rite, or a tendency for the collapsing of the two stages into one, or both. The toing and froing at a Kallar wedding, much of which takes place at the bride's house, and which involves acts performed at the Sadanku in Terku Vandanam, does indeed suggest a tendency for the second stage to take over some of the functions associated elsewhere with the first, but is hardly conclusive. It is at least clear that Kallars have a greater exo-orientation than Sinhalese. Their respective puberty rites have similar structures, and both involve the MB, but the extravagant prestations expected of him in the Kallar case differentiate the two. On the other hand, Kallar puberty rites do not in any way resemble weddings.

Kallars thus express their exo-bias quite differently from the Tirunelveli or Central Indian groups. Another aspect of this is their practice of circumcising adolescent boys. What are the implications of the fact that Kallars have in effect a *male* as well as a female puberty rite? Brahmans also have such rites, of course, in the form of the tying of the sacred thread (see 11.8, above). Although this has no overt connection with physical puberty, it does mark the acquisition of twice-born adult status (Stevenson 1971: 27; Subramaniam 1974: 52). It is consistent with Yalman's (1963) argument that patrilineal groups should display an interest in male puberty too, as the male is clearly the principal status-transmitting parent in such cases. For example, Tamil Brahmans display the rudiments of a system of patrilineal hypergamy. In short, I suggest that Kallar patrilineality manifests itself more in their treatment of male, than female sexuality.

Coorgs, too, are strongly patrilineal, so it comes as no surprise to find that they have a male initiation ritual, the ear-boring ceremony. Like Kallars, their marriage ceremony involves several movements back and forth between the homes of the bride and groom, keeping their respective families largely apart. If the amount of space Srinivas devotes to them can be taken as evidence, the emphasis seems very much on the wedding rather than the girl's puberty rite. Even the male ear-boring seems more important than the latter. In short, there is an even stronger emphasis on the second stage of the female puberty–marriage cycle than in the Kallar case, and—despite its less exotic nature—a similar tendency to stress male at the expense of female sexual maturity.

Finally, Batticaloa Tamils are matrilineal, and marriage is monogamous and isogamous. Couples live uxorilocally, but the wife's parents move out, leaving the couple in possession of her share of the estate. Overall, they seem to fall in between *binna* Sinhalese and Sudra Nayars, so the extent to which affines participate in puberty rites ought also to be intermediate.

The female cross-cousin of a Batticaloa girl is involved in her puberty rite, as in Terku Vandanam, but as a 'companion' rather than a 'groom'. Moreover, her genealogical identity is not specified, so it is merely her terminological category which is relevant. Even this cannot be said of all female participants in the rite: they are required to be auspicious, married women with living husbands, but their precise identities are not important. Officiants are not exclusively drawn from members, or wives of members, of the girl's matrilineage, and need not even be relatives (McGilvray 1982*b*: 36). Wedding officiants are not precisely specified either, though the MBW/FZ may be involved.

This evidence seems to conform to expectations. On one hand, Batticaloa Tamils attach far more importance than Nayars to affinal relationships, not only ritually but also in the more conventional relationship between H and W thereafter. On the other hand, although the puberty rite resembles the Sadanku in form, 'affinity' is not only more vaguely defined than in Terku Vandanam but much less important. The officiants can equally well be 'kin' or 'affines'—however one chooses to apply these epithets to women in matrilineal contexts! Even Sinhalese are more concerned with involving specific affines (*māmā*, *nenda*) in their rites, and so are closer to the exo-pole.

15.4 Conclusions

As the exo-orientation increases, in other words as the ritual cycle—particularly its first stage, the 'puberty rite'—puts more emphasis upon resolution of the girl's status *vis-à-vis* her marital relatives, the affinal role in the puberty rite becomes greater, and more genealogically precise. An increasing exo-orientation is also associated with more pronounced patrilineality, a greater stress on the giving of dowry, and an increasing tendency for post-marital residence to be viri-patrilocal. The second stage of the cycle, the 'wedding', may become more elaborate relative to the first, and may ultimately absorb it entirely. Matrilineal and patrilineal hypergamy, respectively, become more likely as one approaches the endo- and exo-poles. Finally, among strongly patrilineal groups a male puberty rite co-exists with, or even replaces, the female-oriented ceremonies found in most instances. Figure 15.1 displays the relative orientations of the various societies considered, in the light of the foregoing discussion.

In the last few chapters, many seemingly diverse practices involving the legitimation or control of female sexuality have been examined. It was argued that all are concomitants of the caste system, and the concern to maintain unambiguous caste identity. Some of the reported cultural differences are purely contingent, in that alternative but equally felicitous and efficacious procedures are used to achieve similar aims. On the other hand, the studied groups differ in key socio-structural respects, with regard to lineality, isogamy, rules of residence, inheritance, and so on. These structural differences seem to correlate fairly well with changes in the emphases and purposes of the various stages in the overall ritual cycle.

It would be interesting to know how widely this model can be applied within the South Asian region. The practices of Muslims and Christians are likely to be of great interest, while North India seems strongly exo-oriented, and sociologically significant female puberty rites are generally absent. This wider project cannot be undertaken here, partly because much of the necessary field-research remains to be done. However, by confining discussion to the South Indian and Sri Lankan region—wherein, despite obvious linguistic and other differences, there are clear uniformities in social structure—it has proved possible to carry forward the project initiated by Dumont (1983 [1961*a*]: 132), of showing how, and to what extent, Nayar

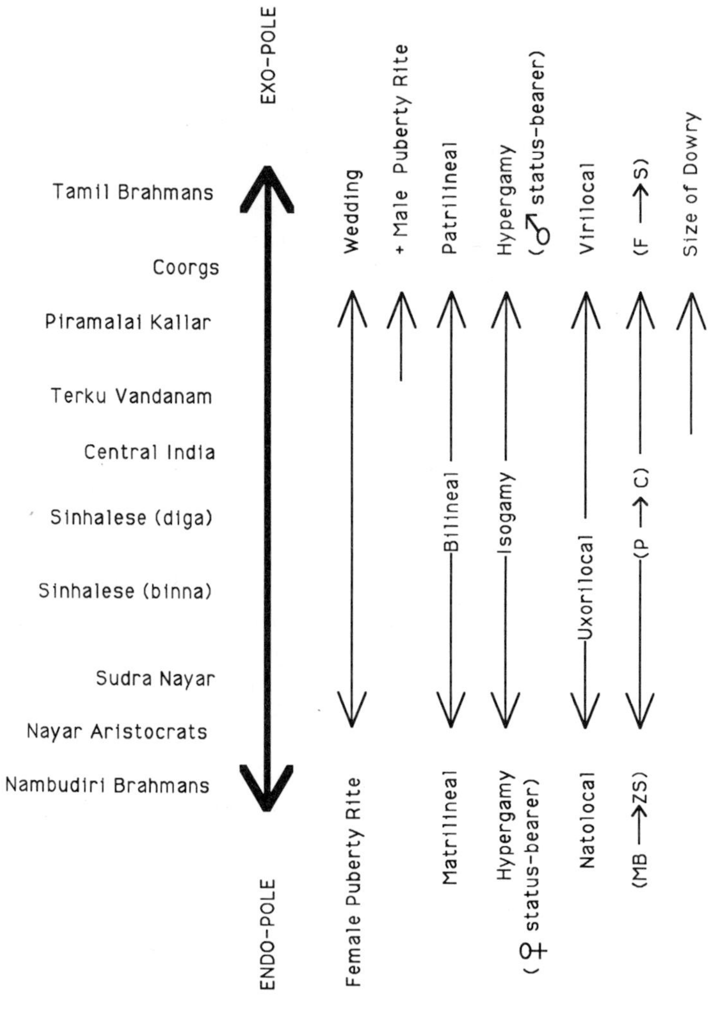

FIG. 15.1 The Endo-/Exo-Continuum in South India and Sri Lanka

tāli-tyings and Terku Vandanam Sadankus can, indeed, both be seen as genuinely *Indian* facts.

More generally, I hope also to have demonstrated the potential of controlled regional comparison. Such comparative syntheses are becoming increasingly necessary to the advancement of anthropological study, particularly in regions lying within the orbit of major literate civilizations. It is, however, worth repeating that this analysis, though based upon structural features, differs from earlier structural-functional approaches in that the indices of comparison are polythetically, rather than substantively, defined.

As explained earlier (12.2), such structural studies are necessary precursors to any interpretative, culturally oriented analysis. Now that the underlying socio-structural unity of the region has been demonstrated, however, it is justifiable to attempt an analysis of the latter, currently more fashionable, type. Most previous writing in this vein has taken an ethno-physiological approach to kinship, procreation and social identity, but in the final chapter I shall try instead to shed light on human puberty and marriage rites by comparing them to the marriage ceremonies of Hindu gods.

16
Divine Marriage

16.1 Introduction

The discussion so far has adopted a structural and sociological perspective, in order first to justify and then to conduct the desired regional comparison. This final chapter is intended to shed a rather different light on rituals of puberty and marriage by describing the wedding ceremonies of Hindu deities, and considering their cultural significance.[1]

Indigenous South Asian theories about marriageability and reproductive processes are very varied, and are often self-contradictory even within a single locality (see 12.2, above). The ideas to be dealt with in the present chapter have a rather better claim to transcend the bewildering diversity of opinions and practices found within the region. For obvious reasons the ritual details of divine weddings prove, as we shall see, to be most directly comparable with the marriages of Brahmans (see 11.8, above). At a deeper level, though, such ceremonies are of significance for *all* southern Hindus and Buddhists.[2] After all, the myths and rituals associated with the presiding deities of the large Brahmanic temples which are so important a feature of urban South India, are directed not at particular castes or localities, but at all worshippers, whatever their social and geographical background.

16.2 Temple Worship

In many South Indian temples, the marriage of the presiding deity is the highlight of the ritual cycle and a key episode in local mythology

[1] For a complete description of these ceremonies, setting them more fully into mythological context, see Good 1989.

[2] Buddhists in Sri Lanka worship Hindu deities too. On these grounds at least, it therefore seems justifiable to extend the following interpretation to the Sinhalese also.

(cf. Shulman 1980: 138). I shall illustrate this by describing the annual wedding rituals in the temple at Kalugumalai, a town some 30 miles north-west of Terku Vandanam.

Below a hill at the edge of Kalugumalai town is a temple to Kalukacalamurtti—a form of Murukan, the younger son of Siva (Fig. 16.1). The temple liturgy, of a fairly standard Saivite kind, is performed by a lineage of hereditary Brahman Priests (*paṭṭar*), helped by four Temple Servants (*paricārakar*), and a Chanter (*sāṣtiri*) of Sanskrit scriptures. Other staff include a Singer (*ōduvār*) of Tamil hymns, and various Musicians.

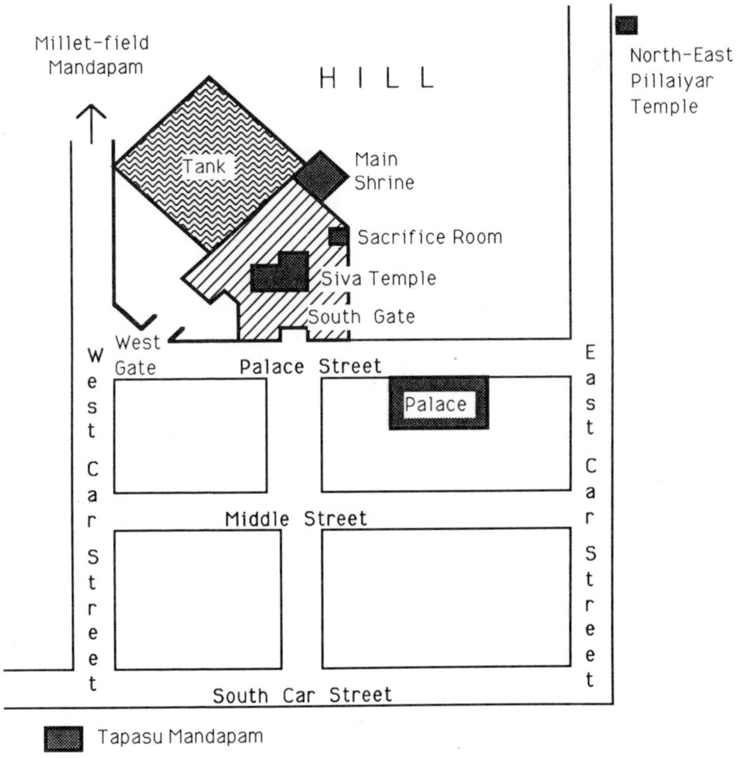

FIG. 16.1 Kalugumalai and its Temple

Temple worship focuses on the stone images (*mūla mūrtti*) of the gods, especially the Main Image of Murukan himself, whose shrine is a cave in the hill. Temple worship (*pūja*) includes six services every day, and many periodic festivals.[3] Vinayakar, Siva, and Akilandisvari—who all occupy a separate temple within the main building—are worshipped at the start of every service, and Murukan at the end. Vinayakar is another name for Pillaiyar, Murukan's elephant-headed elder brother. As explained earlier (Ch. 8 n. 2, above), he is always worshipped before auspicious events. Siva is of course their father, and Akilandisvari is the local name of Siva's wife, Parvati.

Important deities also have bronze Festival Images (*uṛsava mūrtti*) which are used in processions. Another relevant feature of the liturgy is that Siva and Murukan cohabit with their consorts each night. Special images of the gods and goddesses are carried to their respective bedchambers before the temple closes, and returned to their shrines next morning.

16.3 The Kanda Sasti Festival

Two weddings are held each year in Kalugumalai temple, at the Kanda Sasti and Pankuni Uttiram festivals. Kanda Sasti, which happens in November, enacts the story of Murukan's war with the *Sūraṉ* demons, the forces of disorder who continually menace the universe (Dessigane and Pattabiramin 1967; Clothey 1983: 93–4).[4]

16.3.1 *The Myth*

The gods beg Siva to father a child who will destroy Surapadma, king of the Surans. Six sparks fall from Siva's third eye, and are carried off by Agni (Fire) and Vayu (Wind), to be immersed in the Ganges. Nymphs find six babies there, which combine into one child with six heads. Siva and Parvati claim him, and his six heads merge into one. They present their son Murukan with a lance, and the gods anoint

[3] Details of the structure of daily worship, and a summary of the complex festival calendar, are included in Good 1987*a*.

[4] The version of the myth given here is based primarily not on printed textual versions, but on 27 narrative paintings displayed in Kalugumalai temple itself.

and worship him. Two goddesses resolve to wed him, and meditate to gain spiritual power (*tapasu*).

Murukan kills Tarakan, Surapadma's elephant-headed brother. Surapadma himself refuses to submit, even when Murukan fights and kills the remaining Surans. He disguises himself as a tree, but Murukan splits it with his lance. Surapadma repents and begs for pardon, so the god turns him into a peacock, Murukan's vehicle, and a cock, the emblem on his battle flag. Murukan then marries Deyvayanai, daughter of god Indra. Later, he meets the tribal girl, Valli, as she guards the millet harvest. He saves her from a wild elephant in return for a promise of marriage.

16.3.2 *The Battle against the Surans*

The Kanda Sasti festival begins with Murukan's coronation (*makuṭāpisēkam*; Good 1987*b*). Next day, at a Vinayakar temple north-east of the hill, the officiating festival Priest worships the earth goddess, Budevi, collects a pot of soil, and brings it back to the temple's Sacrifice Room (*yākasālai*; cf. Brunner-Lachaux 1968: pl. 1–6). The main deities are represented by pots of consecrated water (*kumpam*) on the central platform of this room. The Priest sows nine kinds of seed in nine small trays, using the earth from outside. He places these on another platform, around a pot representing Brahma, god of creation. The trays are covered, so that the seedlings grow in darkness throughout the festival.

On each of the next five mornings and evenings, there is a fire sacrifice in this room. Murukan then meets the Surans, represented by huge papier mâché models carried by hereditary dancers, and asks them, in vain, to release the gods. All of them then go in procession round the town.

On the fifth morning Murukan slays Tarakan. A wooden elephant head is impaled on a lance and a prone devotee, representing the Suran, is carried thrice around Murukan's Festival Image. On the sixth night, Murukan kills the other Surans, ending with Surapadma. The peacock vehicle on which the Festival Image is riding is then uncovered, a white cock is freed, and a temple servant, in the role of the reformed Suran, circles three times around Murukan to worship him.

16.3.3 Deyvayanai's Wedding

Next morning the Main Image is anointed, using the water-pots from the Sacrifice Room. It is then draped with the seedlings grown there, and worshipped elaborately.

That evening Deyvayanai meditates in a Hall at the south-west corner of town, to gain the power (*tapasu*) needed to win her groom. Murukan is carried there on a silver peacock for their first glimpse (*kāṭci*) of each other. Garlands are exchanged and Deyvayanai goes round him three times, clockwise.

Next evening, Deyvayanai goes round town in the bride's procession (*peṇ alaippu*), and is then given an unction named *kaḍirviḷippu puṇṇiyākavāsaṉam*, after the ceremony performed when a Brahman girl reaches puberty (cf. 11.8, above).

Murukan and Deyvayanai are put on a swing and their garlands are exchanged three times. They are moved to the Wedding Hall. Deyvayanai's dowry, a set of silver ornaments, is put in front of Murukan. A pair of silver slippers represent Murukan during the rite, and two silver pots represent the couple. The Priest ties the *tāli* round Deyvayanai's neck. He puts the slippers on a grindstone near the sacrificial fire. Two Servants carry the silver Pots thrice around the fire, touching them against the slippers each time. This represents the 'seven steps' ritual (see 11.8, above). The couple are then worshipped.

16.4 Pankuni Uttiram and Valli's Wedding

The Pankuni Uttiram festival is in March. The earth-bringing and seed-sprouting rites are similar to those at Kanda Sasti. There is no coronation, but the festival begins with a complex flag-raising ritual at the temple Flagstaff. On every morning and evening for the next nine days there is a fire sacrifice, offerings are made to altars out in the streets, and the Festival Images go out in procession. The climax comes on the ninth day, when thousands of worshippers haul the Images around the streets in the huge wooden temple car.

On the tenth night there is a ritual sponsored by the local Veduvar tribal community, to which Valli is said to have belonged. At a Millet-field (*tiṉaippuṉam*) Hall north-west of the hill, Valli and

Murukan have their first glimpse of each other, garlands are exchanged, and Valli is taken clockwise around Murukan. Next evening Murukan marries Valli in a rite almost identical to his earlier marriage to Deyvayanai.

16.5 Human and Divine Weddings

There are obvious close similarities between Murukan's weddings and those of Tamil Brahmans, in both broad structure and ritual detail. These resemblances are reciprocal, because all brides and grooms are temporarily deified during their weddings, which are partly acts of worship towards them. I shall compare human and divine weddings briefly, and then consider the two divine marriages themselves.

Murukan's weddings begin with the bride's procession and her puberty ceremony. At Brahman weddings it is the groom who goes in procession: moreover, as Brahman brides formerly reached puberty only after marriage, the timing of Deyvayanai's menstrual purification is strange. There is no such anomaly for the tribal girl Valli, who would be expected to have attained puberty before marriage.

The exchange of garlands between god and goddess on the swing clearly corresponds to the Brahman betrothal ceremony. At Brahman weddings seeds are placed in trays and watered, whereas in the temple this is done at the very start of the festival. The imagery of fertility is clearly appropriate in both cases.

One crucial stage of a Brahman wedding—'giving a virgin' by pouring water over the couple's hands—is completely absent from divine weddings at Kalugumalai, although it does occur at the marriage of the goddess Minaksi in Madurai temple (C. J. Fuller, pers. com.). The *tāli*-tying and seven steps around the sacrificial fire happen just as at a Brahman wedding, however.

Most differences between the two divine weddings themselves are minor, and purely contingent. The different circumstances of the couples' initial meetings are more significant, but in order to appreciate why Valli's meditation occurs out in the wilderness, we must first understand the significance of divine marriage in general. In particular, why do gods so often have *two* wives, one of whom is autochthonous to the territory in which the temple is sited?

16.6 The Significance of Divine Marriage

Every South Indian temple marks the site of a unique manifestation of divinity (Shulman 1980), and has its own myth (*ṣtalapurāṇam*) describing the coming of the deity and the subsequent history of the shrine. Deities are therefore strongly localized, and yet insulated from the impure violence of worldly life by the protection of the temple walls. But whereas the power of a shrine arises from its isolation, it becomes accessible to devotees only in so far as that isolation is breached. The various mythical resolutions of this paradox reflect a theologically complex set of ideas about the source of divine power.

Classically, power was seen as arising from sacrifice, which forcibly induced the process of creation (Gonda 1970: 27). In particular, the power of shrines was seen as stemming from the god's sacrifice by the goddess, from whom he was later reborn. Later, in Shulman's view, the rise of Tamil devotionalism (*bhakti*) made it impossible for deities to be explicitly tainted in this way, and led to a decline in the sacrificial nature of worship (1980: 92). By contrast, Biardeau argues that violence is only superficially eradicated from Tamil shrines, so that worship remains essentially sacrificial (1976: 139–40).[5]

The difficulty presented by sacrificial violence is resolved in Hindu mythology and iconography largely by means of divisions and duplications in the divine pantheon. Its most basic division—into male and female, Siva and *sakti*—seems at first sight to provide a straightforward explanation for the importance of divine marriage. The violence of sacrifice can thereby, it seems, be replaced by the nightly cohabitation of god and goddess, allowing creation to be portrayed more acceptably, as divine sexual intercourse within wedlock. Things are actually less simple, however, as the mythical permutations of divine marriage show. In many shrines, for example, the goddess is portrayed as autochthonous, and therefore identified with both fertility and death (Shulman 1980: 139). This duality is often resolved by means of a further bifurcation, whereby Siva

[5] More radically, Fuller (1988: 24) argues that whatever its historical origins, *pūja*, the central act of temple worship, is nowadays clearly distinguished conceptually from sacrifices (*bali*) such as the offerings to the street altars during Pankuni Uttiram, which have only secondary importance in contemporary Hindu liturgy.

acquires *two* wives, one benevolent and passive, the other violent and capricious, but also fertile and maternal (pp. 267–8).

Orthodox sexual intercourse would diminish her powers, so this creatrix must still kill her spouse in order to give birth to him again (p. 224). Siva's roles, too, tend therefore to be subdivided, and a 'demon-devotee' is sacrificed in his place. This surrogate, who gained power through devotion but misused it, is thereby led to a truer devotion no longer linked to the lust for power. The fate of the demon thus expresses the potential incompatibility of power and purity (p. 348).

This is further illustrated by the case of the goddess. In some myths purity triumphs in the form of a virgin goddess, epitomizing 'power sealed within limits' (p. 349). This rarely provides a satisfactory solution to the mythical dilemma, however, because it is ultimately sterile. More usually the myths tell how the shrine is eventually breached by eroticism, and the chaste virgin reluctantly marries (pp. 144–66).

In fact, although virgin goddesses are indeed particularly powerful, the Tamil notion of chastity (*kaṟpu*) covers marital fidelity too. Mythical expressions of divine chastity therefore also include many stories of goddesses whose devotion to their husbands or husbands-to-be is put to the test (pp. 157–8), as when the two goddesses meditate to win Murukan's hand. Other myths stress the power of the shrine, personified by a sexually active goddess or a bride who slays her demon lover, as in the myth of the goddess and the buffalo-demon (Shulman 1980: 176, 234). Here her eroticism and violence are emphasized.

Collectively, these myths present a closed cycle. Purity brings power, but exercise of that power diminishes purity: conversely, power is potentially impure and violent, and must be restrained.

16.7 Murukan's Weddings

Many of these general points apply directly or indirectly to Murukan. Firstly, his localization is emphasized to an unusual degree. There are conventionally said to be six Murukan temples, each associated with a particular event in his life. Five of these are major contemporary pilgrimage centres, but the sixth has no single site, and is represented by every hilltop in the entire Tamil region, including, of course, the hill at Kalugumalai. Secondly, the Surans at Kanda Sasti are archetypal 'demon-devotees'. The similarities between Surapadma and Murukan,[6] and their final hierarchical identification, hint that yet again the real sacrificial victim is god himself.

Murukan also has unique features, though, which allow him to transcend the divisions and duplications discussed above. The central shrine of every temple is a locus of bounded creative power, hence its name 'womb-chamber' (*garbhagṛha* in Sanskrit). This is emphasized in Siva temples by his representation as a phallic *liṅkam*, but his unimaginably great power is normally accessible to devotees only via his wife, as *sakti*. In temples like that of Minaksi at Madurai, on the other hand, it is the autochthonous goddess who possesses excessive creative powers, which only her marriage tames and regulates (Shulman 1980: 141). Thus, Minaksi was born with three breasts, representing an excess of dangerous feminine power (cf. 9.6, above). She set out to conquer the world, only for her third breast to disappear when she met her future husband Siva on the battle field (Shulman 1980: 192–211; Dessigane, *et al.* 1960: 1; Fuller 1984: 1).

In contrast to both these cases, Murukan combines the power of his father Siva with the *sakti* of his mother Parvati, which is represented in iconography and myth by his lance. Goddesses too can be asked to assist with worldly problems, but clearly a male who also embodies *sakti* is a culturally more manageable entity, a more fitting object of male *bhakti*, than an unsubmissive female displaying violence and aggression. This helps explain Murukan's enormous popularity in the region.

Local legend states that Murukan's image once occupied the Kalugumalai shrine all alone, but his wives had to be added to moderate its intense power (*The Hindu*, 1 May 1988). Clearly this is one important purpose of his two divine weddings.

Both of Murukan's wives are really daughters of Visnu. One is reborn as Deyvayanai in the court of Indra, whose elephant brings her up. Her marriage is arranged by Indra in orthodox fashion, once Murukan has shown his worthiness by defeating the Surans. The other goddess, Valli, is born into a furrow as the child of a doe, and is raised by forest hunters. She is glimpsed by Murukan as she guards the crops, and seized by him against the initial opposition of her

[6] Each has an elephant-headed brother, for instance.

tribal father (Dessigane and Pattabiramin 1967: 221; Shulman 1980: 281–2; Clothey 1978: 84). Valli is thus clearly autochthonous, yet it is her timidity rather than her ferocity which is emphasized. As for Deyvayanai, she is also known as Deyvasena ('army of the gods'), indicating her fierce nature. Just as Murukan conflates Siva and *sakti*, so therefore do Deyvayanai and Valli conflate the two goddess personae described earlier.

Consequently, although one would expect the weddings of Deyvayanai and Valli to be 'orthodox' and 'unorthodox', respectively, given the apparent social identities of the two brides, the two ceremonies are actually very similar. At both Kanda Sasti and Pankuni Uttiram, the earth-goddess is worshipped, and the fertility of the territory is encapsulated in the seedlings grown during the festival. This fertility is explicitly linked with Murukan and *both* his wives, who are all draped in seedlings during the unctions before each marriage.

Tamils regard Parvati as Visnu's sister (Fuller 1984: 7), so Siva and Visnu are brothers-in-law and the goddesses are Murukan's cross-cousins (MBDs)—pre-eminently marriageable. Finally, the earth goddess, Budevi, is a wife of Lord Visnu, and hence Murukan's mother-in-law. In all these ways, Murukan establishes his connection with, and sovereignty over, the local territory, while simultaneously reaffirming Siva and Visnu as archetypal affinal relatives. Not surprisingly, this view of the relationship between the two great gods is characteristically and uniquely South Indian.

16.8 The Social Context

So divine marriages both mimic human ceremonies, and reveal some of the most potent cosmological notions of southern Hinduism. They can therefore help us understand the meanings of the rituals practised in contemporary society.

The link being proposed here, between temple weddings and human views on marriage, sexuality, and fertility, is not merely an analytical imposition from the outside. S. B. Daniel has shown, for example, how the different relationships between Siva and his consort, as portrayed in famous southern temples, are used by some Tamils to epitomize certain types of relationship between mortal husbands and wives (1980: 64). Thus, the superiority of Siva in Chidambaram temple points to the superiority enjoyed as of right by the husband. The case of Minaksi hints, however, that this is mere public show, and that women exercise the true power behind the scenes. A third view, which cites androgynous forms of Siva like that found, for example, in Sankarankovil temple near Kalugumalai, is that neither partner enjoys a monopoly of good qualities, so that marriage ideally involves a proper balance between the two. Any or all of these divine exemplars might be invoked by Daniel's informants —depending on the context—to explain, justify, or criticize the behaviour of themselves or others (1980: 85).

Moreover, as mentioned briefly at the start (1.3, above), Tamils distinguish clearly between four particular female statuses (Reynolds 1980: 36): (1) virgin (*kaṉṉi*), having capricious but auspicious power; (2) married woman (*sumaṅkali*), epitomizing auspicious power and fertility; (3) barren woman (*malaṭi*), inauspicious and potentially malevolent; and (4) widow (*vitavai*), with capricious, highly inauspicious power. Female power is thus seen as capricious if not controlled by men, but this has two aspects. A virgin's power is very auspicious, whereas that of a widow—who 'escapes' male control after the death (= sacrifice?) of her husband—is quite the reverse. A similar dichotomy is apparent among women who *are* under male control. Just as *sakti* is essential for realizing the power of the god, so is a wife vital to male social status. On the other hand, a barren wife prevents full expression of her husband's status and power (barrenness is always blamed on her, of course).

Reynolds postulates a straightforward congruence between human and divine female roles. She argues that married women and virgins correspond, respectively, to goddesses like Minaksi, who bestow well-being, and to village goddesses who both inflict and cure suffering. Barren women and widows correspond to demons, detrimental to human welfare (1980: 37). This rather crudely Durkheimian view of Hinduism separates the two aspects of the goddess's nature, associating her benevolence with Brahmanic worship and her ferocity with the worship of village goddesses. Such a position seems untenable in the light of Shulman's work, however.

In general, goddesses do not statically embody benevolent or demonic qualities; rather, different traits come to the fore at different times during their mythical histories. Indeed, these tensions are essential to the mythology's demonstration that divine creative power can be an ordering moral force only when properly controlled. For example, Minaksi's power threatened the cosmos until it was tamed by her marriage to Siva.

Likewise, the fertility of women is dangerous unless it is properly controlled and regulated by men. The four roles are not alternatives, but *stages* in the lives of all women. All begin adulthood as virgins; all should marry; in every marriage barrenness is an initial cause for anxiety; and every woman should outlive her husband. Indeed, the rituals which we have been studying serve, precisely, to mark and effect transitions from one such stage to the next.

Preservation of caste identity is crucial to social life, so female sexual relationships must be strictly regulated. This is universally true, but just as the myths offer different solutions to the problem of creative sacrifice, so different South Indian groups control female sexuality in ways congruent with other aspects of social structure.

Puberal girls are secluded until their newly acquired fertility can be properly controlled by means of rites which often mimic marriage. This suggests the mythic theme of the sealed shrine, which only the god/husband may safely breach. The allusion seems even clearer for those Nambudiri Brahman girls who are confined within their natal households throughout life. Conversely, like Minaksi whose marriage prevented the untrammelled exercise of her power, Tamil Brahman girls used to be married before the onset of puberty. Responsibility for their sexuality was thereby transferred to their husbands, and their potentially dangerous power was circumscribed in advance.

Throughout their lives, the socio-sexual status of South Indian women is publicly and permanently displayed by styles of dress, in a way that is simply not true of men. An immature girl wears a blouse and skirt, whereas a biologically and/or socially mature woman wears a sari in colours denoting auspiciousness and fertility. Saris are publicly presented to her by potential or actual marriage partners, first by her MB as 'principal affine' and later by her husband, who may of course also be her MB, and is in any case terminologically equated with one for most people in Terku Vandanam. Wifely status is marked by the wearing of the *tāli*. Once donned, this is never removed until her husband's death, when a woman adopts the white clothing and unkempt appearance of a widow. In short, the everyday clothing of all females—first donned in the course of ritual—serves to define and limit their behaviour and their potentiality.

These spectacular and expensive rituals thus serve to display, celebrate, control, or transfer the sexuality of South Indian women. Since women—again unlike men—are defined socially primarily in terms of that sexuality, the rituals also establish their social statuses in a broader sense.

References

AIYAPPAN, A. (1934), 'Cross-Cousin and Uncle-Niece Marriages in South India', *Congrès international des sciences anthropologiques et ethnologiques* (London: RAI), pp. 281–2.

—— (1944), 'Iravas and Culture Change', *Bulletin of the Madras Government Museum* (NS), gen. sect., 5/1.

ALLEN, N. J. (1974), 'The Ritual Journey: A Pattern Underlying Certain Nepalese Rituals', in C. von Furer-Haimendorf (ed.), *Contributions to the Anthropology of Nepal* (Warminster: Aris & Phillips), pp. 6–22.

—— (1975) 'Byansi Kinship Terminology: A Study in Symmetry', *Man* (NS), 10, 80–94.

AUSTIN, J. L. (1976), *How to Do Things with Words*, 2nd edn. (Oxford: OUP).

BABB, L. A. (1975), *The Divine Hierarchy: Popular Hinduism in Central India* (New York and London: Columbia Univ. Press).

BANKS, M. Y. (1957), 'The Social Organisation of the Jaffna Tamils of North Ceylon, with Special Reference to Kinship, Marriage and Inheritance', Ph.D. thesis (Cambridge).

BARNARD, A. J., and GOOD, A. (1984), *Research Practices in the Study of Kinship*, ASA Research Methods in Social Anthropology, 2 (London: Academic Press).

BARNETT, S. A. (1976), 'Coconuts and Gold: Relational Identity in a South Indian Caste', *Contributions to Indian Sociology* (NS) 10, 133–56.

BARTH, F. (1975), *Ritual and Knowledge among the Baktaman of New Guinea* (New Haven, Conn.: Yale Univ. Press).

BASHAM, A. L. (1967), *The Wonder that was India*, 3rd edn. (London: Sidgwick & Jackson).

BECK, B. E. F. (n.d.), 'Sister's Daughter Marriage in South India', unpub. MS.

—— (1969), 'Colour and Heat in South Indian Ritual', *Man* (NS) 4, 553–72.

—— (1972), *Peasant Society in Koṅku* (Vancouver: Univ. of British Columbia Press).

—— (1974), 'The Kin Nucleus in Tamil Folk-lore', in T. R. Trautmann (ed.), *Kinship and History in South Asia*, Michigan Papers on South and South-East Asia, 7 (Ann Arbor, Mich.: Univ. of Michigan Press), pp. 1–28.

BENSON, J. (1977), 'A South Indian Jajmānī System', *Ethnology*, **16**, 239–50.

BETEILLE, A. (1971), *Caste, Class and Power: Changing Patterns of Stratification in a Tanjore Village* (Berkeley, Calif.: Univ. of California Press).

BHATTACHARYA, J. (1893), *Commentaries on the Hindu Law* (Calcutta: Thacker, Spink & Co.).

BHATTACHARYYA, N. N. (1968), *Indian Puberty Rites* (Calcutta: Indian Studies Past and Present).

BIARDEAU, M., and MALAMOUD, B. (1976), *Le Sacrifice dans l'Inde ancienne* (Paris: Presses Universitaires de France).

BOURDIEU, P. (1977), *Outline of a Theory of Practice* (Cambridge: CUP).

BRUNNER-LACHAUX, H. (1968), *Somasambhupaddhati, Pt. 2: Rituels occasionnels* (Pondicherry: Institut français d'Indologie).

CALDWELL, R. (1881), *A Political and General History of the District of Tinnevelly* (Madras: Government Press).

CARMAN, J. B., and MARGLIN, F. A. (eds.) (1985), *Purity and Auspiciousness in Indian Society* (Leiden: E. J. Brill).

CARTER, A. T. (1973), 'A Comparative Analysis of Systems of Kinship and Marriage in South Asia', *Proceedings of the Royal Anthropological Institute*, pp. 29–54.

Chambers Twentieth Century Dictionary (Edinburgh: W. & R. Chambers, 1973).

CHETTIAR, S. M. L. (1973), *Folklore of Tamil Nadu* (Delhi: National Book Trust).

CLOTHEY, F. W. (1978), *The Many Faces of Murukan: The History and Meaning of a South Indian God* (Paris and The Hague: Mouton).

—— (1983), *Rhythm and Intent: Ritual Studies from South India* (Bombay: Blackie & Son).

COMAROFF, J. L. (1980), 'Introduction', in J. L. Comaroff (ed.), *The Meaning of Marriage Payments* (London: Academic Press), pp. 1–48.

DANIEL, E. V. (1984), *Fluid Signs: Being a Person the Tamil Way* (Berkeley, Calif.: Univ. of California Press).

DANIEL, S. B. (1980), 'Marriage in Tamil Culture: The Problem of Conflicting "Models"', in Wadley 1980: 61–91.

DAS, V. (1977), 'On the Categorisation of Space in Hindu Ritual', in R. K. Jain (ed.), *Text and Context: The Social Anthropology of Tradition*, ASA Essays, 2 (Philadelphia, Pa.: Institute for the Study of Human Issues), pp. 9–27.

—— (1982), *Structure and Cognition: Aspects of Hindu Caste and Ritual* (Delhi: OUP).

DAVID, K. (1973), 'Until Marriage Do Us Part: A Cultural Account of Jaffna Tamil Categories for Kinsman', *Man* (NS), 8, 521–35.

—— (1974), 'And Never the Twain Shall Meet? Mediating the Structural Approaches to Caste Ranking', in H. M. Buck and G. E. Yocum (eds.), *Structural Approaches to South India Studies* (Chambersburg, Pa.: Wilson Books), pp. 43–80.
—— (ed.), (1977*a*), *The New Wind: Changing Identities in South Asia* (Paris and The Hague: Mouton).
—— (1977*b*), 'Hierarchy and Equivalence in Jaffna, North Sri Lanka: Normative Codes as Mediator', in David 1977*a*: 179–226.
DESSIGANE, R., and PATTABIRAMIN, P. Z. (1967), *La Légende de Skanda selon le Kandapuranam tamoul et l'iconographie* (Pondicherry: Institut français d'Indologie).
—— —— and FILLIOZAT, J. (1960), *La Légende des jeux de Civa à Madurai: D'après les textes et les peintures* (Pondicherry: Institut français d'Indologie).
DJURFELDT, G., and LINDBERG, S. (1975), *Behind Poverty: The Social Formation in a Tamil Village*, Scandinavian Institute of Asian Studies Monographs, 22 (London: Curzon Press).
D'OYLY, Sir J. (1975 [1929]), *A Sketch of the Constitution of the Kandyan Kingdom*, 2nd edn. (Dehiwala: Tisara Prakasakayo).
DUBE, S. C. (1953), 'Token Pre-Puberty Marriage in Middle India', *Man*, 53, 18–19.
DUBOIS, Abbé J. A. (1879), *A Description of the Character, Manners and Customs of the People of India*, 3rd edn. (Madras: Higginbotham).
DUMONT, L. (1950), 'Kinship and Alliance among the Pramalai Kallar', *Eastern Anthropologist*, 4, 3–26.
—— (1953*a*), 'The Dravidian Kinship Terminology as an Expression of Marriage', *Man*, 53, 34–9 (repr. Dumont 1983: 3–17).
—— (1953*b*), 'Dravidian Kinship Terminology', *Man*, 53, 143 (repr. Dumont 1983: 20–3).
—— (1957*a*), *Hierarchy and Alliance in South Indian Kinship*, RAI Occasional Paper, 12 (London: RAI) (repr. Dumont 1983: 36–104).
—— (1957*b*), *Une Sous-caste de l'Inde du sud: Organisation sociale et religion des Pramalai Kallar* (Paris and The Hague: Mouton).
—— (1957*c*), 'For a Sociology of India', *Contributions to Indian Sociology*, 1, 7–22 (repr. Dumont 1970: 2–18).
—— (1959), 'A Structural Definition of a Folk Deity of Tamil Nad: Aiyanar the Lord', *Contributions to Indian Sociology*, 3, 75–87 (repr. Dumont 1970: 20–32).
—— (1961*a*), 'Les mariages Nayar comme faits Indiens', *L'Homme*, 1, 11–36 (trans. Dumont 1983: 105–36).
—— (1961*b*), 'Marriage in India: The Present State of the Question, pt. i. Marriage Alliance in South-East India and Ceylon', *Contributions to Indian Sociology*, 5, 75–95.

DUMONT, L. (1963), 'Distribution of some Maravar Sub-Castes', in B. Ratnam (ed.), *Anthropology on the March* (Madras: Book Centre), pp. 297–305.
—— (1964), 'Marriage in India: The Present State of the Question: Post-script to Pt. i. ii. Marriage and Status; Nayar and Newar', *Contributions to Indian Sociology*, 7, 77–98.
—— (1970), *Religion/Politics and History in India* (Paris and The Hague: Mouton).
—— (1975), *Dravidien et Kariera: L'Alliance de mariage dans l'Inde du Sud, et en Australie* (Paris and The Hague: Mouton).
—— (1980), *Homo Hierarchicus: The Caste System and its Implications* (Chicago, Ill.: Chicago Univ. Press).
—— (1983), *Affinity as a Value* (Chicago, Ill.: Chicago Univ. Press).
—— and POCOCK, D. F. (1957), 'Village Studies', *Contributions to Indian Sociology*, 1, 23–41.
—— (1959), 'Pure and Impure', *Contributions to Indian Sociology*, 3, 9–39.
DYSON, T., and MOORE, M. (1983), 'On Kinship Structure, Female Autonomy, and Demographic Behaviour in India', *Population and Development Review*, 9, 35–60.
ELIADE, M. (1955), *The Myth of the Eternal Return* (London: Routledge & Kegan Paul).
—— (1964), *Shamanism: Archaic Techniques of Ecstasy* (New York: Bollingen Foundation).
EMENEAU, M. B. (1967), *Collected Papers: Dravidian Linguistics, Ethnology and Folktales*, Department of Linguistics Publications, 8 (Annamalai: Annamalai Univ. Press).
EVANS-PRITCHARD, E. E. (1951), *Kinship and Marriage among the Nuer* (Oxford: Clarendon Press).
FABRICIUS, J. P. (1972 [1779]), *Tamil and English Dictionary*, 4th edn. (Tranquebar: Evangelical Lutheran Mission Publishing House).
FAWCETT, F. (1903), 'The Kondaiyamkottai Maravars: A Dravidian Tribe of Tinnevelly, Southern India', *Journal of the Royal Anthropological Institute*, 33, 57–65.
FERRO-LUZZI, G. E. (1974), 'Women's Pollution Periods in Tamilnadu', *Anthropos*, 69, 113–61.
FORTES, M. (1970), *Time and Social Structure, and other Essays* (London: Athlone Press).
FOX, R. (1967), *Kinship and Marriage* (Harmondsworth: Penguin).
FREED, R. S., and FREED, S. A. (1980), 'Rites of Passage in Shanti Nagar', *Anthropological Papers of the American Museum of Natural History*, 56, 323–554.
FUKUZAWA, H. (1972), 'Rural Servants in the Eighteenth-Century Maharashtrian Village: Demiurgic or Jajmani System?' *Hitotsubashi Journal of Economics*, 12, 14–40.

FULLER, C. J. (1976), *The Nayars Today* (Cambridge: CUP).
—— (1977), 'British India or Traditional India? An Anthropological Problem', *Ethnos*, 95–121.
—— (1984), *Servants of the Goddess: The Priests of a South Indian Temple* (Cambridge: CUP).
—— (1988), 'The Hindu Pantheon and the Legitimation of Hierarchy', *Man* (NS), **23**, 19–39.
—— (1989), 'Misconceiving the Grain Heap: A Critique of the Concept of the Indian Jajmani System', in J. P. Parry and M. Bloch (eds.), *Money and the Morality of Exchange* (Cambridge: CUP), pp. 33–63.
GOMBRICH, R. F. (1971), *Precept and Practice: Traditional Buddhism in the Rural Highlands of Ceylon* (Oxford: Clarendon Press).
GONDA, J. (1970), *Visnuism and Sivaism: A Comparison* (London: Athlone Press).
GOOD, A. (1978*a*), 'Kinship and Ritual in a South Indian Micro-Region', Ph.D. thesis (Durham).
—— (1978*b*), 'The Principle of Reciprocal Sets', *Man* (NS), **13**, 128–30.
—— (1980*a*), 'Only Siva is in the Cemetery: Death and its Consequences in a Tamil Micro-Region', in B. T. Quayle (ed.), *Hindu Death and the Ritual Journey*, Durham Univ. Working Papers in Anthropology, 4, pp. 129–81.
—— (1980*b*), 'Elder Sister's Daughter Marriage in South Asia', *Journal of Anthropological Research*, **36**, 474–500.
—— (1981), 'Prescription, Preference and Practice: Marriage Patterns among the Kondaiyankottai Maravar of South India', *Man* (NS), **16**, 108–29.
—— (1982*a*), 'The Female Bridegroom: Rituals of Puberty and Marriage in South India and Sri Lanka', *Social Analysis*, **11**, 35–55.
—— (1982*b*), 'The Actor and the Act: Categories of Prestation in South India', *Man* (NS), **17**, 23–41.
—— (1983), 'A Symbolic Type and its Transformations: The Case of South Indian Poṅkal', *Contributions to Indian Sociology* (NS), **17**, 223–44.
—— (1985*a*), 'The Annual Goddess Festival in a South Indian Village', *South Asian Social Scientist*, **1**, 119–67.
—— (1985*b*), 'Markedness and Extensions: The Tamil Case', *Man* (NS), **20**, 545–7.
—— (1987*a*), 'The Religious, Economic and Social Organization of a South Indian Temple', *Quarterly Journal of Social Affairs*, **3**, 1–25.
—— (1987*b*), 'Divine Coronation in a South Indian Temple', in Sudarsen, *et al.* 1987: 37–71.
—— (in press), 'Divine Marriage in a South Indian Temple', in A. J. Barnard and K. Maddock (eds.), *Kinship and Cosmology* (Sydney: Anthropological Society of New South Wales).
GOODY, J. R. (ed.) (1971), *Kinship* (Harmondsworth: Penguin).
GOUGH, E. K. (1952), 'Changing Kinship Usages in the Setting of Political

and Economic Change among the Nayars of Malabar', *Journal of the Royal Anthropological Institute*, 82, 71–87.

GOUGH, E. K. (1955), 'Female Initiation Rites on the Malabar Coast', *Journal of the Royal Anthropological Institute*, 85, 45–80.

—— (1956), 'Brahmin Kinship in a Tamil Village', *American Anthropologist*, 58, 826–53.

—— (1959*a*), 'The Nayars and the Definition of Marriage', *Journal of the Royal Anthropological Institute*, 89, 23–34.

—— (1959*b*), 'Cults of the Dead among the Nayars', in M. Singer (ed.), *Traditional India: Structure and Change* (Philadelphia, Pa.: American Folklore Society), pp. 240–72.

—— (1961), 'Nayar: Central Kerala', in D. M. Schneider and E. K. Gough (eds.), *Matrilineal Kinship* (Berkeley, Calif.: Univ. of California Press), pp. 298–384.

—— (1965), 'A Note on Nayar Marriage', *Man*, 65, 8–11.

—— (1979), 'Dravidian Kinship and Modes of Production', *Contributions to Indian Sociology* (NS), 13, 265–91.

Government of India (1972*a*), *Census of India 1971: Tamil Nadu*, Pt. X–A, *District Census Handbook, Tirunelveli District: Village and Town Directory* (Madras: Government Press).

—— (1972*b*), *Census of India 1971: Tamil Nadu*, Pt. X–B, *District Census Handbook, Tirunelveli District: Primary Census Abstract*, 2 vols. (Madras: Government Press).

HARDGRAVE, R. L. (1969), *The Nadars of Tamilnad* (Berkeley, Calif.: Univ. of California Press).

HART, G. L. (1973), 'Women and the Sacred in Ancient Tamilnad', *Journal of Ancient Studies*, 32, 233–50.

Hindu Marriage Act 1955 (as amended 1976) (1976) (Allahabad: Central Law Agency).

HOCART, A. M. (1927), 'The Indo-European Kinship System', *Ceylon Journal of Science*, G/1, 179–204.

—— (1968), *Caste* (New York: Russell & Russell).

INDEN, R. B., and NICHOLAS, R. W. (1977), *Kinship in Bengali Culture* (Chicago, Ill.: Chicago Univ. Press).

IYER, L. K. A. K. (1909–12), *The Cochin Tribes and Castes*, 2 vols. (Madras: Government Press).

JAMES, V. (1974), 'First Menstruation Ceremonies among the Parayans of a Nilgiri Village', *Man in India*, 54, 161–72.

KADHIRVEL, S. (1977), *A History of the Maravas, 1700–1802* (Madurai: Madurai Publishing House).

KALAM, M. A. (1987), 'Okka of the Coorgs: Lineage or Joint Family?' in Sudarsen, *et al.* 1987: 195–219.

KANE, P. V. (1941), *History of Dharmasastra*, ii. pt. 1 (Poona: Bhandarkar Oriental Institute).

KAPFERER, B. (1977), 'First Class to Maradana: Secular Drama in Sinhalese Healing Rites', in S. F. Moore and B. G. Myerhoff (eds.), *Secular Ritual* (Assen: Van Gorcum), pp. 91–123.

—— (1979*a*), 'Ritual Process and the Transformation of Context', *Social Analysis*, 1, 3–19.

—— (1979*b*), 'Entertaining Demons: Comedy, Interaction and Meaning in a Sinhalese Healing Ritual', *Social Analysis*, 1, 108–52.

KEARNS, J. F. (1868), *Kalyāna Shatanku, or, the Marriage Ceremonies of the Hindus of South India* (Madras: Higginbotham).

KHARE, R. S. (1977), 'Prestations and Prayers: Two Homologous Systems in Northern India', in David 1977*a*: 105–32.

KOLENDA, P. M. (1959), 'A Multiple Scaling Technique for Caste Ranking', *Man in India*, 39, 127–47.

—— (1984), 'Woman as Tribute, Woman as Flower: Images of "Woman" in Weddings in North and South India', *American Ethnologist*, 11, 98–117.

LAVE, J. C. (1966), 'A Formal Analysis of Preferential Marriage with the Sister's Daughter', *Man* (NS), 1, 185–200.

LEACH, E. R. (1954), *Political Systems of Highland Burma: A Study of Kachin Social Structure* (London: Athlone Press).

—— (1960*a*), *Aspects of Caste in South India, Ceylon and North-West Pakistan* (Cambridge: CUP).

—— (1960*b*), 'Introduction', in Leach 1960*a*: 1–10.

—— (1960*c*), 'The Sinhalese of the Dry Zone of Central Ceylon', in G. P. Murdock (ed.), *Social Structure in South-East Asia* (Chicago, Ill.: Aldine), pp. 116–27.

—— (1961*a*), *Rethinking Anthropology* (London: Athlone Press).

—— (1961*b*), *Pul Eliya: A Village in Ceylon* (Cambridge: CUP).

—— (1970), 'A Critique of Yalman's Interpretation of Sinhalese Girl's Puberty Ceremonial', in J. Pouillon and P. Maranda (eds.), *Échanges et communications*, ii (Paris and The Hague: Mouton), pp. 819–28.

—— (1971), 'More about "Mama" and "Papa"', in Needham 1971*a*: 75–98.

—— (1976), *Culture and Communication: The Logic by which Symbols are Connected* (Cambridge: CUP).

—— (1982), *Social Anthropology* (London: Fontana).

LÉVI-STRAUSS, C. (1969), *The Elementary Structures of Kinship* (London: Eyre & Spottiswoode).

LOGAN, P. (1980), 'Domestic Worship and the Festival Cycle in the South Indian City of Madurai', Ph.D. thesis (Manchester).

Ludden, D. E. (1985), *Peasant History in South India* (Princeton, NJ.: Princeton Univ. Press).

Macdonald, A. W. (1953), 'Juggernaut reconstruit', *Journal Asiatique*, 487–528 (trans. Macdonald 1984: 27–59).

—— (1984), *Essays on the Ethnology of Nepal and South Asia* (Kathmandu: Ratna Pustak Bhandar).

McGilvray, D. B. (1982*a*), 'Mukkuvar Vannimai: Tamil Caste and Matriclan Ideology in Batticaloa, Sri Lanka', id. (ed.), *Caste Ideology and Interaction* (Cambridge: CUP), pp. 34–97.

—— (1982*b*), 'Sexual Power and Fertility in Sri Lanka: Batticaloa Tamils and Moors', in C. P. MacCormack (ed.), *Ethnography of Fertility and Birth* (London: Academic Press), pp. 25–73.

Mandelbaum, D. G. (1970), *Society in India*, i. *Continuity and Change* (Berkeley, Calif.: Univ. of California Press).

Marglin, F. A. (1985*a*), 'Introduction', in Carman and Marglin 1985: 1–10.

—— (1985*b*), *Wives of the God-King: The Rituals of the Devadasis of Puri* (Delhi: OUP).

Marriott, M. (1959), 'Interactional and Attributional Theories of Caste Ranking', *Man in India*, **39**, 92–107.

—— (1968), 'Caste Ranking and Food Transactions: A Matrix Analysis', in M. Singer and B. S. Cohn (eds.), *Structure and Change in Indian Society* (Chicago, Ill.: Aldine), pp. 133–71.

—— (1976), 'Interpreting Indian Society: A Monistic Alternative to Dumont's Dualism', *Journal of Asian Studies*, **36**, 189–95.

—— and Inden, R. B. (1974), 'Caste Systems', *Encyclopaedia Britannica*, 15th edn. (Chicago, Ill.), iii. 982–91.

—— (1977), 'Towards an Ethnosociology of South Asian Caste Systems', in David 1977*a*: 227–38.

Maybury-Lewis, D. H. P. (1965), 'Prescriptive Marriage Systems', *Southwestern Journal of Anthropology*, **21**, 207–30.

Mayer, A. C. (1958), 'The Dominant Caste in a Region of Central India', *Southwestern Journal of Anthropology*, **14**, 407–27.

—— (1960), *Caste and Kinship in Central India* (London: Routledge & Kegan Paul).

Mencher, J. P., and Goldberg, H. (1967), 'Kinship and Marriage Regulations among the Namboodiri Brahmans of Kerala', *Man* (NS), **2**, 87–106.

Miller, D. (1986), 'Exchange and Alienation in the *Jajmani* System', *Journal of Anthropological Research*, **42**, 535–56.

Morgan, L. H. (1871), *Systems of Consanguinity and Affinity of the Human Family* (Washington, DC: Smithsonian Institution).

Mudiraj, G. N. R. 'Caste-Sect Dichotomy in Telengana Villages', *Man in India*, **50**, 280–8.

MUS, P. (1935), *Barabadur: Esquisse d'une histoire du Bouddhisme fondée sur la critique archéologique des textes*, 2 vols. (Hanoi: Imprimerie d'Extrême-Orient).

NARAYANAN, V. (1985), 'The Two Levels of Auspiciousness in Srivaisnava Ritual and Literature', in Carman and Marglin 1985: 55–64.

NEEDHAM, R. (1967), 'Terminology and Alliance, II—Mapuche; Conclusions', *Sociologus*, **17**, 39–53.

—— (ed.) (1971*a*), *Rethinking Kinship and Marriage*, ASA Monographs, 11 (London: Tavistock).

—— (1971*b*), 'Remarks on the Analysis of Kinship and Marriage', in Needham 1971*a*: 1–34.

—— (1973), 'Prescription', *Oceania*, **42**, 166–81.

—— (1975), 'Polythetic Classification: Convergence and Consequences', *Man* (NS), **10**, 349–69.

O'FLAHERTY, W. D. (1973), *Asceticism and Eroticism in the Mythology of Siva* (London: OUP).

PARRY, J. P. (1980), 'Ghosts, Greed and Sin: The Occupational Identity of the Benares Funeral Priests', *Man* (NS), **15**, 88–111.

—— (1986), 'The Gift, the Indian Gift and the "Indian Gift" ', *Man*, (NS), **21**, 453–73.

PATE, H. R. (1917), *Madras District Gazetteers: Tinnevelly*, i (Madras: Government Press).

POCOCK, D. F. (1973), *Mind, Body and Wealth* (Oxford: Basil Blackwell).

PUTHENKALAM, Fr. J. (1977), *Marriage and Family in Kerala, with Special Reference to Matrilineal Castes* (Calgary: Journal of Comparative Family Studies Monograph Series).

RADCLIFFE-BROWN, A. R. (1953), 'Dravidian Kinship Terminology', *Man*, 53, 112 (repr. Dumont 1983: 18–20).

RAHEJA, G. (1988), *The Poison in the Gift: Ritual, Prestation, and the Dominant Caste in a North Indian Village* (Chicago, Ill.: Chicago Univ. Press).

—— (1989), 'Centrality, Mutuality and Hierarchy: Shifting Aspects of Inter-Caste Relationships in North India', *Contributions to Indian Sociology* (NS), **23**, 79–101.

RAJAYYAN, K. (1974), *Rise and Fall of the Poligars of Tamilnadu* (Madras: Madras Univ. Press).

REINICHE, M. L. (1975), 'Les "Démons" et leur culte dans la structure du panthéon d'un village de Tirunelveli', *Purusartha*, 2, 173–203.

—— (1977), 'La Notion de "Jajmānī": Qualification abusive ou principe d'intégration?', *Purusartha*, 3, 71–107.

—— (1979), *Les Dieux et les hommes: études des cultes d'un village du Tirunelveli, Inde du sud* (Paris and The Hague: Mouton).

REYNOLDS, H. B. (1980), 'The Auspicious Married Woman', in Wadley 1980: 35–60.

RIVERS, W. H. R. (1907), 'The Marriage of Cousins in India', *Journal of the Royal Asiatic Society*, 611–40.

—— (1924), *Social Organization* (London: Kegan Paul, Trench and Trubner).

RIVIÈRE, P. G. (1966*a*), 'Oblique Discontinuous Exchange: A New Formal Type of Prescriptive Alliance', *American Anthropologist*, **68**, 738–40.

—— (1966*b*), 'A Note on Marriage with the Sister's Daughter', *Man* (NS), **1**, 550–6.

ROBINSON, M. S. (1968), 'Some Observations on the Kandyan Sinhalese Kinship System', *Man* (NS), **3**, 402–23.

RYAN, B. (1958), *Sinhalese Village* (Coral Gables, Fla.: Univ. of Miami Press).

SAHLINS, M. D. (1965), 'On the Ideology and Composition of Descent Groups', *Man*, **65**, 104–7.

SARASWATHI, S. (1973), *The Madras Panchayat System*, i (Delhi: Impex).

SCHEFFLER, H. W. (1966), 'Ancestor Worship in Anthropology: Or, Observations on Descent and Descent Groups', *Current Anthropology*, **7**, 541–51.

—— (1977), 'Kinship and Alliance in South India and Australia', *American Anthropologist*, **79**, 869–82.

—— (1984), 'Markedness and Extensions: The Tamil Case', *Man* (NS), **19**, 557–74.

—— (1985), 'Markedness and Extensions: The Tamil Case', *Man* (NS), **20**, 547.

—— and LOUNSBURY, F. G. (1971), *A Study in Structural Semantics: The Sirionо Kinship System* (Englewood Cliffs, NJ: Prentice-Hall).

SCHNEIDER, D. M. (1968), *American Kinship: A Cultural Account* (Englewood Cliffs, NJ: Prentice-Hall).

SCOTT, Sir J. G. ['SHWAY YOE'] (1927), *The Burman, his Life and Notions* (London: Macmillan).

SHAPIRO, W. (1966), 'Secondary Unions and Kinship Terminology: The Case of Avuncular Marriage', *Bijdragen tot de Taal-, Land- en Volkenkunde*, **122**, 82–9.

SHULMAN, D. D. (1980), *Tamil Temple Myths: Sacrifice and Divine Marriage in the South Indian Saiva Tradition* (Princeton, NJ: Princeton Univ. Press).

SOUTHWOLD, M. (1978*a*), 'Definition and its Problems in Social Anthropology', in E. Schwimmer (ed.), *The Yearbook of Symbolic Anthropology*, i (London: C. Hurst).

—— (1978*b*), 'Buddhism and the Definition of Religion', *Man* (NS), **13**, 362–79.

SPATE, O. K., and LEARMONTH, A. T. A. (1967), *India and Pakistan*, 3rd edn. (London: Methuen).

SPERBER, D. (1975), *Rethinking Symbolism* (Cambridge: CUP).

SRINIVAS, M. N. (1952), *Religion and Society among the Coorgs of South India* (London: Clarendon Press).

—— (1955), 'The Social System of a Mysore Village', in M. Marriott (ed.), *Village India* (Chicago, Ill.: Chicago Univ. Press), pp. 1–35 (repr. Srinivas 1987: 60–95).

—— (1959), 'The Dominant Caste in Rampura', *American Anthropologist*, 61, 1–16 (repr. Srinivas 1987: 96–115).

—— (1975), 'The Indian Village: Myth and Reality', in J. H. M. Beattie and R. G. Lienhardt (eds.), *Studies in Social Anthropology: Essays in Memory of E. E. Evans-Pritchard* (Oxford: OUP) (repr. Srinivas 1987: 20–59).

—— (1987), *The Dominant Caste and other Essays* (Delhi: Oxford Univ. Press).

STEIN, B. S. (1980), *Peasant State and Society in Medieval South India* (Delhi: Oxford Univ. Press).

STEVENSON, S. (1971 [1920]), *The Rites of the Twice-Born* (New Delhi: Oriental Books Reprint Corporation).

SUBRAMANIAM, K. (1974), *Brahmin Priest of Tamil Nadu* (New Delhi: Wiley Eastern).

SUDARSEN, V., REDDY, G. P., and SURYANARAYANA, M. (eds.) (1987), *Religion and Society in South India* (Delhi: BR Publishing Corporation).

TAMBIAH, S. J. (1965), 'Kinship Fact and Fiction in Relation to the Kandyan Sinhalese', *Journal of the Royal Anthropological Institute*, 95, 131–73.

—— (1973*a*), 'Form and Meaning of Magical Acts: A Point of View', in R. Horton and R. Finnegan (eds.), *Modes of Thought* (London: Faber & Faber), pp. 199–229.

—— (1973*b*), 'Dowry and Bridewealth, and the Property Rights of Women in South Asia', in J. Goody and S. J. Tambiah, *Bridewealth and Dowry* (Cambridge: CUP), pp. 59–169.

—— (1979), 'A Performative Approach to Ritual', *Proceedings of the British Academy*, 65, 113–69.

TAPPER, B. E. (1979), 'Widows and Goddesses: Female Roles in Deity Symbolism in a South Indian Village', *Contributions to Indian Sociology* (NS), 13, 1–31.

THOMAS, E. J. (1949), *The Life of Buddha as Legend and History*, 3rd edn. (London: Routledge & Kegan Paul).

THURSTON, E. (1906), *Ethnographic Notes in Southern India* (Madras: Government Press).

—— and RANGACHARI, K. (1909), *Castes and Tribes of Southern India*, 7 vols. (Madras: Government Press).

TRAUTMANN, T. R. (1981), *Dravidian Kinship* (Cambridge: CUP).
TURNER, V. W. (1967), *The Forest of Symbols* (London and Ithaca, NY: Cornell Univ. Press).
VAN GENNEP, A. (1960), *The Rites of Passage* (London: Routledge & Kegan Paul).
WADLEY, S. S. (ed.) (1980), *The Powers of Tamil Women* (Syracuse, NY: Maxwell School of Citizenship & Public Affairs).
WINSLOW, D. (1980), 'Rituals of First Menstruation in Sri Lanka', *Man* (NS), 15, 603–25.
WINSLOW, M. (1981 [1862]), *A Comprehensive Tamil and English Dictionary* (New Delhi: Asian Educational Services).
WIRZ, P. (1954), *Exorcism and the Art of Healing in Ceylon* (Leiden: E. J. Brill).
WISER, W. H. (1936), *The Hindu Jajmani System* (Lucknow: Lucknow Publishing House).
YALMAN, N. (1960), 'The Flexibility of Caste Principles in a Kandyan Community', in Leach 1960*a*: 78–112.
—— (1962), 'The Structure of the Sinhalese Kindred: A Re-examination of the Dravidian Terminology', *American Anthropologist*, **64**, 548–75.
—— (1963), 'On the Purity of Women in the Castes of Ceylon and Malabar', *Journal of the Royal Anthropological Institute*, **93**, 25–58.
—— (1969), 'The Semantics of Kinship in South India and Ceylon', in T. A. Sebeok (ed.), *Current Trends in Linguistics*, 5, *Linguistics in South Asia* (Paris and The Hague: Mouton), pp. 607–26.
—— (1971), *Under the Bo Tree: Studies in Caste, Kinship and Marriage in the Interior of Ceylon* (Berkeley, Calif.: Univ. of California Press).

Glossary

Important Tamil words used in the main text are listed below. Proper names and kinship terms are mostly not included: the latter are given in Tables 5.1 and 5.2. The words are listed in English alphabetical order except that short vowels take precedence over long vowels throughout.

ammaṉ: goddess
ālatti: an honorific tray of auspicious objects
jāti: caste, sub-caste; genus
kalikuḍam uḍaittal: the ceremony of breaking a water-pot over a funeral pyre
kaliyāṇam: an auspicious ceremony; a wedding
karṇam: a village land-accountant
karumāti: a purificatory rite ending death ritual
kavalai: a bucket for raising water from a well
kāppu: amulets or charms against evil eye
kiḷai: 'a branch'; an exogamous group
kottu: an exogamous group among Maravar
kōṭṭai: a fort; 110 kg of paddy
kōttiram: a clan, often endogamous
kōvil: a Hindu temple
kuḍimakaṉ: 'village son'; a Washerman or Barber
kuladeyvam: a family deity
kulam: a family, lineage, or clan
kuḷam: an irrigation tank
kuṅkumam: kumkum, a red cosmetic used in worship
kuṛukkam: an area of 0.97 acres of dry land
kuruvai: a ululating cry made by women to mark auspicious transitions
maṇḍapam: the pillared entrance-hall of a temple
marakkāl: an area of 1/12 acre of 'wet' land; the amount of seed required by such an area
maritēr: a funeral bier
mālai: a flower-garland
māṉiyam: a gift to a specialist; land held on usufruct by virtue of office
māppiḷḷai: a male cross-cousin; a bridegroom

moy: a list, especially of donations at a life-crisis rite
mukūrttakal: a post erected prior to a wedding
muṉsīp: a village revenue official
nañcai: 'wet' rice-growing land
nāḍu: a country or region
nākaṣvaram: an oboe-like reed instrument
nīrmālai: the bathing of mourners before a funeral
paḍi: a volume of grain (about 1.5 kg)
pakkā: a volume of grain (about 1.0 kg); a 'big' *pakkā* is equivalent to 1 *paḍi*, q.v.
pandal: a hut of bamboo and palmyrah required on ceremonial occasions
paṅkāḷi: heirs; a group of male parallel relatives
paramparai: succession from father to son
parisam: a wedding prestation, designed to obtain the bride's consent
pavaḷam: an exogamous Maravar group; part of a Maravar woman's *tāli*, q.v.
pāḷaiyakkāraṉ: a Poligar, or traditional chieftain
peṇ: girl; bride
poṅkal: ceremonially boiled rice, cooked at a temple; a temple festival
puḍam: a truncated square-pyramid of masonry, representing a deity
puñcai: 'dry', unirrigated, agricultural land
puṛampōkku: waste or common land
pūja: worship; a religious service
pūsāri: a temple priest
saḍaṅku: a rite associated with female puberty
sammandakkāraṉ: affinal relatives
sammandi, *sampandi*: affines
sampaḷam: wage, pay for work done
sandōsam: mutual satisfaction in fair transactions
sāmi: a deity
sāmiyāḍi: a person possessed by a temple deity
sāṣtiram: specialized knowledge; obligation, right; prestation to or by a specialist
sīdaṉam: a prestation to a bride from her father; 'dowry'
sokkāraṉ: an ego-centred group of male parallel relatives
sondam: relatives in general
sōṛu: boiled grain
suḍukāḍu: a cemetery
sumaitāṅki: a stone erected in the name of a woman dying in childbirth
suruḷ: a rolled-up betel leaf; a name for various wedding prestations
talaiyāri: village policeman, Munsip's assistant
tāli: the ornament on a marriage necklace
tāymāmāṉ: senior MB

teṭcaṇai: a gift to a specialist (Skt. *dakṣiṇā*)
tēṅkāy: a coconut
tiṭṭu: impurity
tōṭṭam: 'garden' land, irrigated by wells
tōṭṭi: a messenger associated with funerals
urimai: a right; especially of first refusal in marriage of a specified relative
varattusampaḷam: wages, salary
vāḍar, *vāḍai*: an exogamous Reddiyar group
vēppilai: leaves of the margosa tree (*Azadirachta Indica*)
vēṣṭi: a dhoti, the main male garment
vēṭṭiyaṉ: a grave-digger or funeral attendant

Index